On Whitman

On Whitman

The Best from *American Literature*

Edited by Edwin H. Cady and Louis J. Budd

Duke University Press   Durham 1987

© 1987 Duke University Press
All rights reserved
Printed in the United States of America
on acid-free paper ∞
Library of Congress Cataloging in Publication Data
appears on the last printed page of this book.

Contents

Series Introduction

From Vol. 1, no. 1, in March 1929 to the latest issue, the front cover of *American Literature* has proclaimed that it is published "with the Cooperation of the American Literature Section [earlier Group] of the Modern Language Association." Though not easy to explain simply, the facts behind that statement have deeply influenced the conduct and contents of the journal for five decades and more. The journal has never been the "official" or "authorized" organ of any professional organization. Neither, however, has it been an independent expression of the tastes or ideas of Jay B. Hubbell, Clarence Gohdes, or Arlin Turner, for example. Historically, it was first in its field, designedly so. But its character has been unique, too.

Part of the tradition of the journal says that Hubbell in founding it intended a journal that should "hold the mirror up to the profession"—reflecting steadily its current interests and (ideally) at least sampling the best work being done by historians, critics, and bibliographers of American literature during any given year. Such remains the intent of the editors based at Duke University; such also through the decades has been the intent of the Board of Editors elected by the vote of members of the professional association—"Group" or "Section."

The operative point lies in the provisions of the constitutional "Agreements" between the now "Section" and the journal. One of these provides that the journal shall publish no article not approved by two readers from the elected Board. Another provides that the Chairman of the Board or, if one has been appointed and is acting in the editorial capacity at Duke, the Managing Editor need publish no article not judged worthy of the journal. Historically, again, the members of the successive Boards and the Duke editor have seen eye-to-eye. The Board has tended to approve fewer than one out of every ten submissions. The tradition of the journal dictates that it keep a slim back-log. With however much revision, therefore, the journal publishes practically everything the Board approves.

Founder Hubbell set an example from the start by achieving the

almost total participation of the profession in the first five numbers
of *American Literature*. Cairns, Murdock, Pattee, and Rusk were
involved in Vol. 1, no. 1, along with Boynton, Killis Campbell,
Foerster, George Philip Krapp, Leisy, Mabbott, Parrington, Bliss
Perry, Louise Pound, Quinn, Spiller, Frederick Jackson Turner, and
Stanley Williams on the editorial side. Spiller, Tremaine McDowell,
Gohdes, and George B. Stewart contributed essays. Canby, George
McLean Harper, Gregory Paine, and Howard Mumford Jones appeared as reviewers. Harry Hayden Clark and Allan Gilbert entered
in Vol. 1, no. 2. Frederic I. Carpenter, Napier Wilt, Merle Curti,
and Grant C. Knight in Vol. 1, no. 3; Clarence Faust, Granville
Hicks, and Robert Morss Lovett in Vol. 1, no. 4; Walter Fuller Taylor, Orians, and Paul Shorey in Vol. 2, no. 1.

Who, among the founders of the profession, was missing? On
the other hand, if the reader belongs to the profession and does not
know those present, she or he probably does not know enough.
With very few notable exceptions, the movers and shakers of the
profession have since the beginning joined in cooperating to create
and sustain the journal.

The foregoing facts lend a special distinction to the best articles
in *American Literature*. They represent the many, often tumultuous
winds of doctrine which have blown from the beginnings through
the years of the decade next to last in this century. Those articles
often became the firm footings upon which present structures of understanding rest. Looking backward, one finds that the argonauts
were doughty. Though we know a great deal more than they, they
are a great deal of what we know. Typically, the old best authors
wrote well—better than most of us. Conceptually, even ideologi-
cally, we still wrestle with ideas they created. And every now and
again one finds of course that certain of the latest work has rein-
vented the wheel one time more. Every now and again one finds
a sunburst idea which present scholarship has forgotten. Then it appears that we have receded into mist or darkness by comparison.

Historical change, not always for the better, also shows itself in
methods (and their implied theories) of how to present evidence,
structure an argument, craft a scholarly article. The old masters
were far from agreed—much to the contrary—about these matters.

But they are worth knowing in their own variety as well as in their instructive differences from us.

On the other hand, the majority of *American Literature*'s authors of the best remain among us, working, teaching, writing. One testimony to the quality of their masterliness is the frequency with which the journal gets requests from the makers of textbooks or collections of commentary to reprint from its pages. Now the opportunity presents itself to select without concern for permissions fees what seems the best about a number of authors and topics from the whole sweep of *American Literature*.

The fundamental reason for this series, in other words, lies in the intrinsic, enduring value of articles that have appeared in *American Literature* since 1929. The compilers, with humility, have accepted the challenge of choosing the best from well over a thousand articles and notes. By "best" is meant original yet sound, interesting, and useful for the study and teaching of an author, intellectual movement, motif, or genre.

The articles chosen for each volume of this series are given simply in the order of their first publication, thus speaking for themselves and entirely making their own points rather than serving the compilers' view of literary or philosophical or historical patterns. Happily, a chronological order has the virtues of displaying both the development of insight into a particular author, text, or motif and the shifts of scholarly and critical emphasis since 1929. But comparisons or trend-watching or a genetic approach should not blur the individual excellence of the articles reprinted. Each has opened a fresh line of inquiry, established a major perspective on a familiar problem, or settled a question that had bedeviled the experts. The compilers aim neither to demonstrate nor undermine any orthodoxy, still less to justify a preference for research over explication, for instance. In the original and still current subtitle, *American Literature* honors literary history and criticism equally—along with bibliography. To the compilers this series does demonstrate that any worthwhile author or text or problem can generate a variety of challenging perspectives. Collectively, the articles in its volumes have helped to raise contemporary standards of scholarship and criticism.

This series is planned to serve as a live resource, not as a homage to once vibrant but petrifying achievements in the past. For several sound reasons, its volumes prove to be weighted toward the more recent articles, but none of those reasons includes a presumed superiority of insight or of guiding doctrine among the most recent generations. Some of the older articles could benefit now from a minor revision, but the compilers have decided to reprint all of them exactly as they first appeared. In their time they met fully the standards of first-class research and judgment. Today's scholar and critic, their fortunate heir, should hope that rising generations will esteem his or her work so highly.

Many of the articles published in *American Literature* have actually come (and continue to come) from younger, even new members of the profession. Because many of those authors climb on to prominence in the field, the fact is worth emphasizing. Brief notes on the contributors in the volumes of their series may help readers to discover other biographical or cultural patterns.

Edwin H. Cady
Louis J. Budd

On Whitman

Main Drifts in Whitman's Poetry*
Floyd Stovall

IT IS a mistake to suppose, as some do, that Whitman had reached his full stature as a poet in 1855. On the contrary, he was at that time, notwithstanding his thirty-six years, relatively immature. His experiences during the next decade developed his character and his poetic faculties enormously. This development, as it is reflected in *Leaves of Grass,* is both progressive and, in the main, consistent. It falls roughly into three periods, the approximate limits of which are determined by the composition of four major poems, here designated key-poems because they are most characteristic of their respective periods. In this essay I shall attempt to trace this development through Whitman's characteristic ideas and to indicate the main drifts or persistent tendencies according to which these ideas were modified.

I

The first period covers the time approximately from 1855 to 1859, and its key-poem is "Song of Myself." In its amorphous structure and in its arrogant tone it exemplifies the dominant principle it incorporates: the love of freedom. Concurrently with the announcement of this principle, Whitman began more noticeably to follow it in his personal conduct. "I wear my hat as I please," he boasts, "indoors or out."[1] He approves what he calls the pioneer's "boundless impatience of restraint,"[2] and declares himself the spokesman of those "whom laws, theories, conventions can never master."[3]

For this assumption of freedom he finds both authority and example in nature. "I see that the elementary laws never apologize,"

---

* The conclusions of this essay are based on what I conceive to be the predominant trends of thought in Whitman's poetry. I think of them as a kind of majority report. A minority report might also be made, with other conclusions. I see no hope of reducing Whitman's thought to a system harmonious in every detail. *Leaves of Grass* is like the Bible in this, that its general import is of more significance to the intelligent reader than any particular text, however emphatic, that may appear to be inconsistent with it.

[1] "Song of Myself" (1855), p. 40. All references are to Emory Holloway's Inclusive Edition of *Leaves of Grass* (New York, 1925). The date in parentheses, except when otherwise specified, is the date of first publication as given by Holloway.

[2] "Song of the Broad-Axe" (1856), p. 157.

[3] "By Blue Ontario's Shore" (1856), p. 297.

he remarks.[4] He sometimes envies the animals because he attributes
their apparent happiness to their freedom from social responsibility.

> They do not lie awake in the dark and weep for their sins,
> They do not make me sick discussing their duty to God
>
> .   .   .
>
> Not one is respectable or unhappy over the whole earth.[5]

Nature, he believes, is not only free, but also good. "How perfect is
the earth," he exclaims, "and the minutest thing upon it!"[6] He imagines that man might be similarly perfect if he were similarly free,
and resolves therefore to throw away man-made standards and habits and to live according to nature:

> I harbor for good or bad, I permit to speak at every hazard,
> Nature without check with original energy.[7]

Since all natural things are equally good, the body is for him as
much an object of reverence as the soul, and every part and function
of the body shares in this holiness. "Not an inch," he says, "nor a
particle of an inch is vile, and none shall be less familiar than the
rest."[8] For him, therefore, sex and the entire process of generation
were suitable and necessary subjects for poetry. By segregating his
sex poems, however, and publishing them under the separate title
of *Children of Adam*,[9] he ascribed to sex a special importance that is
hardly normal in nature. This overemphasis was due, I think, not
mainly to what Professor Bliss Perry calls Whitman's "endeavor to
express the spirit in terms of the flesh,"[10] but rather to his effort to
find in the cloisters of the spirit a sanctuary for the flesh after it has
sinned against some moral law that persists in the conscience long
after the mind has repudiated it. When the flesh offends the spirit,
the mind seeks to make peace by asserting the identity of body and
soul, as Whitman did in these poems.[11] It may be that his theory
of the sanctity of sex was a consequence of previous sexual indul-

---

[4] "Song of Myself," p. 40.

[5] *Ibid.*, p. 50. Original reading, "industrious" for "unhappy," p. 570.

[6] "To Think of Time" (1855), p. 368.

[7] "Song of Myself," p. 24.   [8] *Ibid.*, p. 26.

[9] Though these poems were not given this group title until 1860, they properly belong
to the first period; several were published in 1855 and 1856.

[10] *Walt Whitman: His Life and Work*, p. 80.

[11] "I Sing the Body Electric" (1855), p. 79.

gence. When the period of indulgence was definitely passed, the theory, being no longer useful as a defense of conduct, became dormant except as it was recalled to justify the early poems.

That the sexual frankness of *Children of Adam* was not intended merely to illustrate a theory but expressed the inherent sensuality of Whitman's nature is apparent from the fact that sensual ideas and images unconnected with sex appear frequently in his verse, and in the most unexpected places. "I believe in the flesh and the appetites," he avers.[12] His images often seem inappropriate, as in these lines describing an attractive personality:

> Toward the fluid and attaching character exudes the sweat
>   of the love of young and old,
>
>   .   .   .
>
> Toward it heaves the shuddering longing ache of contact.[13]

Some lines are nothing short of disgusting; for example,

> The scent of these arm-pits aroma finer than prayer.[14]

In a description of the dawn otherwise free of association with sex, we find the following figure of speech:

> Something I cannot see puts upward libidinous prongs,
> Seas of bright juice suffuse heaven.[15]

Not only was Whitman a sensualist, but he was also at this period of his life primarily a materialist. It is true that he proclaims himself the poet of the soul as well as the poet of the body,[16] and asserts that the spiritual is equally true with the material,[17] yet the tone and subject matter of his poetry do not bear out these statements. In theory he was the poet of the soul, but in fact he was as yet the poet of the body almost exclusively. The supernatural he held of no account;[18] and though he said, "I know I am deathless,"[19] he also said that immortality was no more wonderful than eyesight or any other fact in nature,[20] thus indicating the materialistic basis of his conception of immortality. He was, in fact, as nearly pure pantheist

---

[12] "Song of Myself," p. 44.
[13] "Song of the Open Road" (1856), p. 128.
[14] "Song of Myself," p. 45.   [17] "With Antecedents" (1860), p. 204.
[15] "Song of Myself," p. 46.   [18] "Song of Myself," p. 64.
[16] *Ibid.*, p. 41.   [19] *Ibid.*, p. 40.
[20] "Who Learns My Lesson Complete" (1855), p. 330.

as anything else. Identity, as he conceived it, pertains to the body only:

> I too had been struck from the float forever held in solution,
> I too had receiv'd identity by my body,
> That I was I knew was of my body, and what I should be I
>   knew I should be of my body.[21]

Nothing remains of this identity after death except what is absorbed in nature. Thus he writes at the close of the "Song of Myself":

> I bequeath myself to the dirt to grow from the grass I love,
> If you want me again look for me under your boot-soles.[22]

Since everything in nature is perfect in its time and place, Whitman accepted his own world as the best possible world under the circumstances. "I will show," he declares, "that there is no imperfection in the present, and can be none in the future."[23] If the world were reduced again to its primordial condition, it would "surely bring up again where we now stand, and surely go as much farther."[24] The human race shares the same blessing of irrepressible progress.[25] This view of the world is closer to the eighteenth-century conception of progress than to the evolutionism of Darwin; for having outgrown the past, Whitman seems to think he can dispense with it and forget it. He examines his inheritance, admires it, then dismisses it to stand in his own place in the present.[26]

For one holding such a philosophy it was easy to be an egotist, and to think himself potentially if not actually superior to his antecedents. Thus he writes,

> I sat studying at the feet of the great masters,
> Now if eligible O that the great masters might return and study me.[27]

Again he writes, "I am an acme of things accomplish'd, and I an encloser of things to be."[28] Though his "I" is here typical or generic, it is not always so, as when he writes, "I bathe and admire

---

[21] "Crossing Brooklyn Ferry" (1856), p. 136.
[22] "Song of Myself," p. 76.
[23] "Starting from Paumanok" (1860), p. 18.
[24] "Song of Myself," p. 70.
[25] *Ibid.*, p. 71.
[26] "Starting from Paumanok," p. 14.
[27] *Ibid.*, p. 14.
[28] "Song of Myself," p. 68.

myself,"[29] or "I dote on myself,"[30] or "I find no sweeter fat than sticks to my own bones."[31] And he confesses, "I know perfectly well my own egotism."[32] In 1858, while preparing for a lecture, he wrote in his notebook: "Washington made free the body of America, for that was first in order. . . . Now comes one who will make free the American soul."[33] Thus he charms more by his honesty than by his modesty.

Whitman was not only an egotist himself, but he would establish a democracy of egotists, himself their poet. "I will effuse egotism . . . I will be the bard of personality," he announces.[34] But he also proclaims with convincing vehemence, "By God! I will accept nothing which all cannot have their counterpart of on the same terms."[35] This principle of equality was of major importance in Whitman's teaching, but it is hard to see how he could reconcile it with the principle of egotism, or individuality.[36] His desire for equality extended to the offices of government, and he expected to see the day "when qualified mechanics and young men will reach Congress and other official stations, sent in their working costumes, fresh from their benches and tools, and returning to them again with dignity."[37] In his journalistic years before *Leaves of Grass* he had been an active Democrat and states' rights advocate,[38] as well as an equalitarian, and later he became a staunch Lincoln unionist; we may assume, therefore, that his ideas of equalitarianism and individualism were philosophical rather than political.

The effect of this poetry of the first period of *Leaves of Grass* is to exalt the individual man and his physical nature, the poet himself standing as the type. This individual possesses some admirable traits, but is lacking in all those qualities which derive chiefly from social cultivation and self-restraint. He is a splendid animal, but

---

[29] *Ibid.*, p. 26.

[30] *Ibid.*, p. 45.

[31] *Ibid.*, p. 40.

[32] *Ibid.*, p. 66.

[33] Clifton J. Furness, *Walt Whitman's Workshop*, p. 35.

[34] "Starting from Paumanok," p. 18.

[35] "Song of Myself," p. 44.

[36] In "A Backward Glance o'er Travel'd Roads" (1888) Whitman said he had stressed individuality as a counterpoise to the leveling tendency of democracy. See Holloway's *Leaves of Grass*, p. 532.

[37] Quoted by Furness in *Walt Whitman's Workshop*, p. 81, from a manuscript dated 1856.

[38] See *ibid.*, p. 225.

little more. Obviously, then, Whitman had not yet given full expression to his personality. Years afterwards, in the Preface to the edition of 1872, Whitman said that from the beginning of *Leaves of Grass* the religious purpose underlay all others; yet I am of the opinion that if he had such a purpose in 1855 it must have been still only a theory without the support of natural feeling, and hence incapable of affecting his poetry deeply at that time. I can find no slightest trace of a religious purpose in these early poems, unless the joyous and sensuous love of life may be called religious.

II

In the second period of Whitman's poetical development, extending from 1859 to 1865, his barbaric yawp is silenced, and in its place are heard the softer song of love and the melancholy chant of death. These themes, illustrated in the key-poems, "Out of the Cradle Endlessly Rocking" and "When Lilacs Last in the Dooryard Bloom'd," which mark the beginning and conclusion respectively of the period, give to it a predominantly elegiac tone. The change from the joyous to the pensive mood, while not completed and confirmed until he had learned to forget himself in the army hospital at Washington, had its origin probably in some more intimate experience that reached a crisis in 1859. "Out of the Cradle Endlessly Rocking," first published near the close of that year, has all the characteristics of a lament for the loss, by death or permanent separation, of a beloved companion and mistress. It is the first and only true love poem that Whitman ever wrote; this fact in itself gives it special significance. It is, moreover, his first poem that is tragic in tone and that is concerned seriously with death. It is difficult to account for this sudden change in mood except on the supposition of such an emotional upheaval as might be caused by the loss of a lover.

Some justification of this supposition is to be found in Whitman's numerous allusions, both in his poetry and in conversations reported by Horace Traubel, to a serious love entanglement with a woman of the South. On one occasion he told Traubel that he had "sacred, precious memories" of friends in the South;[39] and at another time he spoke of "the one big factor, entanglement (I may almost say tragedy) of my life about which I have not so far talked freely with

[39] Horace Traubel, *Walt Whitman in Camden*, III, 43.

you."[40] We here see that though Whitman professed to have been intimate with more than one woman he remembers only one as a "big factor" in his life. The word "tragedy" is significant. He promised over and over to tell Traubel this big secret, but never did. So far as this poem is concerned, it does not matter whether or not Whitman had a normal sexual life; it may be, as many believe, that he was "romancing" in his famous letter to Symonds about his six children. Nevertheless he could have felt the agony of a bereaved lover, even as Poe felt it, and out of that agony produced a poem.[41]

Whether the experience that gave rise to it was real or imaginary, the poem unquestionably reveals a definite modification in the style and subject matter of *Leaves of Grass.* It has an intensity of feeling, a beauty of phrase and rhythm, and a definiteness of structure almost entirely lacking in Whitman's earlier work. In the experience here related he first discovered the true nature and meaning of the songs he should sing. The mocking bird is the symbol of the genius or daemon (spelled *demon* by Whitman) of the poet's soul.

> Demon or bird! (said the boy's soul,)
> Is it indeed toward your mate you sing? or is it really to me?
> For I, that was a child, my tongue's use sleeping, now I have
>   heard you,
> Now in a moment I know what I am for, I awake,
> And already a thousand singers, a thousand songs, clearer,
>   louder and more sorrowful than yours,
> A thousand warbling echoes have started to life within me,
>   never to die.

The child of the poem is perhaps symbolic of the immaturity of the poet of the first *Leaves.* The awakening here described certainly does not refer to his real childhood. Nor do I believe it refers to the original conception of *Leaves of Grass,* for the songs that the

---

[40] *Ibid.,* II, 543.

[41] Emory Holloway thinks the poem was inspired by the death, shortly before the poem was composed, of a woman whom he loved. See *Walt Whitman: An Interpretation in Narrative,* p. 164.

Clara Barrus, in her recent book *Whitman and Burroughs: Comrades,* seems to think Whitman's story of six children a pathological fabrication (p. 337). Yet in a footnote (p. 338) she quotes from a letter from Whitman to Bucke, May 23, 1891, in which he said: "I have two deceased children (young man and woman—illegitimate of course) that I much desired to bury here with me—but have abandoned the plan on account of angry litigation and fuss generally, and disinterment from down South."

bird taught him were all sorrowful, whereas the first *Leaves* were joyous.

The songs are sorrowful because they spring from "unsatisfied love" which "the messenger there arous'd, the fire, the sweet hell within, the unknown want, the destiny of me." How shall this untold want be satisfied, the fire of unfulfilled love be quenched? Surely there is some solution, some solace for this pain, some hope that he can weave into his song. He looks to the sea, symbolic of the mystery of eternity, and pleads for a clue, a key-word, that will help him in his perplexity.

> Whereto answering, the sea
> Delaying not, hurrying not,
> Whisper'd me through the night, and very plainly before daybreak,
> Lisp'd to me the low and delicious word death,
> And again death, death, death, death,
> Hissing melodious, neither like the bird nor like my arous'd
>   child's heart,
> But edging near as privately for me rustling at my feet,
> Creeping thence steadily up to my ears and laving me softly all over,
> Death, death, death, death, death.

Death is the consoler, the clue to man's destiny, because it is the divine complement of human imperfection, through which love is made complete and immortal. The poignant emotions associated with this revelation awakened Whitman's latent æsthetic sense, and he turned away from his former poetry of theory and animal sensation and began to chant the sorrowful songs that now started to life within him, of which "Out of the Cradle Endlessly Rocking" was the first.

As a consequence of this awakening there came a change in Whitman's view of life and nature. The self receded, and the community loomed larger in his view than before. He began to perceive that the individual cannot escape the law of the group that "all must have reference to the ensemble of the world."[42] But he attains this view only after passing through a period of spiritual upheaval and profound dejection. He who in 1855 was an untamed egotist, joyous and sensual, has become humble, melancholy, and perplexed.

[42] "Laws for Creations" (1860), p. 324.

O baffled, balk'd, bent to the very earth,
Oppress'd with myself that I have dared to open my mouth,
Aware now that amid all that blab whose echoes recoil upon me
    I have not once had the least idea who or what I am,
But that before all my arrogant poems the real Me stands yet
    untouch'd, untold, altogether unreach'd,
Withdrawn far, mocking me with mock-congratulatory signs and
    bows,
With peals of distant ironical laughter at every word I have
    written,
Pointing in silence to these songs, and then to the sand beneath.[43]

He who was so free, so proud, so wholesome now sees himself (as
in a mirror) a slave, diseased, and mentally abased. "Such a result,"
he cries, "so soon—and from such a beginning!"[44] His optimism
is gone; the perfectionist sees the ills of the world—sorrow, pain,
cruelty—but he has no remedy:

All these—all the meanness and agony without end I sitting look
    out upon,
See, hear, and am silent.[45]

Having perceived the inadequacy of love and the imperfection of
life without the fulfilment of death, he began to feel as a reality
what at first he had conceived only as a theory; namely, that he was
to be the poet of death and the soul as well as of life and the body.

Give me your tone therefore O death, that I may accord with it,
Give me yourself, for I see that you belong to me now above all,
    and are folded inseparably together, you love and death are.[46]

He understands now better than ever the value of companion-
ship, and considers himself especially qualified to be the poet of the
love of comrades. "For who but I," he says, "should understand
lovers and all their sorrow and joy?"[47] He recognizes two degrees
of love. One, a kind of benevolence, which he bestows upon all
without condition, he symbolizes by gifts of lilac, pine, moss, laurel,
and other herbs and flowers; the other is special, a jealous love which

[43] "As I Ebb'd with the Ocean of Life" (1860), pp. 216-217.
[44] "A Hand-Mirror" (1860), pp. 228-229.
[45] "I Sit and Look Out" (1860), p. 232.
[46] "Scented Herbage of My Breast" (1860), pp. 96-97.
[47] "These I Singing in Spring" (1860), p. 99.

he reserves for those who love as he himself is capable of loving, and its symbol is the calamus root.[48] The peculiar expression of this special love in the *Calamus* poems, which were probably begun in the latter part of 1859,[49] has led some readers of Whitman to suspect him of sexual abnormality; yet it seems to me possible to explain the distinction here referred to without reference to such abnormality. The calamus root was for his intimate friends, the companions of his body, whom he loved with a sense of possession, and of whom he demanded an equally exclusive love; the other symbolic herbs were for the friends whom he reached or hoped to reach through his poems, including the whole world if possible, and who therefore could not all return his affection in kind.

He dreamed of arousing America to engage with him in a crusade to establish throughout the world the institution of the love of comrades as he proclaimed it.[50] Politically, he imagines the world of the future as a democratic hegemony with America in the leading rôle, "a new race dominating previous ones."[51] His enthusiastic support of the North during the Civil War, in spite of some Southern sympathies and ties, was doubtless due to his belief that a victory for the North would advance his own plan to revolutionize society through the love of comrades. To him the North represented the new America, while the South represented the forces of the past. But above all, like Lincoln, he hoped that the union might be maintained.

His benevolent spirit naturally led him to the hospitals instead of the army camp. This move is to be construed as a sign of strength, not of weakness; a weaker man would have become hard and bitter in self-defense against the harrowing scenes he witnessed, but Whitman became more gentle than ever. In fact, as I have already suggested, his hospital experience only completed the emotional development that had commenced in 1859 and that culminated in the full expansion of one of the tenderest and deepest natures ever recorded in the literature of the world. For the second time he is made acquainted with death; this time he is not prostrated as one who suffers an unexpected personal loss, but softened and purified

[48] *Ibid.*, pp. 99-100.   [49] See "In Paths Untrodden," p. 95.
[50] "States," published in 1860, later rejected, though most of its original lines are retained in other poems. See Holloway's *Leaves,* p. 402.
[51] "Starting from Paumanok," p. 22.

in mind and spirit by the power of sympathy. In the generous service of those who had no means of making an equal return he discovered in himself at last a love which transcended even the love of
comrades because it was the love of man. In this situation he found
it difficult to play the part of war poet:

> Arous'd and angry, I'd thought to beat the alarum, and urge
>   relentless war,
> But soon my fingers fail'd me, my face droop'd and I resign'd
>   myself,
> To sit by the wounded and soothe them, or silently watch
>   the dead.[52]

Though not less firmly convinced than before of the justness of the
Northern cause, he finds it difficult to maintain his enthusiasm, for
these wounded and dead of whom he writes were both Northern
and Southern soldiers, and he had attended them impartially. At
the end of the war he comes forth spiritually enriched though sad-
dened. Nothing could be less arrogant or more tender than this
brief poem called "Reconciliation":

> Word over all, beautiful as the sky,
> Beautiful that war and all its deeds of carnage must in time be
>   utterly lost,
> That the hands of the sisters Death and Night incessantly softly
>   wash again, and ever again, this soil'd world;
> For my enemy is dead, a man divine as myself is dead,
> I look where he lies white-faced and still in the coffin—
>   I draw near,
> Bend down and touch lightly with my lips the white face in
>   the coffin.[53]

As the beginning of the second period of Whitman's poetic development was marked by the composition of the key-poem, "Out
of the Cradle Endlessly Rocking," an elegy commemorating the
death of one personally beloved, so its close was distinguished by
the writing of another key-poem, "When Lilacs Last in the Dooryard Bloom'd," an elegy also, though not merely personal, but representative of a nation's grief at the loss of its friend and hero,
Lincoln. Both poems are remarkable for a perfection of form which

---

[52] "The Wound-Dresser" (1865), p. 261.   [53] P. 271.

the poet achieved in no other work. I do not mean that the lines are regular, for they are not; but each poem is an artistic whole, finely proportioned in structure and unified in thought and feeling. Undoubtedly they were struck off under great emotional and imaginative excitement, and I believe that it was this extraordinary excitement and not any meticulous craftsman's labor that accounted for their artistic superiority.

But Whitman could not have written this elegy if he had not previously gone through the various experiences reflected in the poems of this period—poems of friendship, sympathy, suffering, and death in many moods; poems of enthusiasm and pride and partisan fury; poems, at last, of melancholy victory and tender reconciliation. For in Lincoln, somehow, he personified the otherwise incompatible ideals of individualism, democracy, and unionism; and in the poem written in his memory he fused the three great themes of the poetry of this period: love, death, and nationalism. Yet he keeps the tone of the poem personal, avoids the grandiose in style, and throws over all an atmosphere mingled of fresh fields and the solemn and mystic night.

Here as in "Out of the Cradle Endlessly Rocking" a bird is the symbol of the poet's soul, only in this case it is a hermit thrush instead of a mocking bird. Two other symbols are used: the star, standing for Lincoln, and the lilac, standing for enduring love. Though Whitman calls Lincoln "my departing comrade," it is clear that the love here symbolized by the lilac is different from that elsewhere symbolized by the calamus-root. He was not personally acquainted with the President, but he uses the language of friendship because for the moment he is the representative of the bereaved millions who had loved Lincoln as an ideal "big brother," which is the democratic fashion of hero-worship. This broadening of the sentiment of love from a purely personal to a national scope was the result chiefly, though not altogether, of the war and its attendant circumstances. The idea of death, too, is more fully developed in this poem than in the earlier elegy, where it is named as the key to man's "unknown want," but not elucidated. In the Lincoln poem Whitman explicitly states that death is greater than life and joy and love because it brings freedom, comfort, and certainty to the harassed soul, delivering it from the difficulties it faces in the "fathomless universe." In a vision he beholds those who have died, and they are fully at rest.

In structure his poem is much like the conventional elegy, consisting of the two main divisions, the lament for the dead and the consolation. But the manner in which the thrush, which is to sing the consolatory carol of death, is introduced at the beginning and twice thereafter mentioned, yet held in reserve until the end of the section of lamentation, is unlike the conventional elegy and superior to it, because it gives to the poem a greater effect of unity and intensity. Technically speaking, the poem is not without flaw, for it contains some absurd jingles and some flat commonplaces; but, taken as a whole, it is artistically perhaps the finest of Whitman's poems.

III

In the third period of Whitman's development, the period from 1866 to his death, all the principal ideas introduced into *Leaves of Grass* in the second period were retained and expanded. Poems in praise of death led to the making of poems on immortality, which became the dominant theme of this last period. Love, already national in scope, now reached out to include the entire world. The poet grew more conservative, but remained fundamentally a democrat; and from a nationalist he tended more and more to look towards an eventual union of all the nations of the world in politics as well as in commerce and culture. In the poems on death there is an important change in the point of view. Before, he had written as one who mourns the death of a friend, but now he records the thoughts and feelings that arise from the anticipation of his own death.

Though he is now never so terribly depressed as he had been after his first great sorrow and disillusionment in 1859, he is keenly aware of the perpetual struggle by which alone one may hope to release his higher impulses from the lower. In the early *Leaves* he had declared the good and evil of human nature equally acceptable, but now he desires the triumph of the good and pins his faith upon it.

You degradations, you tussle with passions and appetites

. . .

Ah think not you finally triumph, my real self has yet to come forth,
It shall yet march forth o'ermastering, till all lies beneath me.[54]

[54] "Ah Poverties, Wincings, and Sulky Retreats" (1865-6), p. 398.

The ego of former years, though not dead, is now reduced to the conservative virtue of self-reliance, by which he defends the soul against a world of uncertain values:

> When shows break up what but One's-Self is sure?[55]

Sometimes, too, his religious nature breaks through old reserves of theory and produces a poem, like "The Singer in the Prison,"[56] that for its reverence and tenderness is almost a paradox in *Leaves of Grass*. He is more than ever convinced that his soul's restlessness, "the untold want," can be satisfied only through death;[57] that life, in fact, is the tillage and death the harvest according,[58] the only true life coming after death;[59] and that death is after all but a sleep in camp breaking the forward march of the spirit.[60] He now requires of man an idealism which shall assist him in seeking the good and avoiding the evil, since only the best, the ideal, the divine is worthy of being called God.[61] The body pertains merely to the life of sensation, which can never fulfill the desires of the idealist, for life's mystery baffles him and its struggles beat down his hope.[62]

He is impressed with the evanescence of human life:

> To-day gives place, and fades—the cities, farms, factories fade:
> A muffled sonorous sound, a wailing word is borne through
>   the air for a moment
> Then blank and gone and still, and utterly lost.[63]

Life has meaning only when viewed as a part of God's plan, and the individual has value only as he partakes of the divine character and function. Of his own particular case Whitman writes:

> My three-score years of life summ'd up, and more, and past,
> By any grand ideal tried, intentionless, the whole a nothing,
> And haply yet some drop within God's scheme's ensemble—
>   some wave, or part of wave,
> Like one of yours, ye multitudinous ocean.[64]

He had thought to solve the problem of life and death by giving them a place in nature, but now he knows they are never solved—

---

[55] "Quicksand Years" (1865), p. 374.
[56] "The Singer in the Prison" (1869), p. 316.
[57] "The Untold Want" (1871), p. 415.
[58] "As I Watch'd the Ploughman Ploughing" (1871), p. 378.
[59] "Pensive and Faltering" (1868), p. 378.
[60] "Camps of Green" (1865), p. 414.   [62] "Life" (1888), p. 433.
[61] "Gods" (1870), p. 229.   [63] "Yonnondio" (1887), p. 433.
[64] "By that Long Scan of Waves" (1885), p. 427.

> By each successive age insoluble, pass'd on,
> To ours to-day—and we pass on the same.[65]

Through all the changes of nature nothing is lost or in vain, for all things move imperceptibly through infinite cycles of growth and decay to some ultimate goal, certain yet undiscerned.[66] With all his dreams and his enterprise man cannot hasten this process much, but it is reassuring to Whitman to reflect

> That coursing on, whate'er men's speculations,
> Amid the changing schools, theologies, philosophies,
> And the bawling presentations new and old,
> The round earth's silent vital laws, facts, modes continue.[67]

It is clear that law had now become a more important word than freedom in his philosophy of life. Only the soul dares to be free; it points the way to perfection, but the body, which must abide by the laws that govern the progress of this world, lags behind. Thus death is for the soul a joyful release, frequently compared by Whitman to the launching of a ship for a long-awaited voyage to some wonderful unknown land.

Thus we see that Whitman in old age turned even more definitely to thoughts of the spiritual side of life than poets ordinarily do in old age. It is the more remarkable because of his early materialism. All the forms of the material world, grand as they are, at last seem to him as nothing without the soul, which is more vast, multiform, and puzzling than they.[68] Even his great pride in America is not proof against this change. America's "proudest material civilization," he writes, "must remain in vain" until it attains also a "moral wealth and civilization."[69] She lacks also what he calls the greatest gift of all—the gift of "beauty, health, completion."[70] He foresees the day when his beloved land shall have all these—the moral and æsthetic as well as the material accomplishments, all in perfect proportion—but that time is not yet.

As Whitman grew older, his interests and attachments expanded until they became fairly international in scope. This expansion is

---

[65] "Life and Death" (1888), p. 435.
[66] See "Continuities" (1888), p. 432, and " 'Going Somewhere' " (1887), p. 433.
[67] "The Calming Thought of All" (1888), p. 435.
[68] "Grand is the Seen" (1891), p. 457.
[69] "Thou Mother with Thy Equal Brood" (1872), p. 382.
[70] "With All Thy Gifts" (1876), p. 335.

reflected in his poetry. He wrote a sympathetic and encouraging poem to France in the midst of her tragic ordeal of 1871,[71] and two years later addressed a poem to Spain welcoming her among the nations exalting the flag of liberty.[72] When Brazil abandoned the monarchical for the republican form of government, Whitman, speaking for the United States, greeted her with congratulatory verses.[73] Nor was his interest restricted to movements towards democracy, but extended even to the most conservative nations, as indicated by his admiration for Frederick William, Emperor of Germany, on whose death he wrote a brief poem "mourning a good old man—a faithful shepherd, patriot."[74]

He perceived that America had much to learn from the elder nations, which, in the pride of her youth, she was in danger of forgetting. Thus in 1871 he wrote:

> Not to repel or destroy so much as accept, fuse, rehabilitate,
> To obey as well as command, to follow more than to lead,
> These also are the lessons of our New World;
> While how little the New after all, how much the Old, Old World![75]

In "Proud Music of the Storm" he records a dream in which he hears, blended in the music of the blast, the songs of all lands and times, which he understands to be for his instruction in the writing of poems "bridging the way from Life to Death."[76] Here he clearly recognizes his obligation to write poetry that shall pertain not to America alone, but to all the world.

"Passage to India" is very likely one of those "poems bridging the way from Life to Death" that had been "vaguely wafted" to him in his dream.[77] The poem was inspired, however, by two material achievements: the opening of the Suez Canal and the completion of the Union Pacific Railroad. These two improvements made India and the Orient commercially accessible to Europe and America as they had never been before.

This is the key-poem of Whitman's third and last period. Since it did not appear at the beginning of that period, but rather sums

[71] "O Star of France" (1871), p. 331. [73] "A Christmas Greeting" (1889), p. 450.
[72] "Spain, 1873-1874," p. 400. [74] "The Dead Emperor' (1888), p. 450.
[75] "Song of the Exposition" (1871), p. 166.
[76] See pp. 337-342. Composed, according to Holloway, in 1868. First published in 1871.
[77] See pp. 343-351. Composed, according to Holloway, in 1868. First published in 1871.

up and fuses most of the themes of his later poetry, I have reserved it for final analysis. Though inferior in form to the two elegies, perhaps, it is in my opinion the most profound and characteristic work of his life.

"Passage to India" has a three-fold meaning, physical, intellectual, and spiritual. In the first place, it celebrates the physical union of the nations of the earth. Life began, the poet presumes, somewhere in Asia, possibly in India itself. Thence man spread eastward and westward until the two movements came together in America and so completed the circle of the earth. The American nation, therefore, may expect to become the greatest in the world, being the culmination of a long process of political and economic evolution:

> Lands found and nations born, thou born America,
> For purpose vast, man's long probation fill'd,
> Thou rondure of the world at last accomplish'd.

From this physical union of East and West there should follow eventually an intellectual union. Indeed, such a union is essential to the fulfillment of the vast purpose he assigns to America,

> For what is the present after all but a growth out of the past?

In the development of the ideal man the marvels of modern science will do much, but not all. The Western mind must also hold commerce with the mind of the East, and returning to the place of its origin, recover what has been lost in its long progress; it must return

> To reason's early paradise,
> Back, back to wisdom's birth, to innocent intuitions,
> Again with fair creation.

But even more than for the body and the mind, India has food for the soul of man, and it too must return "to the realms of budding bibles," to the "teeming spiritual darkness" in search of an answer to its eternal questions: *"Wherefore unsatisfied soul? and Whither O mocking life?"* After the world shall have been thus unified, the true poet shall arrive, "the true son of God shall come singing his songs." Then indeed,

> All these hearts as of fretted children shall be sooth'd,
>   .   .   . the secret shall be told,
>   .   .   .

The whole earth, this cold, impassive, voiceless earth, shall be
   completely justified,
Trinitas divine shall be gloriously accomplish'd and compacted
   by the true son of God, the poet,
(He shall indeed pass the straits and conquer the mountains,
He shall double the cape of Good Hope to some purpose,)
Nature and Man shall be disjoin'd and diffused no more,
The true son of God shall absolutely fuse them.

Man's long search for an all-water passage to India is made to typify the soul's long and baffled search for truth and for God, and the discoverer is the type of the poet who plumbs the depths of the spiritual universe. For the soul, then, this voyage is a passage to more than India—

Passage to you, your shores, ye aged fierce enigmas!
Passage to you, to mastership of you, ye strangling problems!
You, strew'd with the wrecks of skeletons, that, living,
   never reach'd you.

And as the body and mind return for completion to the place of their origin, to India and the East, so the soul must return for completion to the place of its origin in God.

Reckoning ahead O soul, when thou, the time achiev'd,
The seas all cross'd, weather'd the capes, the voyage done,
Surrounded, copest, frontest God, yieldest, the aim attain'd,
As fill'd with friendship, love complete, the Elder Brother found,
The Younger melts in fondness in his arms.

This is a far cry from the egotism, sensuality, and materialism of "Song of Myself." And yet there is nothing in "Passage to India" that is not consistent with the basic character and promise of that earlier poem. One emphasizes the spiritual side of man's nature, the other the material. There has been no radical change, but only development through experience. In *Leaves of Grass*, as Whitman often explained, he attempted to express his own personality. Necessarily, then, the character of his poems altered with the alteration in his personality under the stress of circumstance. Hence it would be a mistake to judge his achievement by the early poems only, when he was spiritually and emotionally immature, or by the poems of his old age, after his poetic faculty had passed the summit of its power, which, in my opinion, it reached in "Passage to India." Rather should we estimate his value by his best work, which was mostly completed within the decade from 1859 to 1869.

In concluding this essay I repeat that I attempt to indicate only the main drifts in Whitman's thought and feeling as they are revealed in *Leaves of Grass*. These main drifts covered most of the interests of human life and thought in the America of the nineteenth century. Some of the more important of them may be summarized as follows: (1) in politics, the drift from individualism to nationalism, with strong tendencies toward internationalism; (2) in general philosophy, the drift from love of freedom towards love of law; and (3) in religion, the drift from materialistic pantheism towards a highly spiritualized idealism. The direction of his development is also apparent in the changing themes that dominate his poetry from time to time. In the first period of the *Leaves* he was moved to poetic activity almost exclusively by his interest in life, especially life as sensation and spectacle. In the second period he was moved chiefly by the thought of death, and in the third period by the hope of immortality. The extent of his progress is clearly shown in his changing view of love as it is illustrated in the four key-poems of *Leaves of Grass*. Of these, the "Song of Myself" celebrates man's self-love and arrogant pride in the possession of all life's material blessings, whereas the other three are concerned with unselfish love as manifested in some relation to death. "Out of the Cradle Endlessly Rocking" describes how death by intensifying makes pure the love of man for woman; "When Lilacs Last in the Dooryard Bloom'd" shows how death may exalt and consecrate the love of man for his fellowman; and "Passage to India" reveals how in death the love of man for God is consummated and brought to fruition. These key-poems therefore mark the progress of a special personality, incorrectly supposed by Whitman to be typical, from youth to old age, and from love of self to love of God.

Walt Whitman on Timber Creek
Sculley Bradley

READERS of *Leaves of Grass* who admire Whitman as a poet of nature are generally well acquainted also with the admirable prose sketches in his *Specimen Days*. As nature-sketches they compare favorably with the writings of the poet's great friend, John Burroughs, who admired them so much. Every reader of Whitman knows that they were written along Timber Creek, New Jersey, for the poet tells us so himself. However, this is far from constituting an exact location; and in view of the importance of the place in the later life of the poet it deserves to be accurately known. If Thoreau's Walden Pond should be visited, why not Whitman's creek and pond? There he fought his first battle against death and paralysis, and came off victorious, with a reprieve of sixteen years in which to write *Specimen Days* and *November Boughs* and *Good-Bye My Fancy,* and to revise and enlarge *Leaves of Grass* twice before the so-called "Complete Edition" of 1892. Much of this work was actually done on Timber Creek during successive summers. The place repays a visit better than Walden, because it is less changed from the scene described by the poet. The sight of Thoreau's pond is now generally disappointing to those who have preconceived it from reading *Walden,* but one can still, after half a century, take a copy of Whitman's *Specimen Days* for a guide-book and follow his footsteps down the farm-lane from the old Stafford house, and thence to the creek, to the spring and marl pit, the scene of the famous mud-baths and sun-baths, and farther on to the pond, with its pond-lilies and calamus and hawks, still today almost as Whitman described it.

The first difficulty confronting the student is to find the place. In *Specimen Days* the poet gives its location merely as on Timber Creek, a meandering stream with several small tributaries which enters the Delaware River about ten miles below Camden. The biographers are not of great assistance. Apparently Binns visited the

* This article is supplementary to an essay entitled "Mr. Walter Whitman," published in *The Bookman* for March, 1933.

scene in 1904, since his photographs bear that date and his description is accurate.[1]   One is led to believe that subsequent biographers have in general relied upon his convincing picture; at least there is no evidence of first-hand information in any other of the various biographies, nor any description that does not seem a direct reflection of Whitman's own notes in *Specimen Days*.   Neither Binns nor any other writer locates the place with sufficient accuracy to be of assistance to the student who wishes to find it today, and none of them place sufficient emphasis on the crucial nature of the events which occurred there or the influence of these experiences on Whitman's future work. Several of the commentators who wrote the various memoirs,[2] especially Donaldson, Johnston and Wallace, Burroughs and Morris, reveal a personal knowledge of the spot, but none of them are of great assistance to the explorer. Similarly, in the more ambitious biographies the references are too casual to be of value.   De Selincourt, Rogers, Bailey, and Barrus, in this respect, are negligible.[3]   Carpenter[4] locates the Stafford farm simply as "near Whitehorse."   Bazalgette,[5] having permitted himself a reference to Camden as "a wretched corner of New Jersey . . . a workingman's suburb" of Philadelphia, goes on to place Whitman's summer retreat as "a suburb in New Jersey twelve or fifteen miles from Camden . . . called Whitehorse."   Holloway[6] in 1926 might have been more explicit than to call it "Whitehorse, a hamlet ten or twelve miles from Camden, toward the sea."   For it is not Whitehorse, nor is it decidedly toward the sea, unless one thinks of going by way of the Delaware River.

On a modern map the Stafford farmhouse would be located in the town of Laurel Springs, New Jersey. In 1876 Laurel Springs was a mere post office about two miles from the hamlet called Whitehorse Tavern in designation of its principal building. In the

---

[1] H. B. Binns, *A Life of Walt Whitman* (London, 1905), pp. 259-260.

[2] See Thomas Donaldson, *Walt Whitman, the Man* (N. Y., 1896), p. 40; John Johnston, and J. W. Wallace, *Visits to Walt Whitman in 1890-1891* (London, 1917), pp. 187-190; and Harrison S. Morris, *Walt Whitman* (Cambridge, Mass., 1929), p. 75.

[3] See Basil De Selincourt, *Walt Whitman* (N. Y., 1914); Cameron Rogers, *The Magnificent Idler* (N. Y., 1926); John Bailey, *Walt Whitman* (London, 1926); and Clara Barrus, *Whitman and Burroughs, Comrades* (N. Y., 1931).

[4] George R. Carpenter, *Walt Whitman* (N. Y., 1909), p. 144.

[5] Léon Bazalgette, *Walt Whitman: The Man and his Work*, trans. by Ellen Fitzgerald (N. Y., 1920), p. 260.

[6] Emory Holloway, *Whitman* (N. Y., 1926), p. 282.

interval the present town has grown up and absorbed the Stafford land; and Whitehorse is known only as the name of the turnpike which passes hard by and conducts the thousands of hurrying motor cars to Atlantic City, fifty miles away. Following the White-horse Pike from the toll-house in Camden exactly twelve miles, one observes a cross-road marked Laurel Springs. The town is scarcely visible, for it lies one-quarter of a mile to the south, among trees.

The Stafford farm now forms the southern portion of the town. The Stafford land has been subdivided into generous building lots for suburban dwellers and the "farm lane" of *Specimen Days* is now Maple Avenue. The Stafford farmhouse still stands, the oldest struc-ture in the neighborhood. Its date cannot be ascertained because of the fire which destroyed the early records of the township. It was an old house at the time of the earliest recorded conveyance in 1812. In spite of a modern wing at the rear, it is still a lovely old house, of white frame, with well proportioned gable-ends and an air of restful simplicity. The ancient floors within are built on several levels and the rooms are spacious. The handhewn planks, the venerable ma-sonry and the occasional remnant of antique hardware attest the age of the structure. Three patriarchal maples shade the lawn, and there are lilacs in the dooryard—an old hedge of them across the front.

It must be stressed that the reasons for a record of this place are not entirely sentimental. So much nonsense has been written about the insincerity of Whitman's biographical notes that it seems valu-able to substantiate them wherever possible. Besides this, there have been persistent efforts on the part of Whitman's detractors to in-validate his inspiration from nature, frequently on the ground that he lived most of his life in the city. This point of view fails to con-sider his boyhood on Long Island and his frequent visits to the home countryside as a young man; it also fails to take into account the summers on Timber Creek during a period when *Leaves of Grass* was in continual revision; yet a critic like Mr. Ernest Boyd could be beguiled into his recent statement that Whitman "surveyed nature from the top of a Broadway omnibus."

Those who hold such views should be forced, for their sins, to visit the Stafford farm with a copy of *Specimen Days* in their hands, and to see how accurately and minutely the poet described his environment there. Not only the lane, the creek, and the pond, but even some of the very trees, are still entirely recognizable these many years later. If we find such fidelity in the prose passages, may we not reason that the poet was equally faithful and sincere in his record of other natural experiences which we cannot substantiate? This, if proof were needed. Anyone who has ever watched birds, or loved flowers, or known the stretch of sand between the tides, would find the evidence of sincere experience in the leaves of grass which are the man. But apparently still the "trippers and askers" torment his memory as they tormented his life.

In 1876, as was said, the village of Laurel Springs was merely a post office at a cross-roads. Even today the Stafford house is on the outermost fringe of the tiny village, and the streets that have been opened through the old farm have brought but few houses to that end of the hamlet. Maple Avenue, which now passes before the house, is little more than the farm lane described in *Specimen Days*. A block westward, across the rustic wooden bridge over the railroad, it reverts suddenly to its earlier condition, and as one pursues it across the field and down the hillside toward the creek, there is little difficulty in identifying the place as described by the poet:[7]

A real farm-lane fenced by old chestnut-rails gray-green with dabs of moss and lichen, copious weeds and briars growing in spots athwart the heaps of stray-pick'd stones at the fence bases—irregular paths worn between, and horse and cow tracks—all characteristic accompaniments marking and scenting the neighborhood in their season—apple-tree blossoms in forward April—pigs, poultry, a field of August buckwheat, and in another the long flapping tassels of maize—and so to the pond, the expansion of the creek, the secluded-beautiful, with young and old trees, and such recesses and vistas.

There have been changes in a half-century, to be sure. The paths, the fruit-trees, the weeds and briars are still there, but the fields are now untilled and a profusion of wild flowers has replaced the maize and buckwheat, and the pigs are apparently without descendants. The general impression of the place is preserved, however. As one reaches the creek, and, turning to the right, follows

[7] *Prose Works* (Philadelphia, David McKay, n.d.), p. 118.

the path down to the pond, the foliage and trees become more and more dense. Here the passing years have not wrought very great changes. On the way one passes the spring already described and emerges, in a few hundred feet, on the shore of the pond. It is, as Whitman said, an "expansion of the creek" about a quarter of a mile broad and perhaps three-quarters of a mile long, but its margins are tortuous and indented with shy and sudden recesses, and the banks rise on every side in gentle and thickly-wooded hills. Across the pond a few summer cottages, perhaps a half-dozen, have been built, but the whole impression of the spot is still one of solitude only a little less deep than that described by the poet:[8]

The fervent heat, but so much more endurable in this pure air—the white and pink pond-blossoms, with great heart-shaped leaves; the glassy waters of the creek, the banks, with dense bushery, and the picturesque beeches and shade and turf; the tremulous, reedy call of some bird from recesses, breaking the warm, indolent, half-voluptuous silence; an occasional wasp, hornet, honey-bee or bumble (they hover near my hands or face, yet annoy me not, nor I them, as they appear to examine, find nothing, and away they go)—the vast space of the sky overhead so clear, and the buzzard up there sailing his slow whirl in majestic spirals and discs; just over the surface of the pond two large slate-color'd dragon-flies, with wings of lace, circling and darting and occasionally balancing themselves quite still, their wings quivering all the time (are they not showing off for my amusement?)—the pond itself, with the sword-shaped calamus; the water-snakes—occasionally a flittering blackbird, with red dabs on his shoulders, as he darts slantingly by—the sounds that bring out the solitude, warmth, light, shade—the quawk of some pond duck—(the crickets and grasshoppers are mute in the noon heat, but I hear the song of the first cicadas;)—then at some distance the rattle and whirr of a reaping machine as the horses draw it through a rye field on the opposite side of the creek—(what was the yellow or light-brown bird, large as a young hen, with short neck and long-stretched legs I just saw, in flapping and awkward flight over there through the trees?)—the prevailing delicate, yet palpable, spicy, grassy, clovery perfume to my nostrils; and over all, encircling all, to my sight and soul, the free space of the sky, transparent and blue—and hovering there in the west, a mass of white-gray fleecy clouds the sailors call "shoals of mackerel"—the sky, with silver swirls like locks of toss'd hair, spreading, expanding—a vast, voiceless, formless

[8] *Ibid.*, p. 88.

simulacrum—yet may-be the real reality and formulator of everything—
who knows?

Thus on a July day in 1877 the pond seemed to Walt Whitman;
and thus on another July day fifty-five years later it still appeared,
in spite of the thousands of automobiles that tore past this solitude
oblivious on the highway not two miles away. Hills and water,
dragon flies and bees, pond-lilies and clover perfume were there
unchanged. Even for a moment, dimly among the trees of the
farther shore, flitted the ghost of a mysterious light-brown bird.

It was a physical calamity that brought the good gray poet there,
an invalid, in 1876, at the age of fifty-seven. His exposures as a
volunteer hospital nurse during the Civil War had resulted in an
infection and a serious illness that weakened his stalwart constitution. Subsequently he had suffered a severe emotional shock which
resulted in paralysis. It was necessary for him to seek a leave of
absence from his clerical duties in Washington. It was then that
Camden, New Jersey, found a place on the American literary map.
Those who passed the window of George Whitman's house on
Stevens Street caught an impressive glimpse of the hair and beard
which were to mark the most picturesque citizen of Camden during
the next eighteen years.

This poet who had so courageously written, "I laugh at what
you call dissolution," would probably have been called upon to
resign life at its prime had it not been for the serene and healing
influence of nature which he experienced during the following summers on Timber Creek. What fortunate chance led him to find
the place and the hospitable family of George Stafford we do not
know, but in *Specimen Days*[9] he states his belief that they were
instrumental in his partial recovery and in the same passage he acknowledges the healing of nature as his final resource in his extremity. "After you have exhausted what there is," he wrote, "in
business, politics, conviviality, love—have found that none of these
finally satisfy or permanently wear—what remains? Nature remains; to bring out from the torpid recesses the affinities of a man
or woman with the open air, the trees, fields, the change of seasons—
the sun by day and the stars of heaven by night." In view of his

[9] *Ibid.*, pp. 81-82.

own testimony it seems important to record what can be learned from the few still alive who knew the poet in this place of healing, and to describe the place.

There were seven members of the Stafford family, including two daughters and three sons, Edwin, Harry, and Vandoran.[10] Mrs. Browning,[11] the younger of the two daughters, is still alive and resides in the neighborhood a few miles from the old farm. She has a great store of memories of this old time, now a half-century away; she, and others like Wesley Stafford, a cousin, and John Rowan,[12] now eighty-two, who worked on the Stafford farm as a young man. Their testimony substantiates the record of the poet in *Specimen Days*. But one also derives from conversation with these kindly old people a portrait of the poet himself as he survives in their memories: a serene, quiet, thoughtful man, gentle and sympathetic, who came to them from far places with a mind stored with information that they could not comprehend but that they respected, who dwelt in a realm of philosophical thought far above them, yet shared their lives and their thoughts as an equal as well. They all loved him. Apparently his serenity was undisturbed unless his privacy was invaded, and they were quick to respond to his need. Day after day they moved his chair farther from the house, down the long lane toward the creek,[13] and he marked his progress by trees. There they left him to himself. His strong spirit and the healing of nature accomplished the miracle. He recovered, very slowly, but perceptibly.

The mellowness of his nature in this affliction was the more remarkable when one considers the irony which he must have felt in the spectacle of his magnificent body prematurely broken. He had announced himself the "teacher of athletes," the poet of "the body equally with the soul." His philosophy had centered in the sublime rapport of body and spirit, until the two became merged, and he wrote,

And if the body were not the soul, what is the soul?

---

[10] John Johnston and J. W. Wallace, *op. cit.*, p. 184.

[11] *Ibid.*, p. 185.

[12] See Sculley Bradley, "Mr. Walter Whitman," *The Bookman*, LXXVI, 227-232 (March, 1933).

[13] John Johnston and J. W. Wallace, *op. cit.*, p. 187.

One might have expected a certain irritation from a man who had announced such doctrines, only to find his own body shattered and incapable, while his soul still abounded in energy for further flights. This was the poet, too, who had written of old age as the beautiful crown of life accomplished, who had welcomed "old age superbly rising" and the "ineffable grace of dying days." The old athlete could surely find little grace of any sort in his tottering and shrunken frame doomed to a wheel-chair and slow ossification.

In this extremity he fell back upon his enormous capacity for human love and poured out the best of himself upon the simple people whom he found in the Stafford family and among their neighbors. He realized fully that portrait of himself which he had drawn a score of years before as the friend "who was not proud of his songs, but of the measureless ocean of love within him, and freely poured it forth." It has seldom fallen to the lot of a philo-sophical poet to be put so thoroughly to the test of his theory and to survive the ordeal so successfully.

It has been said that he was greatly assisted by his love of nature, by a capacity for the observation of the minutest miracles of plant and animal life such as only Thoreau and Burroughs among his con-temporaries possessed. It was well that he was able to perceive even the simple leaves of grass as "so many uttering tongues," for at first his orbit was a small one. Yet within this orbit he observed closely and with returning strength he recorded his observations in the notes which later formed his prose sketches. He dwelt upon mul-leins and wild bees, blackberries and birds, the liquid syllables of the spring, clover and clouds, oaks and poplars and willows, butter-flies, and the "haughty, white-bodied, dark-wing'd hawk." These he incorporated into *Specimen Days*[14] as he stored his spirit with their strength.

Before the summer had passed he had progressed down the long lane by stages to the very brink of the brook[15] where he began to pull himself up with the help of the overarching branches of trees and to try his own legs for a few steps. Before long he was able to hobble a few yards down the stream, still on the Stafford farm, to the place where a fluent spring[16] of sweet water made a three-foot

[14] *Prose Works,* pp. 82-94.
[15] *Ibid.,* p. 94, "Nov. 14, as I sit here by the creek, resting after my walk. . . ."
[16] *Ibid.,* p. 83.

leap down a marl-bank into a boggy bed.   There, in the privacy of the thick shrubbery, he inaugurated the habit of nude sun-bathing and mud-bathing[17] that his physician had recommended. Removing his clothing with the aid of one of the Stafford boys,[18] he would bask in the sun, then cover himself with the rich mud and bake a while, and finally complete his ablutions beneath the icy cataract. In time this eccentricity gave rise to shocked rumors in the neighborhood.[19]   As poet or as man it was Whitman's fate to be ever too much in advance of the times.

The spring is dried up now, its waters diverted by the wells that have been sunk for the homes on the hills above.   But the stone arch and basin yet remain in the bank, the willows, shrubbery, and blackberry bushes are still thick; and as one stands there ankle-deep in the mud, which seems in every respect unimpaired, there is small difficulty in visualizing the place as Whitman gave it in *Specimen Days*:[20]

To the spring under the willows—musical as soft clinking glasses—pouring a sizeable stream, thick as my neck, pure and clear, out from its vent where the bank arches over like a great shaggy eye-brow or mouth-roof gurgling, gurgling ceaselessly—meaning, saying something, of course (if one could only translate it)—always gurgling there, the whole year through—never giving out—oceans of mint, blackberries in summer—choice of light and shade—just the place for my July sun-baths and water-baths too—but mainly the inimitable soft sound-gurgles of it, as I sit there on hot afternoons. How they and all grow into me, day after day—everything in keeping—the wild, just-palpable perfume, and the dapple of leaf-shadows, and all the natural-medicinal elemental-moral influences of the spot.

By the end of the summer of 1876 his condition was remarkably improved, and after a winter spent chiefly in the chair behind George Whitman's window in Camden, he returned in the spring of 1877 to the Staffords.[21]   Summer after summer he continued to return, and sometimes in the winter also, to restore his soul and his body by learning over again the simple ways that he had known as a boy on the farms and beaches of Long Island. Even amid the fret of

[17] *Ibid.*, pp. 103-104.
[18] Testimony of Mrs. Browning and John Rowan.
[19] *Ibid.*   [20] *Prose Works*, p. 83.
[21] *Ibid.*, Feb. 20 (p. 98), April 6 (p. 98), Feb. 22 (p. 99), May 21, and Aug. 26 (p. 101).

newspaper offices, the pungent and sickening odors of army hospitals, or the drab monotony of a clerk's life, these realities had never been far from his consciousness and had formed the rich sub-stratum from which his leaves of grass sprang so luxuriantly. It was through the dusty window of an editor's office that the poet had looked, twenty years earlier, as the chimney-pots faded into visions of his father's farm, and he had written,

> I am enamored of growing out-doors,
> Of men that live among cattle and taste of the ocean
> or woods.

Now once again he could realize the wish that he had expressed those many years before.

> I think I could turn and live with animals, they're so
> placid and self-contained,
> I stand and look at them long and long.
>
> They do not sweat and whine about their condition,
> They do not lie awake in the dark and weep for their
> sins,
> They do not make me sick discussing their duty to God,
> Not one is dissatisfied, not one is demented with the
> mania of owning things,
> Not one kneels to another, nor to his kind that lived
> thousands of years ago,
> Not one is respectable or unhappy over the whole earth.

Again "the procreant urge of the world" entered his blood and kindled his energies. In the second summer he devised an appropriate exercise for the development of his returning faculties, although he was again observed by the local gossips who were further confirmed in their opinion that this gentle eccentric "was not quite all there." He began to wrestle with trees.[22]

Once again we can find the record in a characteristic passage in *Specimen Days*. In order to understand the amazement of the local wits one has only to imagine what his own reactions might be were he to come suddenly in the woods upon the spectacle of a venerable gentleman with the hair and beard of Michaelangelo's

[22] *Ibid.*, pp. 98, 105.

Moses, engaged in single combat with a sapling and splitting the air with wild song. But so the poet describes it:[23]

A solitary and pleasant sundown hour at the pond, exercising arms, chest, my whole body, by a tough oak sapling thick as my wrist, twelve feet high—pulling and pushing, inspiring the good air. After I wrestle with the tree awhile, I can feel its young sap and virtue welling up out of the ground and tingling through me from crown to toe, like health's wine. Then for addition and variety I launch forth in my vocalism; shout declamatory pieces, sentiments, sorrow, anger, &c., from the stock poets or plays—or inflate my lungs and sing the wild tunes and refrains I heard of the blacks down south, or patriotic songs I learn'd in the army. I make the echoes ring, I tell you! As the twilight fell, in a pause of these ebullitions, an owl somewhere the other side of the creek sounded *too-oo-oo-oo-oo,* soft and pensive (and I fancied a little sarcastic) repeated four or five times. Either to applaud the negro songs—or perhaps an ironical comment on the sorrow, anger, or style of the stock poets.

As Whitman's strength returned and he began to go about unaided, if slowly, he took refuge again in his studying and his writings, composing many of the prose sketches which later appeared as *Specimen Days* and *Collect* in 1882.[24] He absorbed nature into himself and lived again. In a moment of ineffable beauty one of a beloved grove of trees leaned down to him to whisper, "We do all this on the present occasion, exceptionally, just for you." He became at one again with the "bare-bosomed night of the large few stars" and recorded in prose as he had in verse its perfection. "Perfect, or nearly perfect days, I notice, are not so very uncommon," he wrote. "But the combinations that make perfect nights are few, even in a life-time."[25] These, and other moods of nature he observed and recorded along Timber Creek. And here also he worked over, for two successive editions, the text of *Leaves of Grass*. At the Stafford house he received many guests. Traubel and Bucke and Harned and Donaldson were there frequently, and John Burroughs also came, as well as visitors from abroad, like Edward Carpenter, Mrs. Gilchrist, and others. Apparently the Stafford farm was as important a focus for the later life of the poet as the well-known house on Mickle Street, Camden.

[23] *Ibid.,* p. 98.
[24] Testimony of Mrs. Browning. [25] *Prose Works,* p. 118.

He continued going there for long vacations during ten years, and, according to Mrs. Browning and John Rowan, he brought with him the manuscripts on which he happened at the time to be engaged. Undoubtedly the serene influence of the spot, which he felt so keenly, entered into much of his revision and creation there. Even after George Stafford gave up the farm, about 1885, and went to keep store at Glendale, a cross-roads about four miles away, Whitman still continued to visit the family, and sent friends like Johnston and Wallace down to see them. When the Glendale house was destroyed by fire, early in 1933, it was erroneously reported in local papers that the "Whitman house" had gone. But a few with longer memories knew that the important landmark still stood.

One might expand much further the experiences of Walt Whitman with nature in this place—the birds and flowers and trees he listed, observed and studied, the days and nights he described—but they are all recorded in *Specimen Days*. But impermanent and perishable is the memory of Whitman still treasured by those few simple folk in the countryside who knew him well in the Timber Creek days. They have not read *Leaves of Grass,* or, like Peter Doyle and Whitman's mother and the other members of the great "en-masse" for whom he set out to write, they were forced to abandon the book as incomprehensible to them. But without at all knowing the reason for the questions asked them about Whitman's life in that place, they substantiated by their testimony his own record of his manner of life among them.[26] They knew him as one who loved them and whom they loved in spite of certain eccentricities which they could not understand. They still remember long conversations they had with him—his wisdom and his sympathy. The great artist will expect the immortality of his book; but to achieve nearly a half-century of tender memory in the minds of simple men is a much rarer tribute.

[26] See the interview with John Rowan, in "Mr. Walter Whitman," by Sculley Bradley, *The Bookman,* LXXVI, 229-232 (March, 1933).

Whitman's Conception of the Spiritual Democracy, 1855–1856
Henry Alonzo Myers

I

ALTHOUGH more than forty years have passed since Walt Whitman's death, his message has not yet become a part of our national cultural heritage. This loss to America is attributable to the failure of the average reader, and of many critics, to grasp the essential significance, the permanent element, in his writings. The literature of comment and controversy accumulated in his name has sometimes replaced old misinterpretations with new ones; more often it has perpetuated the good gray nonsense of tradition. Whitman's recent fame, like his earlier infamy, has been founded on the sands of changing literary and social conventions, for his notoriety has become fame only as the customs which he ignored have gone out of fashion; and his work, sometimes vilified, sometimes appreciated, has frequently been understood in its relations to other things rather than in its own inner meaning.

It has been his fate to be used as a means rather than to be considered as an end; his effigy, not the true Whitman, served as a central figure in two bloodless civil wars, fought for emancipation from the old literary forms and from the conceptions of sex current in the nineteenth century. A new and an incidental Whitman has been revealed with each change in popular interest, and the true Whitman, who might otherwise have been found in the text of his writings, has been obscured by the smoke of battle raised by his self-appointed disciples. Whitman remains, abroad and at home, the poet of political democracy and social freedom, the advocate of certain strange personal modes of behavior, in spite of the fact that a sober analysis of *Leaves of Grass* proves that the Whitman of 1855, convinced that he had a large mission to fulfill, brought to world literature a new and profound interpretation of life in terms of an inner, spiritual democracy, an interpretation which has often been so completely overlooked that Whitman's brief period of fame as the poet of adolescent America, already past its zenith, seems to approach decline. Nor will he remain the poet of the present and of the future as well as of the past, unless we turn our attention to this spiritual democracy, realizing that he is the poet, not of a social and economic period, but of an America that never dies.

Although few have yet shown an understanding of Whitman's mission and its fulfillment, the better part of the appreciation of his work has been based on a true feeling, an intuitive grasp, of his meaning. Emerson, in view of his lack of warmth toward the reformers of society, could hardly have greeted him warmly, as he did, at the beginning of a great career which was to consist merely of conflicts with convention. Nor could merely accidental elements in his writings have attracted Thoreau, Burroughs, Garland, Tennyson, and Swinburne, who were often repelled by his eccentricities and drawn back only by a feeling of his intrinsic greatness. This feeling indeed has doubtless haunted a host of other commentators, who, through their inability to express in rational discourse the deep meaning which they feel in Whitman's poetry, have been reduced from the position of critics to the level of the aesthetic chatterboxes who must express themselves by such banalities as Homeric or Cosmic.

It may well be that the correct interpretation of Whitman will eventually owe more to the frank opposition to the poet expressed by certain critics than to the often inchoate exposition of his admirers. Certainly, we can take no better starting-point than the question raised over thirty years ago by John Jay Chapman, a question he obviously thought only an idiot could answer in the affirmative: "Can the insulting jumble of ignorance and effrontery, of scientific phrase and French paraphrase, of slang and inspired adjective, which he [Whitman] puts forward with the pretence that it represents thought, be regarded, from any possible point of view, as a philosophy, or a system, or a belief?"[1] This question, since it immediately challenges the essential Whitman, is quite properly the question to have in mind throughout our undertaking.

If we call to mind Bacon's maxim that truth comes out of error more rapidly than out of confusion, we find further help in Santayana's *Interpretations of Poetry and Religion.* There we learn

[1] John Jay Chapman, *Emerson and Other Essays* (New York, 1898), p. 120.

that Whitman "basked in the sunshine of perception and wallowed in the stream of his own sensibility," that for him the world "has no inside," and that in his works "it is a phantasmagoria of continuous visions, vivid, impressive, but monotonous and hard to distinguish in memory."[2] We are indebted to the discrimination which Santayana brought to his task, for these statements are not confusion, but error; they are the exact opposites of the truth, and, as such, they point to the truth as clearly as ever error can.

We have then before us the very questions appropriate to our undertaking. What was Walt Whitman's mission? How did he fulfil it? Is it true that his world has no inside?

Let us first examine the inside of Walt Whitman's world. Most rationalists agree that the inside of the world of appearances or perceptions is not something that would prove tangible if we could reach it, like the kernel of a nut; they believe that the inside of a world of perceptions, always in a state of flux, must be some principle of permanence, for instance, a law or laws. Taking a typical list of perceptions from Walt Whitman, we find the poet looking through them to something akin to the inside of the rationalist's world.

> The sharp-hoofed moose of the north, the cat on the
>   house-sill, the chickadee, the prairie-dog . . .
> I see in them and myself the same old law.[3]

Or turning to the pages of "To Think of Time," we find that Whitman is quite as much given to listing the conceptions which make up the inside of his world as to listing the perceptions of the outside.

> The law of the past cannot be eluded!
> The law of the present and future cannot be eluded!
> The law of the living cannot be eluded—it is eternal!
> The law of promotion and transformation cannot be eluded!
> The law of heroes and good-doers cannot be eluded!
> The law of drunkards, informers, mean persons, cannot be eluded![4]

These verses are in themselves sufficient to show that Whitman lived in a world having an inside as well as an outside, and that he

---

[2] George Santayana, *Interpretations of Poetry and Religion* (New York, 1900), p. 180.
[3] *Leaves of Grass* (Brooklyn, New York, 1856), p. 22. The text of the poetry quoted in this paper, with the exception of the titles, is from this edition.
[4] *Ibid.*, pp. 338-339.

recognized the importance of this inner world. Indeed, we shall
find that this world is uppermost in his thought, that it is the very
reason and justification for the presentation of a world of experience.

His method of communicating this world is that of giving
selected pictures from his own experience. In this method he has
the greatest confidence; although he speaks again and again of "the
same old law" which he finds in his own experience, the thought of
systematically formulating this law never occurs to him. He furnishes us with the materials; we must see the law as he has seen it,
feel it as he has felt it. As he tells us in the preface to *November
Boughs* (1888), his purposes were always implicit rather than explicit. "After completing my poems," he says, "I am curious to
review them in the light of their own (at the time unconscious, or
mostly unconscious) intentions, with certain unfoldings of the thirty
years they seek to embody."[5] And as we read the two important
prefaces to his poems (of 1855 and 1888), we realize that these
purposes never became explicit in his mind, that he could never
formulate them systematically. For this he had no gift; when he
tries to tell us in prose what his purposes are, he is apt to overlook
the significance of his own verses: his attempt at explanatory prose
simply becomes more poetry, as is evident from the ease with which
he recast the 1855 preface into three new poems a year later.

In 1855 indeed he was able to sum up his notion of the function
of the poet, although he was unable to develop his statement sufficiently to make it clear. "Of all mankind," he wrote, "the great
poet is the equable man. Not in him but off from him things are
grotesque or eccentric or fail of their sanity. Nothing out of its
place is good and nothing in its place is bad. He bestows on every
object or quality its fit proportions neither more nor less."[6] This,
which might pass for an expression of democracy or mere indolence,
rightly understood is not far from the genius attributed to Sophocles,
"who saw life steadily and saw it whole." The right interpretation
of this conception of the great poet's function shows us something
far different from a desire to bask in perceptual sunshine; we detect

---

[5] In "Inclusive Edition," *Leaves of Grass,* ed. Emory Holloway (New York, 1927), p.
522. *November Boughs,* 1888, p. 5.
[6] *Leaves of Grass,* ed. Holloway, p. 491.

a yearning to get beyond the evaluations of finite existence and to apprehend the perfection of everything in its place. For who has come closer to Spinoza's *intellectualis amor Dei* than has Whitman in the 1855 preface? "The known universe," he says, "has one complete lover and that is the greatest poet. He consumes an eternal passion and is indifferent which chance happens and which possible contingency of fortune or misfortune and persuades daily and hourly his delicious pay."[7] Certainly, if the world of Whitman has no inside, the world of Spinoza is equally vacuous. But, as we shall see, Whitman's world has an inside warmer in human values than the cold necessity which lies at the heart of Spinoza's.

The importance of the inner world to Whitman is apparent in the fact that he has gone beyond the middle of the 1855 preface before he turns aside to discuss, as a secondary topic, political liberty and equality. It is made further apparent when we note the contrast between the just equality of men proclaimed as an *eternal law* in his poetry and the political inequality discovered by his sober and critical analysis of the American experiment in *Democratic Vistas*. In the preface (1855) Whitman insists again and again that the perfect poet will find all beings equal in his eyes, *not in society,* but in the inner world. In order to discover this equality the poet must pierce through the surface to the inside. "The poets of the kosmos advance through all interpositions and coverings and turmoils and stratagems to first principles."[8] The first principle of equality is to be seen first by the poet (Whitman in this preface compares the poetic faculty to clear vision). He retained this conception of the poet's function in looking back over his completed work. "Whatever may have been the case in years gone by, the true use for the imaginative faculty of modern times is to give ultimate vivification to facts, to science, and to common lives, endowing them with glows and glories and final illustriousness which belong to every real thing, and to real things only."[9] This preoccupation with first principles, this yearning to see all things as they really are, this earnest exhortation to pierce all outward coverings and turmoils is the keynote in the preface to the poetry of a barbarian wallowing in the stream of his own sensibility, a barbarian whose world "has no inside"!

[7] *Ibid.,* p. 494.
[8] *Ibid.,* p. 500.
[9] *Ibid.,* p. 525.

But when we examine the poetry itself, especially the poems of
1855 and 1856, we are grateful to Santayana for turning our attention to the inside of Whitman's world. We rub our eyes. Why
have we so long missed this plainly written message?

II

Giving up the notion that the Civil War brought Whitman to
poetic maturity, let us consider the poems in the 1855 edition in their
proper order, holding in mind Whitman's contention that the poet's
function is to see things clearly and to reveal that *eternal* equality of
beings which may be known by seeing each thing in its place and
as it really is. Here, if anywhere, we shall find the immediate result
of that mental simmering which had recently been brought to a
boil.

The first poem, "Walt Whitman," long famous as the anthem of
provincial egotism, proves a perfect expression of the transcendentalist's method of belief, just as *Cogito, ergo sum* is the starting-point
of Descartes's method of doubt. In the attempt to see things as they
really are, what is more natural than that the poet, like the philosopher, should start with what is nearest at hand, himself? The
poem is a progressive attempt to define or understand one real thing,
Walt Whitman.

"What is a man anyhow? What am I? What are you?"[10] The
answer is well known to anyone who has read the poem. A man is
not something small, contained within an impermeable shell, and
set off against a world order.

I pass death with the dying, and birth with the new-washed babe, and
   am not contained between my hat and boots. . . .[11]

Who is Walt Whitman? He is infinite; he is of the past and of the
present and future, of the old and of the young; his personality
admits no barriers; he sees through good and evil, through space
and time. He pervades everything, becomes everything; he has died
a thousand deaths; he has carefully considered you before you were
born. He will admit no limitations.

This splendid poem proceeds in the most concrete manner imag-
inable through great sweeping enumerations of the things with

[10] *Leaves of Grass* (1856), p. 32.   [11] *Ibid.*, p. 14.

which Whitman identifies himself, not by logical argument, but by a sympathy and understanding which have seldom been equaled. It is splendid poetry; at the same time it comes very close to the most famous philosophical theories of what the self is or ought to be. Putting this imaginative insight into matter-of-fact terms, we find that for Whitman a man is not an empty something that has experiences; a man is rather the sum total of his experiences. A man is as unlimited as his experience; in thought he is the whole world; everything that comes within his experience is a part of him, and even things of which he is not explicitly or immediately aware, the past and the future, are also parts of him. "The world," said Schopenhauer, "is my idea." Were we looking for terms to explain Spinoza's notion of the ideal self or Hegel's notion of the escape from the state of isolation and "unhappy consciousness" by identification of self with reality, we should not need to change any term in Whitman's conception.

Emerson wrote in his diary (1840): "In all my lectures, I have taught one doctrine, namely, the infinitude of the private man."[12] Whitman very probably took over this idea from Emerson without being consciously aware of it; he derived the spirit rather than a formal doctrine from the master, and he embodied this spirit according to his own peculiar talents. It emerges as the infinite and self-contained person, who is the sum total of his experiences. Such is the conception which Whitman sets over against the "featherless biped" of the logicians and the "political animal" of those whose world has a social surface but no inside.

Thus the idea of an unlimited personality is the first principle of *Leaves of Grass*. It is accompanied at every point by the further principle of equality, for it is not only Walt Whitman who is an unlimited, all-embracing personality. The very opening verses make this assertion:

> I celebrate myself,
> And what I assume you shall assume;
> For every atom belonging to me, as good belongs to you.[13]

Taken out from the poetry and set up as theory, the grounds on which he asserts this equality are not illogical. Equality exists only

[12] *Emerson's Journals*, ed. E. W. Emerson and R. W. Forbes (New York, 1911), V, 380.
[13] *Leaves of Grass* (1856), p. 5.

in a world of unlimited personalities. How can one unlimited personality be either more or less than another? This argument, expressed in accordance with his method, may be found in the verses made out of the 1855 preface:

> Have you thought there could be but a single Supreme?
> There can be any number of Supremes—one does not
>   countervail another any more than one eye-sight
>   countervails another, or one life countervails another.[14]

Undoubtedly this concept of equality had its origin in the surface world of American democracy, where it had been an ideal since the Declaration of Independence. But with Whitman equality is much more than a political ideal; it is an *eternal fact* in the real world of unlimited personalities; it is a great first principle.

> In all people I see myself—none more, and not one a barleycorn less,
> And the good or bad I say of myself, I say of them.[15]

Equality of this kind, a real equality between unlimited personalities, is discovered only by piercing through the coverings and turmoils to the insides of beings. Out of the American democracy of 1855, Walt Whitman constructed an inner complement to the outer world, a spiritual democracy governed by two principles, one the unlimited individual, the other the equality of individuals. Finding these principles in the poems is not a matter of judiciously choosing apt quotations; on the contrary, there is nothing in the 1855 and 1856 *Leaves* which does not follow *a priori* from them. Once they are clearly grasped, we soon find that each verse contributes something to them, that each verse is an attempt to read these inner principles through the maze and confusion of life on the surface. Once we grasp the true nature of these principles, realizing that they are, first and foremost, principles of the spiritual democracy and only secondarily slogans of the social democracy, we no longer see Walt Whitman's poems as a mere catalogue of perceptions, nor as a mere satisfaction in his own sensibility; moreover, we discover that many of his themes, which have hitherto seemed related only to his eccentricities, are direct consequents of these principles. Why is he the poet of the body as well as of the soul? Why is he the poet of death

---

[14] *Ibid.*, p. 181.   [15] *Ibid.*, p. 34.

as well as of life? Why is he the poet of evil as well as of good? A further consideration of the poems of 1855 in their proper order answers these questions and reveals Whitman's method of establishing and demonstrating the principles of the inner world.

The second poem, "A Carol of Occupations," presents an antithesis between people as they appear in society and as they really are, an antithesis between the surface classification of people as mechanics, laborers, Presidents, drunkards, thieves, or prostitutes, and people as the equal, infinite personalities of the spiritual democracy. Surface classifications are actual; they mean something; we must not resign ourselves fatalistically to any position or place in society.

I do not affirm what you see beyond is futile—I do not advise you to stop,
I do not say leadings you thought great are not great,
But I say that none lead to greater, sadder, happier, than those lead to.[16]

Nevertheless, we must not lose sight of the inner side of the world, the first principles of infinitude and equality. In society obvious differences exist between the laborer and the President, between the Magdalen and the Madonna; these, however, are the surface turmoils and coverings; underneath them lies the community of equal and infinite souls, equal and infinite in that each soul is commensurate with the world: "you and your soul enclose all things, regardless of estimation. . . ."[17] No occupation can limit the soul; no occupation can deprive it of participation in the principles of the inner world.

In the third poem, "To Think of Time," Whitman faces one of the most difficult problems of his attempt to shadow forth the reality of persons. We cannot think of ourselves as unlimited while we yet look upon ourselves as identified with a particular time, a definite span of years.

Have you guessed you yourself would not continue? Have you dreaded
    these earth-beetles?
Have you feared the future would be nothing to you?[18]

His answer to these questions is in keeping with the best traditions of philosophy; he pierces through the outward antinomy and mystery of time and subjects himself, and all others, to eternal law.

[16] *Ibid.*, p. 138.
[17] *Ibid.*, p. 138.
[18] *Ibid.*, p. 332.

I have dreamed that we are not to be changed so much, nor the law of us
    changed,
I have dreamed that heroes and good-doers shall be under the present and
    past law,
And that murderers, drunkards, liars, shall be under the present and past
    law,
For I have dreamed that the law they are under now is enough.[19]

In bringing the individual under this law, he gets beyond the limitations of the present by including in the individual's present the past
and the future, each governed by the same old law. This eternal
law is in a sense the essence of the soul.

> I swear I think now that every thing has an eternal soul! . . .
> I swear I think there is nothing but immortality![20]

In respect to the spiritual democracy the fourth poem, "The
Sleepers," presents a vision of people, unequal according to surface
classifications, made equal by night and sleep.

The laugher and weeper, the dancer, the midnight widow, the red squaw,
The consumptive, the erysipalite, the idiot, he that is wronged,
The antipodes, and every one between this and them in the dark,
I swear they are averaged now—one is no better than the other,
The night and sleep have likened them and restored them.[21]

In "I Sing the Body Electric," the fifth poem, Whitman looks
through a surface of turmoils and coverings which has largely disappeared since his time. We are less inclined than the men of 1855
to identify ourselves with a soul conceived of as independent of, and
superior to, the body, and it is difficult for us to see why Whitman
should have been condemned for a gross apotheosis of the body.
The fact is that he intends only to make clear his point that nothing,
not even the body, can limit an infinite person or destroy his equality
with other infinite persons. The body is gross and ugly only to
those who will not see their unlimited nature, for the body, as an
experience, becomes a part of the soul, just as the whole world
becomes a part of the soul.

O I think these are not the parts and poems of the body only, but of the
    soul,
O I think these are the soul![22]

---

[19] *Ibid.*, p. 340.
[20] *Ibid.*, p. 342.
[21] *Ibid.*, p. 298.
[22] *Ibid.*, p. 179.

The sixth poem, "Faces," is another concrete expression of the antithesis between the appearances and inequalities of the surface world and the first principles of the inner world.

Sauntering the pavement or riding the country by-road, here then are faces!
Faces of friendship, precision, caution, suavity, ideality. . . .
The ugly face of some beautiful soul, the handsome detested or despised face. . . .[23]

On the surface, if one wallows in perception only, these faces are marked by their inequalities and differences. In the light of the inner meaning of life, however:

Features of my equals, would you trick me with your creased and cadaverous march?
Well, you cannot trick me.
I see your rounded never-erased flow,
I see neath the rims of your haggard and mean disguises.[24]

In the "Song of the Answerer," which in 1856 he called "The Poem of the Poet," he announced the qualities of the perfect poet, which flow naturally from his faith in the inner principles establishing all men as his brothers and equals. The power of the perfect poet lies in his ability to translate all languages into his own and to project himself into the very being of his equals. The perfect poet will be known to the mechanic as a mechanic, to the legislator as a legislator, to the Englishman as an Englishman, to the German as a German. Since his native language is the inner language of eternal principles, he will have the gift of tongues; since his eyes have read the essence of man, he can be to every man what that man is to himself.

Between this poem and the tenth, which returns to the first principles, Whitman inserted the only two poems in the volume which have nothing to do with the unfolding of the spiritual democracy. Both are earlier poems. "Europe," the eighth poem, was written in 1850 to commemorate the recent revolution; "A Boston Ballad," the ninth poem, was written in 1854.

In the tenth poem, "There Was a Child Went Forth," Whitman

---

[23] *Ibid.*, p. 302.   [24] *Ibid.*, p. 304.

recapitulates the principle of the infinitude of the individual by
furnishing a concrete example of the manner in which the soul
absorbs the whole world, in the form of experience, into itself.

There was a child went forth every day,
And the first object he looked upon and received with wonder, pity, love,
    or dread, that object he became . . .
The early lilacs became part of this child . . .
The horizon's edge, the flying sea-crow, the fragrance of salt-marsh and
    shore-mud;
These became part of that child who went forth every day, who now
    goes, and will always go forth every day.[25]

The eleventh poem, "Who Learns my Lesson Complete," is an
affirmation of the mystery and wonder of that eternal law by virtue
of which a man, contained in the life of the surface between hat and
boots, is taken out of himself and placed eternally in the community
of infinite individuals; its purpose is to lead up to the twelfth and
last poem of the 1855 edition, "Great are the Myths." This poem is
an affirmation of the wide world and of all things, rightly understood, that are in it. Great, says Whitman, are all things: myths,
nations, men of all kinds, youth, age, wealth, poverty, life, and
death, for all these things of the surface make manifest the law and
justice of the universe. Great is political democracy because it will
rule the world in imitation of the eternal first principles. The surface of the world shall imitate, as ideals, the eternal laws of the
inner world. "The new rule" (political democracy) "shall rule as
the Soul rules, and as the love, justice, equality" (eternal principles
in the spiritual democracy) "in the Soul rule!" "Great is Law," and
"Great is Justice," for justice is the true meaning of the inner law;
it is the true significance of the equality of infinite individuals. Justice is contained in the principle of the soul; "it is immutable—it
does not depend on majorities."[26]

Thus, in pondering the eternal nature of law and justice, he
reaches the central principle of the inner world. He was not altogether unaware of what he had done. In 1888, looking back over
his work, he could find one "purpose enclosing all, and over and
beneath all." This purpose has ruled all his thought. "Ever since
what might be call'd thought, or the budding of thought, fairly be-

[25] *Ibid.*, pp. 282-285.   [26] *Leaves of Grass*, ed. Holloway, p. 467.

gan in my youthful mind, I had had a desire to attempt some worthy
record of that entire faith and acceptance ('to justify the ways of
God to man' is Milton's well-known and ambitious phrase) which is
the foundation of moral America."[27]

This affirmation of all things grasped as manifestations of eternal
justice brings to a close Whitman's interpretation of life in terms of
an inner, spiritual democracy. Although his remarkably stubborn
and tenacious consistency never permitted him to contradict a single
principle laid down in 1855, he never again painted the picture in its
artistic entirety. He had so completely sketched in the outline of his
system in the poems of the first edition that he could not, without
contradiction, produce anything further, apart from expansion,
repetition, and development. His system of thought—for, to answer
Chapman's helpful question, it is as much a system as any poetic
insight not subjected to logical discipline can be—was as complete
at the end of "Great are the Myths" as was Milton's at the completion of *Paradise Regained;* and the unity of thought manifest in
the ten significant poems of 1855, added to their original lack of
titles, suggests that they might have been woven into one long epic,
if Whitman had not been converted to Poe's theory that long poems
are not suited to modern needs.

His system differs from Milton's as a *cosmodicy* differs from a
theodicy, for Whitman's problem was to justify the ways of the
world to man. In order to justify these ways of the outer world he
produced a picture of that inner world which Santayana was unable
to discover in his poetry, a picture of a community of infinite individuals ruled by an eternal and just law of equality. But we must
not invert Santayana's error by thinking that Whitman lived in an
inner world only. While he maintained that the justice of life is
established by the equality of infinite personalities, he sought also to
see this inner principle always in relation to the surface problems of
society.

Once we realize that Whitman is talking about an inner democracy of the spirit, we eliminate two widely accepted interpretations
of his work. These interpretations presented Whitman as a blind
optimist, as one who could in a poetic trance lose sight of the evil
and imperfection everywhere experienced, as one who could shut

[27] *Ibid.,* p. 534.

his eyes to political corruption and to the cost of the Civil War in order to proclaim that America is the best of all possible societies. He did not, however, think that political democracy had been perfectly instituted in his own time; he did not even have a vision of its future perfection; in Whitman's terminology perfection is not attributed to things of the surface.

Three poems written in 1856 deserve mention. A further point in establishing equality as the inner meaning of the world is made in "Unfolded out of the Folds":

A man is a great thing upon the earth, and through eternity—but every
     jot of the greatness of man is unfolded out of woman,
First the man is shaped in the woman, he can then be shaped in himself.[28]

This poem brings out one aspect of Whitman; namely, his feminism, but it serves the better purpose of pointing out the fallacy of confusing the incidental with the real Whitman, for the poem obviously springs not from devotion to feminism but from a recognition that women also share in the community of equal persons. Whitman never attacked a convention merely for the sake of reform; he attacked only those conventions which stood in the way of his vision of reality.

In "Salut au Monde" Whitman makes it unmistakably clear that the community of infinite persons includes not only the citizens of the United States but all human beings. He leaves the shores of his native land, travels everywhere, and everywhere illustrates his poetic equivalent of the logical argument for equality. He does not say, I am the equal of that man; he says, I am that man; and he says it of all the people of the earth.

My spirit has passed in compassion and determination around the whole
     earth,
I have looked for brothers, sisters, lovers, and found them ready for me
     in all lands. . . .[29]

This power of identifying himself with others is fully revealed in "Crossing Brooklyn Ferry." Truly he can say to men of generations to come that time and space do not keep him from them. He has seen, felt, heard, and touched what they in turn will see, feel, hear, and touch. He is one with each of them, and equal to each,

[28] *Leaves of Grass* (1856), p. 102.   [29] *Ibid.*, p. 120.

for that self-same world of experience has become his very soul which will in turn become the very soul of each of them. He can say to all the items and objects and sensations of the world in his own name and in the name of men of all generations:

We descend upon you and all things, we arrest you all,
We realize the soul only by you, you faithful solids and fluids. . . .
You furnish your parts toward eternity,
Great or small, you furnish your parts toward the soul.[30]

Although Whitman's vision of the inner world grew dimmer as years passed, it rarely grew sufficiently dim to permit self-contradiction. The outlines of the spiritual democracy were so firmly embedded in his art in the years 1855-1856 that they ever afterward demanded a consistency which we do not fail to find in his reaction to the Civil War, in his elegies, and in his general development of *Leaves of Grass*.

[30] *Ibid.*, pp. 221-222.

The Fundamental Metrical Principle in Whitman's Poetry
Sculley Bradley

"THE WORLD," wrote John Burroughs,[1] "always has trouble with its primary men, or with the men who have any primary gifts. . . . The idols of an age are nearly always secondary men: they break no new ground. . . . The primary men disturb us. . . ." According to this standard Whitman's claim to primary rank as an artist is established by seventy-five years of controversy among critics of his verse. Even to this day no general agreement has been reached concerning the exact nature and effect of Whitman's experiments in verse.

Whitman himself realized what a problem his work presented to the critic. "I will certainly elude you," he predicted. He shared with other great artists the instinct to avoid defining himself, knowing that a work of art is indefinable and illimitable in effect. To his notebook he confided the resolve to write "for the five or six grand poets, and the masters of artists. I waste no ink, nor my throat, on the ever-deploying armies of professors, authors, lawyers, teachers and what not. Of them we expect that they be very learned, and nothing more."

Yet the work of the "ever-deploying army" has been ceaseless, and it has contributed to a strengthening of the poet's reputation and to a deeper understanding of his meaning. It would seem that we are now within measurable distance of a satisfactory rationale of Whitman's verse. The general recognition of a fundamental metrical form in his verse will enormously increase the value of Whitman to his readers.

We can at once discard many of the theories advanced in the past and still maintained by certain critics: that he was an artist "by a sort of divine accident" and "equally pleased with himself when . . . he was not an artist or poet at all . . .;[2] that he wrote Ossianic or "prose-poetry";[3] that his line is a sort of "ruined blank-verse";[4] that

[1] *Whitman* (Boston, 1904), pp. 22-23.
[2] John Bailey, *Walt Whitman* (London, 1926), p. 83.
[3] Bliss Perry, *Walt Whitman* (Boston, 1906), pp. 84-86.
[4] *Ibid.*, p. 82.

he substituted for vocalic accent the "pitch-glides of prose";[5] and that he merely wrote in balanced logical units.[6] That the last two theories are in the direction of the truth we shall see. It seems also clear that the many critics who have found the basis for Whitman's verse in oratory[7] or in Hebrew poetry as translated in the English Bible[8] have suggested fundamental principles.

Yet as a rule these writers have confined themselves either to generalizations or to a study of Whitman's obvious use of logical balance and parallelism. No explanation of the rhythmical regularity in his verse, except that accompanied by logical recurrence, has been attempted. Yet it must be clear to any sensitive reader of *Leaves of Grass* that the principle of regularity is operative even when it is not induced by return or repetition of a phrase. Almost no attention has been given to the insistent question: what is the fundamental principle of rhythm or meter which Whitman substituted for syllable-counting in his lines; by what means is this rhythm indicated; how general was his practice of it? I believe it can be shown that the poet employed without deviation the same principle throughout, and that this is the most primitive and persistent characteristic of English poetic rhythm, rather than a new development from prose rhythms.

This view is based upon a fundamental consideration concerning rhythm and meter. It is universally accepted that all speech, whether prose or poetry, has rhythm; that the emotional and imaginative speech of poetry tends toward regularity; and that meter is a highly regulated, patterned or predictable rhythmic recurrence. What has divided the prosodists and frequently puzzled the poets, is the question, *What recurs?* What is the essential rhythmic index of our poetry? Are we to think of a patterned recurrence of long and short syllables as the foundation of meter, or is it rather the regulation of a principal stress or beat, occurring at regular intervals of

[5] Fred N. Scott, "A Note on Whitman's Rhythm," *J. E. G. P.*, VII, 134-153 (1908).

[6] Basil De Selincourt, *Walt Whitman: A Critical Study* (London, 1914), pp. 96-97.

[7] See George R. Carpenter, *Walt Whitman* (New York, 1909), pp. 42-43; Thomas B. Harned, "Walt Whitman and Oratory," *Complete Writings* (10 vols., New York, 1902), *Prose IV;* H. B. Binns, *A Life of Walt Whitman* (London, 1905), p. 98; Clifton J. Furness, *Walt Whitman's Workshop* (Cambridge, Mass., 1928), p. 27; Jean Catel, *Rhythme et langage dans l'édition des "Leaves of Grass," 1855* (Montpellier, 1930).

[8] See Perry, *op. cit.*, pp. 86 and 96; De Selincourt, *op. cit., passim;* A. N. Wiley, "Reiterative Devices in *Leaves of Grass*," *American Literature*, I, 161-170 (May, 1929); Gay W. Allen, *American Prosody* (New York, 1935), "Walt Whitman."

time? Every historian and critic of English poetry is aware of the enormous importance of this fundamental problem. On the surface, the question appears very simple, yet it has been the cause of continuous disagreement among critics and prosodists.

The beginning of the confusion in the case of Whitman, may be traceable to the poet's practice, so natural to a revolutionist, in overestimating the completeness of his revolt. One would think, from certain of his statements, that he had embraced artistic anarchy and lawlessness. "Many trouble themselves about conforming to laws. A great poet is followed by laws—they conform to him."[9] To a generation bred on the idea that conventional, syllabic meter was the absolute outward sign of the inward grace of poetry, Whitman's determined stand against the usual meters, which he likened to "lulling piano-tunes,"[10] his reiterated intention "to let nature speak without check, with original energy," seemed an artistic indecency. Most of his readers—indeed, even most of the critics—were too little acquainted with the true nature and history of English rhythm to recognize, beneath the disguise of innovation, the rugged face of a well-known English ancient.

Again and again Whitman explained his substitute for what he considered arbitrary meter, and affirmed that his rhythmical device was closer to nature. "The truest and greatest poetry, (*while subtly and necessarily always rhythmic,* and distinguishable easily enough) can never again, in the English language, be expressed in arbitrary metre," he declared in *Collect.* He had made a personal memorandum recalling that he had learned the trick of his rhythm by "spouting" Homer and Shakespeare to the waves of the sea.[11] In an unpublished preface, quoted by Bliss Perry,[12] occurs the statement that his lines are apparently "lawless at first perusal, although on closer examination a certain regularity appears, like the recurrence of lesser and larger waves on the sea-shore, rolling in without intermission, and fitfully rising and falling."[13] Burroughs,[14] in his artist's rapport with the spirit of nature, saw that Whitman's rejection of "the old forms," as he called them, was "only equivalent to the abandonment

[9] *Complete Writings* (1902), VI, 39.
[10] "To a Certain Civilian," *Leaves of Grass* (Incl. ed.), p. 272.
[11] Furness, *op. cit.,* p. 28.   [12] *Op. cit.,* p. 207.
[13] An extension of this illustration occurs in Horace Traubel, *With Walt Whitman in Camden,* I, 414-415.
[14] "Walt Whitman and His Art," *Poet Lore,* VI, 64 (Feb., 1894).

of vestments, sacraments and rituals in religion, and relying solely
on the spontaneous motions of the spirit," and Trent[15] pointed out
that the rhythm of Whitman's verses was unlike either prose rhythm
in general or the rhythm of Whitman's prose in particular. Yet the
old error, that Whitman's rhythm is derived from prose, persisted,
and is shown in Bliss Perry's completely mistaken analysis.[16] The
most entirely satisfactory clue to his prosody was given in the very
beginning by the poet himself, in the Preface to the 1855 edition of
Leaves of Grass: "The rhyme and uniformity of perfect poems show
the free growth of metrical laws and bud from them as unerringly
and loosely as lilacs or roses on a bush, and take shapes as compact
as the shapes of chestnuts and oranges and melons and pears, and
shed the perfume impalpable to form."[17]

The poet was not expressing a completely new and original ideal,
although he acted upon it perhaps more fully than any previous
artist had done. The same principle had been inherent in much of
the theory which actuated the earlier romantic movement. Coleridge might have been speaking directly for Whitman in his lecture
on "Shakespeare, a Poet Generally" when, in praise of Shakespeare's
freedom of form, he made his distinction between "mechanic" and
"organic" form. The latter was the mark of truly original greatness.
"The form is mechanic," he wrote, "when on any given material we
impress a pre-determined form, not necessarily arising out of the
properties of the material;—as when to a mass of wet clay we give
whatever shape we wish it to retain when hardened. The organic
form, on the other hand, is innate; it shapes, as it develops, itself
from within, and the fulness of its development is one and the same
with the perfection of its outward form. Such as the life is, such is
the form. Nature, the prime genial artist, inexhaustible in diverse
powers, is equally inexhaustible in forms;—each exterior is the
physiognomy of the being within—its true image reflected and
thrown out from the concave mirror;—and even such is the appropriate excellence of her chosen poet. . . ." This seems to express
completely the ideal which Whitman practiced so steadily to perfect
in the form of his verse.

[15] W. P. Trent, *A History of American Literature* (New York, 1903), p. 494.
[16] *Op. cit.,* pp. 81-96, *passim.*
[17] See, for a similar statement, *In Re Walt Whitman,* ed. Traubel, Bucke and Harned
(Philadelphia, 1893), p. 16.

That the organic theory of compositon had influenced Whitman[18] profoundly is shown by a study of the rhythm of his individual lines. Perhaps even more strikingly it is demonstrated by an analysis of the longer sections of composition which he substituted for more conventional and traditional stanzas. Although he nowhere speaks of his artistic devices as being "organic," he continuously refers to them as being based upon nature itself. It seems clear that the critical principle, originating in the rise of romanticism in Germany, had somehow reached Whitman. It is unlikely that he had derived it directly from such German critics as Herder, Schelling, or Goethe, although his notes refer to the reading of works of Goethe and Friedrich Schlegel. However, the organic theory had such a wide currency in romanticism that the quest for an immediate source is not perhaps necessary. To seek no further, Whitman must have become well aware of this critical attitude in the work of Emerson, Carlyle, and Coleridge, with which he was familiar.

To achieve this impalpable subtlety of form, this rhythmic shape of nature, required endless rewriting and revision, both in manuscript and between successive editions. Every close student of Whitman's manuscripts and of the variorum readings has perceived the poet's increasing sensitiveness to a rhythmical principle. That this principle was rooted in the very nature of English speech, and had been employed in English poetry, especially in popular poetry, continuously since the Old English period, is the fact that seems to have escaped critical attention.

It has been pointed out that so much emphasis has been laid upon the classical ancestry of our English prosody that criticism has frequently lost sight of the earlier and very strong Germanic and Old English ancestry. The classical system employed a rhythm based on the inherent quantity, long or short, contained in the syllables of words. But the English language largely lacked from the beginning, and subsequently lost entirely, the fixed quantities which rendered the classical system rational. Old English poetry did not, and could not, regulate itself by counting syllables. Quantity was

[18] Since this article was written, Mr. Fred W. Lorch has published an article, "Thoreau and the Organic Principle in Poetry," *PMLA*, LIII, 286-302 (March, 1938), in which is given an interesting account of the manner in which identical influences operated in the case of Thoreau.

felt as the duration of time elapsing between stresses, and this
elapsed time was a relatively fixed interval throughout the entire
extent of any composition. Between stresses the number of unstressed syllables was variable. Such a verse as the following, in
which the number of syllables between principal stresses varies from
one to four, is not unusual:

Ic þaet hogode þa ic on holm gestah[19]

What is not generally recognized is that the prosodic principles
represented by that line have survived throughout the history of our
poetry. The amount of freedom in respect to syllabic regularity in
the poetry of various periods of English poetry bears direct relationship to the strength or weakness of classicism at the time. From the
beginning of the romantic movement onward, freedom in respect to
syllabic regularity has increased, partly as a result of the influence
of the popular ballad, in which the Old English tendency persisted
strongly.[20] Walt Whitman's verse merely marked an extreme instance of the general evolution. Unfortunately for the reception of
Leaves of Grass, most critics and prosodists have been of the classical
school. Even so clear an exposition as that of T. S. Omond[21] of the
freedom in English meter resulting from the compromise between
the Old English and the classical prosody, has been lost sight of by
recent writers.

In connection with this entire question it is interesting first to
observe that Whitman obviously intended his lines to be read aloud;
that he wrote for the ear and not for the eye. This, of course, should
be true of all poetry. Yet one observes in English poetry through
the ages that the more "popular" it is, or the more closely connected
with an oral tradition, the more prevalent is the tendency to discard
the counting of syllables and to regulate rhythm by the interval of
elapsed time between stresses—what Mr. Omond conveniently calls
the "period." The first evidence of Whitman's determination to appeal to the ear rather than to the eye, lies in his discarding the verse
or line whose length was arbitrarily fixed by predetermined metrical

[19] *Beowulf,* l. 632.
[20] An interesting analysis of this influence of ballad meters on modern technique of verse
is made in George R. Stewart, Jr., *Modern Metrical Technique as Illustrated by Ballad Meter
(1700-1920)* (New York, 1922).
[21] *A Study of Metre* (London, repub. 1920).

pattern and writing in the unit of the logical clause or sentence. He realized, as Mr. Erskine pointed out,[22] that English readers in oral reading had in large measure ceased to observe line-ends or terminal caesurae in verse unless they represented logical pauses. In his desire to be as natural as possible, therefore, Whitman usually constructed his lines as logical units. It is obvious, however, that the rhythm of such lines is clearly self-conscious, and that, both in respect to rhythm and to length, these verses generally conform to the organic principle as expressed by Coleridge—"such as the life is, such is the form."

Perhaps the connection of such a line with the long tradition of English nonsyllabic, or "periodic," rhythm will be made clearer by the following lines, listed in chronological order, and chosen almost at random from an anthology of standard authors:

Metudes miltse þeah þe he modcearig

> *Wanderer*, l. 2.

Were beth they that biforen us weren

> *Ubi Sunt, anon.* c. 1350.

O father, father, draw your dam!

There's either a mermaid or a milk-white swan!

> *Binnorie*, old ballad.

If hosen and shoon thou gavest nane

The whinnies shall prick thee to the bare bane

> "A Lyke-wake Dirge,"
> *anon.* c. 1475.

Come away, come away death,

And in sad cypress let me be laid.

> Shakespeare, 1599.

Toll for the brave,

The brave that are no more,

> Cowper, 1782.

[22] John Erskine, "A Note on Walt Whitman's Prosody," *Studies in Philology*, XX, 336-344 (July, 1923).

This—all this—was in the olden

Time long ago.

Poe,
"The Haunted Palace," 1839.

I must down to the seas again, to the lonely sea and the sky,

And all I ask is a tall ship and a star to steer her by.

Masefield, c. 1901.

It is obvious that such lines as these are not made by counting so many syllables to a foot. And although Whitman's lines are also marked by other devices, such as parallelism, which these examples do not manifest, they are none the less rhythmically based on the same principle of periodicity. Once the period or interval in such a line has been established the words beat their own time for the verse and establish not only the pattern, but the logical and emotional subtleties which the poet intended. This is an important consideration, for the poet can convey his complete meaning only by his rhythm, which it is therefore necessary for the reader to apprehend exactly.

In his feeling for naturalness of rhythm Whitman also developed another principle already inherent from early times in English poetry and speech. It becomes apparent to the attentive reader of Whitman, especially when reading aloud, that in a great many cases the stress does not fall sharply on a single vowel, but is distributed along the word, or a pair of words, or even a short phrase. This is the familiar phenomenon of the hovering accent, and the reader will find it illustrated above in the second line from the ballad "Binnorie," where the accentual impulse "glides" over the entire adjective "milk-white." Mr. Fred N. Scott called attention to this characteristic in Whitman years ago,[23] but he erroneously supposed that what he calls the "pitch-glide" of prose was the only source for such a practice, when as a matter of fact the phenomenon is inherent in the nature of our English speech, whether prose or verse.

It is difficult to read *Leaves of Grass* without the employment of the hovering accent; it is interesting to note how a sense of naturalness and colloquial ease immediately results when this phenomenon

[23] Scott, *op. cit.*

of our speech is allowed to function. A typical example is found in the four-stress couplet:[24]

> Which of the young men does she like the best?
>
> Ah the homeliest of them is beautiful to her.

If one reads that second line without the "glide," and with strong vocalic accent on the words "them" and "her" the quality and emotional sense are changed, and the line, indeed, becomes jocose instead of pathetic.

Examples could be multiplied to show that Whitman wrote invariably, at his best, in this nonsyllabic meter. Perhaps the proposition is one which each reader will have to test for himself. The present writer can only say that he has found it to be true, in repeated readings of *Leaves of Grass,* except in the very small number of lines in which the conventional syllabic meter appears to survive, perhaps accidentally. A few verses, selected because they manifest such a variety of metrical patterns, will illustrate the general characteristics of Whitman's rhythm:

> To behold the day-break!
>
> The little light fades the immense and diaphanous shadows,
> The air tastes good to my palate.

> Dazzling and tremendous how quick the sunrise would kill me,
> If I could not now and always send sunrise out of me.

> I am he who tauntingly compels men, women, nations,
> Crying, leap from your seats and contend for your lives!

> Whispers of heavenly death murmur'd I hear,
> Labial gossip of night, sibilant chorals,
> Footsteps gently ascending, mystical breezes wafted soft and low. . . .

[24] "Song of Myself," Sec. II, ll. 6-7, Inclusive ed., p. 32.

It is a fact, of course, that the reading of Whitman's lines, or of any meter not based on syllable-counting, requires a greater degree of participation on the part of the reader than does the reading of syllabic verse. That fact did not trouble the poet—on the contrary, such participation by the reader was precisely what he wished to achieve. Once the conception is established of the rhythm as a succession of equal time-intervals marked *either* by vocalic stress or by hovering accent, the reading becomes a natural and simple process. For example, De Selincourt, whose work has much to recommend it, failed[25] to grasp the basic rhythmic principle. He scans the following pair of lines[26] as of six and four stresses. Actually, they constitute a pair in seven stresses, a favorite length with Whitman; and each line is divided by a caesura into two sections of three and four stresses respectively:

A child said *what is the grass?* fetching it to me

with full hands;

How could I answer the child? I do not know what it is

any more than he.

The passage above when scanned by periods reveals a highly developed meter. Each line of a couplet of seven-stress verse is broken by medial caesura at precisely the same point, after the third stress. The rhythmic equivalence between the two lines is striking, and it is not caused by either logical recurrence or the iteration of identical phrases. This purely rhythmic patterning is quite as characteristic of Whitman's writing as the logical balance. It has not apparently been studied by previous writers, some of whom have given valuable data regarding the reiterative parallelism of Whitman's logic. De Selincourt noted the logical balance in 1914.[27] N. A. Wiley[28] later made an exhaustive study of 10,500 lines of *Leaves of Grass* to discover that some form of logical reiteration such as epanaphora (initial) or epanalepsis (within the line) occurred in more than 40 per cent of the lines. Such studies have demonstrated the logical

[25] *Op. cit.*, see, *e.g.*, p. 71.
[26] "Song of Myself," Sec. 6, Inclusive ed., p. 28.
[27] *Op. cit.*, pp. 96-97.
[28] "Reiterative Devices in *Leaves of Grass*," *American Literature*, I, 161-170 (May, 1929).

parallelism of Whitman and have established an inescapable consideration in the comprehension of Whitman's poetics, but it is insufficient to stop there, with De Selincourt's[29] summary: "The identity of the lines in metrical poetry is an identity of pattern. The identity of the lines in *Leaves of Grass* is an identity of substance." For in the majority of the lines of Whitman, which are not brought into equivalence by repetition of substance and phrases, there is still the equivalence of a rhythm regulated by a periodicity of stress so uniformly measured as to constitute a true "meter." It is a device capable of infinite subtlety, and we must understand it fully in order to appreciate the extent of the poet's craftsmanship.

The organic principle, so powerfully operative in Whitman's poetic line, is even more fundamental to his conception of the longer units—the stanzas and odic sections which are so readily perceptible to the eye. It is true that large portions of his poetry, generally those in which the material itself is of a more pedestrian quality, seem to have an organization no more complex than the line-balance, which has already been briefly illustrated. In such passages there frequently is no attempt to build beyond the limits of the single line; or at most, two or three successive lines will be bound together by an arrangement of component rhythmic groups. But where Whitman's material takes wings, and his imagination begins really to soar, we find much larger units, which impress the reader with their organic quality and manifest an obvious unity of form which even the casual reader feels without analysis. These passages rise from the text and take palpable forms with sharp outlines, and substantial, purposeful patterns. The poet has discarded end rime, but obviously he has substituted a more subtle device for controlling his utterance to the shape of his intention. This characteristic is so pronounced and so clearly associated with the greatest of the poet's passages, that numerous attempts have been made to define it. The consensus of opinion has been that such passages are devised on the principle of logical parallelism, borrowed from the English Bible. It becomes apparent on closer examination that this assumption will not satisfactorily explain these longer flights. In the light of the rhythmic principle just discussed, one finds that the organized rhythmic recurrence is even more fundamental and more universally

[29] *Op. cit.,* p. 97.

applied than logical parallelism, not only in the single line, but in longer passages as well.

I do not presume to reject the hypothesis that Whitman, to whom the English Bible was as native as the air of Long Island, frequently employed, in the construction of his larger units, a parallelism and balance of ideas possibly derived from Hebrew poetry. This theory is all the more convincing when one reflects that the English translators employed precisely the same sort of rhythm—periodic instead of syllabic—to which I have drawn attention. Yet more remarkable still is the rhythmical balance through which the poet achieved pattern in stanzas, both long and short, and frequently gave to entire poems a beautiful homogeneity and integrity of construction, even when logical parallelism is reduced to a minimum, or absent altogether.

To understand this clearly it is perhaps necessary to recall the sort of logical construction, similar to that of Bible poetry, which previous writers have illustrated. Perhaps the most careful study is that of Mr. Gay W. Allen in his *American Prosody*.[30] It will be noticed immediately that his conception of Whitman's prosody is based entirely upon logical recurrence—parallelism of thought expressed in parallel construction, and a phonetic recurrence caused solely by repetition of phrases.

Mr. Allen has given valuable attention to Whitman's extensive use of the "envelope," a stanzaic device of biblical prosody in which "the initial line states an idea or a proposition, succeeding lines state parallel thoughts regarding the first line, and the final line states a concluding thought." Frequently the first and last lines are identical, as in "Tears," or equivalent, as in "Quicksand Years." But Mr. Allen, because of his failure to note that the essential rhythm of Whitman's line is caused by something even more fundamental than logical parallelism or phonetic reiteration, does not indicate the amazing subtleties of rhythmic balance to be found in such poems. I could take as examples several scores of poems, but I have selected "Tears"[31] for illustration. To the left of each line I have indicated the number of its stresses. It will be seen that the poem, while a

---

[30] New York, 1935, "Walt Whitman," chap. viii. See also the same writer's "Biblical Analogies for Walt Whitman's Prosody," *Revue Anglo-Américaine*, X, 490-507 (Aug., 1933).

[31] Inclusive ed., p. 218.

remarkably unified organic whole, contains three logical divisions, of five, three, and five lines, respectively, and that each division has its own organic design within the larger pattern:

3 Tears! tears! tears!

3 In the night, in solitude, tears,

5 On the white shore dripping, dripping, sucked in by the sand,

5 Tears, not a star shining, all dark and desolate,

3 Moist tears from the eyes of a muffled head.

5 O who is that ghost? that form in the dark, with tears?

6 What shapeless lump is that, bent, crouched there on the sand?

5 Streaming tears, sobbing tears, throes, choked with wild cries;

6 O storm, embodied, rising, careering with swift steps along the

   beach!

6 O wild and dismal night storm, with wind—O belching and

   desperate!

8 O shade so sedate and decorous by day, with calm countenance

   and regulated pace,

7 But away at night as you fly, none looking—O then the un-

   loosened ocean

3 Of tears! tears! tears!

I hope it is clear that this poem is like a large wave or breaker with three crests. The shape of the entire poem may be interpreted as pyramidal, beginning with a three-stress line, rising to two pinnacles of six and eight stresses, and subsiding again to three stresses in the last line. Similarly, the rhythmic shape of each of the constituent "crests" is pyramidal. The first section of five lines, in which the rain in the night is likened to tears, announces the pyramid in the swell and fall through lines of 3, 3, 5, 5, and 3 stress; in the second, in which the spirit of the world broods over the night, the initial impulse is paralleled more grandly in the succession of 5, 6 and 5 stress; in the final section, in which the identity of an individual weeper merges with the cosmic woe of nature itself, the full rhythmic diapason is unloosed in the great cloudhead, or crest, of 6, 6, 8, 7 and 3 stresses. The artistic integrity of this poem should be clear to anyone who analyzes it rhythmically. When we find similar technical perfection in poem after poem, we must conclude that it is the result of consistent artistic purpose. Sometimes the artist's reach exceeds his grasp, but the great poetic craftsman is always discernible, groping for the ideal organic expression of his thought.

It should be emphasized that such rhythmic "frames" appear continually, whether in connection with the "envelope" form or not; and that similar devices are employed both for the complete organic outline of the short lyric and as stanzaic structures within the body of longer poems. Such shorter lyrics are "A Noiseless, Patient Spider," "Lo, Victress on the Peaks," "A Sight in Camp in the Daybreak Gray and Dim," "Prayer of Columbus," and many others, but no two of them are alike in form. One lyric form which does appear over and over in many variations is presumably based on the logical construction of the Italian sonnet, having the bipartite arrangement into a forward and backward movement of thought with clearly marked division. "By Broad Potomac's Shore"[32] is a beautiful example of this, divided into sections of seven and five lines, respectively. The analysis by rhythmic line-lengths reveals the same sort of construction as that observed in "Tears," although perhaps less dramatic. Each section of the poem is again pyramidal, ascending to an extended impulse in the middle. Strongly marked medial caesurae accentuate the balance of phrase units in parallel patterns of three, four, and five stresses:

5 By broad Potomac's shore, again old tongue

5 (Still uttering, still ejaculating, canst never cease this babble?)

9 Again old heart so gay, again to you, your sense, the full flush

    spring returning,

[32] *Ibid.*, p. 400.

9 Again the freshness and the odors, again Virginia's

   summer sky, pellucid blue and silver,

4 Again the forenoon purple of the hills,

6 Again the deathless grass, so noiseless soft and green,

4 Again the blood-red roses blooming.

5 Perfume this book of mine O blood-red roses!

5 Lave subtly with your waters every line Potomac!

8 Give me of you O spring, before I close, to put between its

   pages!

6 O forenoon purple of the hills, before I close, of you!

3 O deathless grass, of you!

A complete analysis of the wide variety of formal devices employed in Whitman's stanzas should no doubt be made. The present intention is merely to establish the principle that the balance of his lines in longer units is so striking as to indicate conscious effort. Perhaps it will be sufficient at this point to illustrate several of the patterns which recur most frequently in shorter lyrics. Besides those already analyzed—the balanced stanza of "Tears," and the sonnet-like poem as found in "By Broad Potomac's Shores," there are several other prevailing forms. A single stanza based on the pyramid form is the device most frequently employed in every period of Whitman's writing. In the familiar "Quicksand Years,"[33] for example, we find the simple pyramid, in a poem of six lines. The fourth line is the longest, of nine stresses; the others lead up to and away from it in a pattern of 5-8-8-9-8-5 stresses. Reiterative logic appears in only one instance in this poem. Many interesting variants of the pyramid poem occur. The following, "Lo, Victress on the Peaks,"[34] is typical:

2 Lo, Victress on the peaks,

5 Where thou with mighty brow regarding the world,

[33] Ibid., p. 374.   [34] Ibid., p. 273.

5 (The world O Libertad, that vainly conspired against thee,)

6 Out of its countless beleaguering toils, after thwarting them all,

4 Dominant, with the dazzling sun around thee,

9 Flauntest now unharmed in immortal soundness and bloom—

   lo, in these hours supreme,

8 No poem proud, I chanting bring to thee, nor mastery's

   rapturous verse,

5 But a cluster containing night's darkness and blood-dripping

   wounds,

2 And psalms of the dead.

In this poem, the four-stress line, the fifth in a nine-line poem, is
both formally and logically the middle of the poem. There are four
lines before and four after it. The preceding lines increase in stress-
length in stages of 2-5-5 and 6 stresses. The succeeding four lines
decrease in length through the stages of 9-8-5 and 2 stresses, the last
line of the poem being of the same length as the first. Logically considered, this shorter medial line, "Dominant, with the dazzling sun
around thee," marks a moment of emphatic and leisurely reflection,
and serves to divide the material roughly into two parts; the first,
dealing with the power and victory of the nation; and the concluding four lines, dealing with the nature of the poet's song. Certainly
there is a remarkable consistency between the shape of the idea and
the shape of the poem.

Another characteristic variation of the pyramid is seen in the
tender lyric "Reconciliation,"[35] one of the best known of Whitman's
utterances:

4 Word over all, beautiful as the sky,

8 Beautiful that war and all its deeds of carnage must in time

   be utterly lost,

[35] *Ibid.*, p. 271.

12 That the hands of the sisters Death and Night incessantly

    softly wash again and ever again this soiled world;

6 For my enemy is dead, a man divine as myself is dead,

6 I look where he lies white-faced and still in the coffin—

    I draw near,

6 Bend down and touch lightly with my lips the white face in

    the coffin.

In this poem of six lines, the first three, ending in a logical climax, develop the idea of the ultimate banishment of war from the earth. In each of the three lines the emotional intensity increases while the line-lengths mount from four stresses to eight and twelve respectively. The last three lines, given to quiet, reflective reaction, are all in six stresses. Again we are struck by the appropriateness of the form for the ideas expressed.

The pyramid also appears as Whitman's favorite stanza pattern in extended composition. In a poem of several stanzas the lines of each stanza will be arranged in the conventional pyramidal order, yet no two of the stanzas will have lines of exactly the same length. The remarkable poem, "A Noiseless Patient Spider,"[36] illustrates this form. That the stanza pattern is not a mere convention, however, that the poem is truly organic in the fact that each line takes its length inevitably from the nature of its idea, will be clear to the critical observer:

3 A noiseless patient spider,

5 I marked where on a little promontory it stood isolated,

5 Marked how to explore the vacant vast surrounding,

6 It launched forth filament, filament, filament out of itself,

5 Ever unreeling them, ever tirelessly speeding them.

3 And you O my soul where you stand,

[36] *Ibid.*, p. 375.

5 Surrounded, detached, in measureless oceans of space,

7 Ceaselessly musing, venturing, throwing, seeking the spheres
     to connect them,

6 Till the bridge you will need be formed, till the ductile anchor
     hold,

6 Till the gossamer thread you fling catch somewhere, O my soul.

As in the case of all Whitman's greatest poems there are other
elements in this lyric, besides its rhythmic organization, which evoke
respect for his craftsmanship. For example, since earlier mention
has been made of the poet's use of logical repetition in similar
words, we may note the effects of this device in the last two lines of
this poem. Here the two verses, printed as six-stress lines, are in
effect broken down into distichs of three stresses by the reiteration
of the phrases beginning in each case with the words "till the,"
aided by medial caesurae. Thus the rhythm of three stresses, with
which each stanza opens, is subtly returned, with delicate variations,
at the very end of the poem, and the circle is completed.

The principles illustrated in these shorter lyrics are found to be
operative also in the longer poems. In many poems of medium
length, like "Out of the Cradle Endlessly Rocking," "When Lilacs
Last in the Dooryard Bloom'd," or the "Prayer of Columbus," there
is an obvious, conscious shaping of the entire poem as a unified
rhythmic organism, into which the shorter stanzas fall in their
inevitable places, always simple, always consistent with the harmony
of the whole, yet rich with that variety which comes from the
perfect appropriateness of each formal component for the thought
that it conveys.

In the longest poems, even, such as "Song of Myself," "Thou
Mother with thy Equal Brood," and others, in which the material
is usually divided into logical sections of varying lengths depending
upon the amount of material to be presented, the balance and return
of rhythmic patterns are continuously present and obviously controlled with great skill. Sometimes the form is a very simple arrangement of balanced couplets or reiterative parallelism. At other
times a succession of such simple lines will suddenly give way to a

passage of very complex rhythmical counter-point. For example, in Section 21 of "Song of Myself," the familiar line, "I am he that walks with the tender and growing night," announces a passage in which subtle patterns are embroidered upon each other in a manner comparable to that of great symphonic music:

5   I am he that walks with the tender and growing night,

5   I call to the earth and sea half-held by the night.

7   Press close bare-bosom'd night—press close magnetic nourishing

      night!

5   Night of south winds—night of the large few stars!

5   Still nodding night—mad naked summer night.

4   Smile O voluptuous cool-breath'd earth!

4   Earth of the slumbering and liquid trees!

6   Earth of departed sunset—earth of the mountains misty-topt!

6   Earth of the vitreous pour of the full moon just tinged with

      blue!

6   Earth of shine and dark mottling the tide of the river!

7   Earth of the limpid gray of clouds brighter and clearer for my

      sake!

6   Far-swooping elbow'd earth—rich apple-blossom'd earth!

3   Smile, for your lover comes.

7   Prodigal, you have given me love—therefore I to you give love!

3   O unspeakable passionate love.

This beautiful passage stands out from Section 21, which it concludes, as a logical unit with organic structure. Its four logical divisions are carefully balanced as to form. The first and last divisions, each a pair of lines, are logically similar in expressing an initial and final relationship between the poet and the earth. The two internal sections, of three and eight lines, respectively, are likewise similar in material, since each is composed of vocative and descriptive expressions concerning the earth. The rhythmic rise and fall of the lines in the several sections are accomplished by subtle variations of the same pattern, which three times swells to the length of seven stresses and then subsides sharply. The opening is in a couplet of five stresses. The next section bursts at once into a passionate line of seven stresses and then falls away into two lines of five stresses divided into parallel sections by caesurae. The third section, in eight lines, rises more slowly to its climax in the seven-stress line, through a succession of lines in 4-4-6-6 and 6 stresses. From the seven-stress line the falling away is more sharp than before, through two lines of six and three stresses respectively. The fact that this six-stress line is broken into two phrases of three stresses each by strong medial caesura sets up an iteration of three beats, which perhaps renders more telling and dramatic the sudden ending of the passage in the next couplet, with marked decline from a seven-stress to a three-stress line. Of course it is obvious that these rhythmic characteristics are also aided and emphasized by the logical repetitions in parallel construction.

Occasionally the entire section will be thus organically composed. Section 2 of the "Song of Myself," the magnificent parable of the twenty-ninth bather, is a good example of this:

4 Twenty-eight young men bathe by the shore,

4 Twenty-eight young men and all so friendly;

6 Twenty-eight years of womanly life and all so lonesome.

4 She owns the fine house by the rise of the bank,

6 She hides handsome and richly dressed aft the blinds of the window.

4 Which of the young men does she like the best?

4 Ah the homeliest of them is beautiful to her.

4 Where are you off to, lady? for I see you,

6 You splash in the water there, yet stay stock still in your room.

5 Dancing and laughing along the beach came the twenty-ninth

   bather,

5 The rest did not see her, but she saw them and loved them.

6 The beards of the young men glistened with wet, it ran from

   their long hair,

4 Little streams passed all over their bodies.

4 An unseen hand also passed over their bodies,

4 It descended tremblingly from their temples and ribs.

10 The young men float on their backs, their white bellies bulge

   to the sun, they do not ask who seizes fast to them,

7 They do not know who puffs and declines with pendant and

   bending arch,

4 They do not think whom they souse with spray.

Of the eight sections in this poem, the first and last alone are tercets
—the remainder are couplets. The fourth couplet, however, is peculiar: it conveys the climax of the action and is the only one in five
stresses. The other couplets are balanced on each side of this climactic couplet; the complete pattern being:

$$4,4,6—4,6—4,4—4,6—5,5—6,4—4,4—10,7,4$$

It is apparent that the couplets and tercet before the five-stress couplet have the longer line last, and those after this central climax have
the shorter line last—another use of the pyramid. The couplet in
five stresses, in which the woman consummates her rebellion by
running to join the young men in their ocean of life, is clearly set
apart by the dissimilarity of its line-length; and the other two iso-
metric couplets, each in four stresses, are carefully balanced in the
third position before and after the central five-stressed couplet.
Finally, an unmistakable conclusion is given the final tercet by the
extraordinary swell of the first two lines into ten and seven feet,
respectively. Surely the organic principle is convincingly demonstrated in this remarkable passage. Many others, in all portions of
the longer works, are obviously constructed on the same principle.

It would be foolhardy to declare, since we have no direct evidence, that Whitman had rationalized the formal tendencies which
I have illustrated, and that he had organized them into a prosody
which he consciously followed. It has been said that he avoided, for
wise reasons, the concrete declaration of his specific practices. Yet if
such formal perfection as I have shown came merely by the exercise
of artistic instinct during years of revision and rewriting, then surely
that instinct was the mark of a profound artistic genius. In summary there are a few generalizations which it seems important to
make. The first is that, whether instinctively or consciously, the
poet achieved the aspiration revealed in his prefaces: to shape his
words to the exact surface and movement of the spirit in nature or in
truth. By 1876 he knew that he had succeeded, when he wrote in
the Preface of that year, "My form has strictly grown from my
purports and facts, and is the analogy of them." Next it must be
noted that the poet did not completely reject any device of the older
poetry. He made consistent use of assonance, alliteration, stanza,
refrain, return, and even occasional rime.[37] His revolution centered
on three things: a new emphasis, to the point of organic use, upon
ancient repetitive devices, like epanaphora and epanalepsis; the construction of stanzas and larger units on the basis of rhythmic balance
and parallelism; his conscious rejection of syllabic meter in favor of
that more ancient and native English meter based on the rhythmic
"period" between the stresses.

[37] See Lois Ware, "Poetic Conventions in *Leaves of Grass,*" *Studies in Philology,* XXVI,
47-57, *passim* (Jan., 1929).

All of this would have had little point but for the genius by which he was able to transmute his special sense of rhythm into phrases which, as Symonds said,[38] "should exactly suit the matter or the emotion to be expressed. The countless clear and perfect phrases he invented ... are hung, like golden medals of consummate workmanship ... in rich clusters over every poem he produced. And, what he aimed at above all, these phrases are redolent of the very spirit of the emotions they suggest, communicate the breadth and largeness of the natural things they indicate, embody the essence of realities in living words which palpitate and burn forever."

[38] J. A. Symonds, *Walt Whitman: A Study* (London, 1893), p. 150.

Whitman's Triadic Imagery
Alfred H. Marks

MUCH HAS BEEN SAID about the influence of Hegel upon Walt Whitman. In addition to references in practically every biography of Whitman, at least two[1] articles written in the past twenty years deal directly with the problem. Two others[2] treat the general subject of which this relationship is a part and from which it can be extricated only with difficulty: the question of Whitman's acquaintance with German philosophy of the late eighteenth and early nineteenth centuries. Whitman and Hegel have been compared from one principal standpoint. They share an "evolutionary conception of a universe, exhibiting conflict and struggle, yet tending toward a vague divine culmination in the return of the individual souls to the Absolute."[3] But little attention has been paid to Whitman's poetic use of the logical technique which Hegel popularized, the Dialectic. When one notices the number of times Whitman uses the terms "fusing," "blending," "uniting," "joining," so suggestive of the dialectical "synthesis," this neglect seems surprising. The surprise increases when one sees how frequently Whitman calls up paired contradictories or "thesis" and "antithesis" and handles them as if there were no opposition between them. Whitman's statement

> Do I contradict myself?
> Very well then I contradict myself,
> (I am large, I contain multitudes.)

has often been used against him as exemplifying his imputed arrogance and illogicality. When viewed from the standpoint of the Dialectic it becomes one of Whitman's more logical utterances,

---

[1] Mody Boatright, "Whitman and Hegel," *Studies in English* (University of Texas Bulletin), No. 9, pp. 134-150 (July 8, 1929); and Olive W. Parsons, "Whitman the Non-Hegelian," *PMLA*, LVIII, 1073-1093 (Dec., 1943).

[2] Robert P. Falk, "Walt Whitman and German Thought," *Journal of English and Germanic Philology*, XL, 315-330 (July, 1941); W. B. Fulghum, Jr., "Whitman's Debt to Joseph Gostwick," *American Literature*, XII, 491-496 (Jan., 1941).

[3] Robert P. Falk, *op. cit*, p. 329.

meaning: "Although I may seem to contradict myself, there are so many circumstances mitigating those contradictions within me that within my size and complexity they are resolved and synthesized."

The triad, so basic to Dialectic, may be seen reproduced very frequently in *Leaves of Grass*. Characteristically, it presents a grouping in which what might be understood as two separate parts appear actually to be three (and yet one in that the "third" synthesizes and contains "one" and "two"):

> I too with my soul and body,
> We, a curious trio. . . .[4]

Thus, when Whitman said, "I am the poet of the Body and I am the poet of the Soul"[5] he believed that he himself was "triadic." This he underscores in his motto to the *Leaves*,

> COME, SAID MY SOUL,
> SUCH VERSES FOR MY BODY LET US WRITE, (FOR WE ARE ONE,).[6]

The theme of the triadic self is stated many times in the first poem of the work, "One's Self I Sing," in the delineation of that composite self which is the "Modern Man." At least four seemingly contradictory statements are forthrightly presented in this poem, and all are finally seen to be part of that large selfhood which Whitman preached:

> ONE'S SELF I sing, a simple separate person,
> Yet utter the word Democratic, the word En-Masse.

> Of physiology from top to toe I sing,
> Not physiognomy alone nor brain alone is worthy for the Muse, I say
>   the Form complete is worthier far,
> The Female equally with the Male I sing.

Of Life immense in passion, pulse, and power,
Cheerful, for freest action form'd under the laws divine,
The Modern Man I sing.[7]

[4] "Pioneers! O Pioneers!" *Leaves of Grass*, Inclusive Edition, ed. Emory Holloway (Garden City, N. Y., 1948), p. 196. Hereinafter, all page references following titles of Whitman's writings will apply to this edition, unless otherwise stated.
[5] "Song of Myself," p. 41.
[6] Facing p. 1.
[7] "One's Self I Sing," p. 1.

It was important to Whitman, therefore, that he contain contradictions, making himself a synthesis of them:

I am not the poet of goodness only, I do not decline to be the poet of wickedness also.[8]

He cultivated both extremes, balancing each view with its opposite:

I find one side a balance and the antipodal side a balance,[9]

thus advancing to a statement like the following:

I accept Reality and dare not question it,
Materialism first and last imbuing.

Hurrah for positive science! long live exact demonstration . . .
This is the geologist, this works with the scalpel, and this is a mathematician.

Gentlemen, to you the first honors always!
Your facts are useful, and yet they are not my dwelling,
I but enter by them to an area of my dwelling.[10]

Both sides of the dualism are equally important:

I believe in you my soul, the other I am must not abase itself to you,
And you must not be abased to the other.[11]

And the moments when both sides are joined as one are the great, the mystical, the climactic moments of life. This is demonstrated in the love scene of body and soul in "Song of Myself":

I mind how once we lay such a transparent summer morning,
How you settled your head athwart my hips and gently turn'd over upon me,
And parted the shirt from my bosom-bone, and plunged your tongue to my bare-stript heart,
And reach'd till you felt my beard, and reach'd till you held my feet.

Swiftly arose and spread around me the peace and knowledge that pass all the argument of the earth,
And I know that the hand of God is the promise of my own,
And I know that the spirit of God is the brother of my own,
And that all the men ever born are also my brothers, and the women my sisters and lovers.[12]

[8] "Song of Myself," p. 42.   [9] Ibid.
[10] Ibid., p. 43.   [11] Ibid., p. 27.   [12] Ibid., p. 27.

This "Triadic Imagery," as it may be called, is clearly a form of Hegel-like dialectic; but, barring certain exceptions which will be pointed out, it need not be considered as based directly on the form of this logic which Hegel employed.[13] Indeed, the present discussion can be illuminated much more by reference to the writings of Emerson than to those of Hegel.

Several of Emerson's major essays contain discussions of "polarities," the phenomena of essential contradiction upon which the dialectic is based. Whitman's concept of the triadic poet is foreshadowed in Emerson's essay "Plato." Discussing the dualism of unity and variety, Emerson sees that Plato is great because he used both. He says, significantly, "Every great artist has been such by synthesis. . . ."[14] This he explains further:

Art expresses the one or the same by the different. Thought seeks to know unity in unity; poetry to show it by variety; that is, always by an object or symbol. Plato keeps the two vases, one of aether and one of pigment, at his side, and invariably uses both.[15]

Whitman seems to have shared with Emerson the belief expressed in *Nature:*

[13] The problem of the relationship of the writings of Hegel to those of Whitman has had no final and authoritative summation. The reason for this may be the skeptical view toward the pure "influence" study adopted by scholars in the humanities during the past decade or more. Another reason may be the failure of the available material to yield anything more definite about the nature of the relationship.

Aside from Whitman's reference to Joseph Gostwick's *German Literature* (*Complete Poetry and Prose*, II, 203; cf. W. B. Fulghum, *op. cit.*) and another reference by the poet to at least a speaking acquaintance with W. T. Harris, the foremost figure in the St. Louis Hegelian school (*Complete Prose*, Boston, 1898, p. 183), there is no objective evidence to show where Whitman learned anything by or about Hegel.

The comparative studies undertaken by Boatright, however, show in some detail numerous similarities between the ideas expressed by the two men. Boatright, in an article whose real value must not be minimized because in it he tries unsuccessfully to show that Whitman had read Gostwick before 1855, treats the "Triadic I" at some length, although his final conclusion on the subject of triadic logic is "It is more likely, however, that he [Whitman] never mastered the Hegelian dialectic" (*op. cit.*, p. 144). Falk's principal conclusion has been quoted earlier in this article.

The subject is also treated in Richard Riethmueller's "Walt Whitman and the Germans, A Study," *German-American Annals*, Vol. IV (reprinted 1906) and Olive Wrenchel Parson's "Whitman, the Non-Hegelian," *PMLA*, LVIII, 1073-1093 (Dec., 1943), as well as in most of the biographies of Whitman (cf. Robert Falk, *op. cit.*, pp. 315 ff. for detailed bibliography).

[14] *The Complete Works of Ralph Waldo Emerson*, Centenary Edition (New York, 1903), IV, 55.

[15] *Ibid.*, IV, 56.

Philosophically considered, the universe is composed of Nature and the Soul. Strictly speaking, therefore, all that is separate from us, all which Philosophy distinguishes as the NOT ME, that is, both nature and art, all other men and my own body, must be ranked under this name, NATURE.[16]

This would account for the mystical intensity of Whitman's union of body and soul. Since one's soul belongs to one half of the dualism and one's body the other, the self which unifies them is certainly a divine synthesis, both actually and symbolically.

Emerson expands in "Plato" on the ramifications of a great dualism which makes itself visible in different form wherever we turn:

If speculation tends thus to a terrific unity, in which all things are absorbed, action tends directly backwards to diversity. The first is the course or gravitation of mind; the second is the power of nature. Nature is the manifold. The unity absorbs, and melts or reduces. Nature opens and creates. These two principles reappear and interpenetrate all things, all thought; the one, the many. One is being; the other, intellect: one is necessity; the other, freedom: one, rest; the other, motion. . . .[17]

In Whitman the contradictory pairs are also visible: identity and distinction, body and soul, universal and particular, male and female, humanity and deity.

Most striking is Whitman's use of land-and-sea, man-and-companion, man-and-mate, and life-and-death imagery to represent both sides of this dualism. Thus, the shore is seen by him as a great synthesis, "The rim, the sediment that stands for all the water and all the land of the globe."[18] He leaves little doubt as to the importance of the seashore in this prose statement:

Even as a boy, I had the fancy, the wish, to write a piece, perhaps a poem, about the sea-shore—that suggesting, dividing line, contact, junction, the solid marrying the liquid—that curious, lurking something, (as doubtless every objective form finally becomes to the subjective spirit,) which means far more than its mere first sight, grand as that is—blending the real and the ideal, and each made portion of the other. Hours, days, in my Long Island youth and early manhood, I haunted the shores of

---

[16] *Ibid.*, I, 4-5.
[17] *Ibid.*, IV, 51.
[18] "As I Ebb'd with the Ocean of Life," p. 216.

Rockaway or Coney Island, or away east to the Hamptons or Montauk. Once, at the latter place, (by the old lighthouse, nothing but sea-tossings in sight in every direction as far as the eye could reach,) I remember well, I felt that I must one day write a book expressing this liquid, mystic theme. Afterward, I recollect, how it came to me that instead of any special lyrical or epical or literary attempt, the sea-shore should be an invisible *influence*, a pervading gauge and tally for me, in my composition.[19]

In "As I Ebb'd with the Ocean of Life," the poet throws himself on the ground and says, "I throw myself upon your breast my father," and then turns to the ocean and says, "Cease not your moaning you fierce old mother. . . ."[20] Thus, the sides of the dualism receive sexual connotations.

Whitman is quite consistent in his choice of masculine or feminine images to represent either pole. He seldom seems to depart from his own dictum: "The Soul of the Universe is the Male and genital master and the impregnating and animating spirit—Physical matter is Female and Mother and waits. . . ."[21] It is with forethought therefore that the boy and the mockingbird of "Out of the Cradle Endlessly Rocking" and the hermit thrush of "When Lilacs Last in the Dooryard Bloom'd" are males. Save for the woman in "Song of Myself" who yearns toward the twenty-eight bathers (an ambiguous figure who might well be the moon bound to the waters of the earth by the tides of the twenty-eight days of her cycle), there seem to be no questing females in *Leaves of Grass*. Whitman's female symbolizes the Not Me of his universe; she waits, like Nature:

> As I see my soul reflected in Nature,
> As I see through a mist, One with inexpressible completeness, sanity,
>   beauty,
> See the bent head and arms folded over the breast, the Female I see.[22]

Finally, in his treatment of the multiplicities of human life, the occupations, habitats, races, creeds, aspirations, conflicting desires of

[19] *The Complete Poetry and Prose of Walt Whitman*, ed. Malcolm Cowley (New York, 1948), II, 91-92.

[20] "As I Ebb'd with the Ocean of Life," p. 217.

[21] Cited by F. O. Matthiessen in *The American Renaissance: Art and Expression in the Age of Emerson and Whitman* (New York, 1941), pp. 525-526, from a source he does not identify.

[22] "I Sing the Body Electric," p. 82.

hundreds of individuals, all in the name of unity, Whitman reflects again the polarities of thought he seems to be ruled by elsewhere. There are probably few who would claim that Whitman was not the poet of variety and distinction and particularity. Yet no one familiar with his poetry will doubt that he wanted at the same time to be the poet of unity, the one, the universal:

> Still though the one I sing,
> (One, yet of contradictions made,). . . .[23]

Whitman's cultivation of polarities and synthesis in his thought and his poetry was probably based on a conviction that the basic truth of the universe was the progressive realization of such a logical scheme. If so, that conviction was based on someone else's findings. For his triadic imagery is not in itself a device for determining and proving philosophical truths. It operates in the realm of poetic imagery and could be used of itself to prove nothing to a skeptical listener. Hegel, for one, however, did work out a comprehensive philosophy on this basis. And whether he first derived the ideas from Hegel or not, Whitman wrote, about 1870, a résumé of that philosopher's cosmology which is strikingly similar to what one might suppose the poet's own philosophy to be after careful examination of *Leaves of Grass:*

Penetrating beneath the shows and materials of the objective world we find, according to Hegel (though the thought by itself is not new but very antique and both Indian and Grecian) that in respect to human cognition of them, all and several are pervaded by *the only absolute substance* which is SPIRIT, endued with the eternal impetus of development, and producing, from itself the opposing powers and forces of the universe. A curious, triplicate process seems the resultant action; first the positive, then the Negative, then the product of mediation between them; from which product the process is repeated and so goes on without end.[24]

The theme of the poem "Two Rivulets,"[25] the title poem of Vol-

[23] "Still Though the One I Sing," p. 10.

[24] *Notes and Fragments*, ed. Richard Maurice Bucke (London, Canada, 1899), p. 135.

[25] The obvious triadic content of this poem may have motivated Whitman's later rejection of it. It certainly violates his dictum "Without effort and without exposing in the least how it is done the greatest poet brings the spirit of any or all events and passions and scenes and persons some more and some less to bear on your individual character as you hear or read" ("Preface to 1855 Edition," p. 495). This hypothesis is

ume II of the 1876 edition of Whitman's writings, is strictly in
accordance with the doctrine the poet attributes to Hegel.[26]   In this
poem Whitman pictures his universe as consisting of two streams,
both heading for the mystic ocean of spirit where, by just that
"curious triplicate process," life and death, object and subject, real
and ideal, day and night are to be reconciled.   Time is pictured as
a triad, or "trio."   The endless repetition of the process is pictured
in the line "alternate ebb and flow the Days and Nights."   The
partial and incomplete nature of even the highest foreseeable pinnacle is shown by the turn from the "yearnful waves" to the "firm
expanded shore."   Thus, the Hegelian position is re-established, with
the "reality" of the shore seen to be as important to the whole as the
ideality of the mystic ocean.

> Two Rivulets side by side,
> Two blended, parallel, strolling tides,
> Companions, travellers, gossiping as they journey.
>
> For the Eternal Ocean bound,
> These ripples, passing surges, streams of Death and Life,
> Object and Subject hurrying, whirling by,
> The Real and Ideal.
>
> Alternate ebb and flow the Days and Nights,
> (Strands of a Trio twining, Present, Future, Past.)
>
> In You, whoe'er you are, my book perusing,
> In I myself—in all the World—these ripples flow,
> All, all, toward the mystic Ocean tending.
>
> (O yearnful waves! the kisses of your lips!
> Your breast so broad, with open arms, O firm, expanded shore!)[27]

The poem "Thou Mother with Thy Equal Brood" shows to an
even greater extent the influence of Dialectic.   Whitman draws here,
more clearly than elsewhere, the outlines of his view of the universe:

---

supported by the fact that Whitman's reference to the dialectic in the above discussion of
Hegel is suppressed in the version of these notes Whitman finally printed (*Complete Poetry
and Prose*, II, 175 ff.).

[26] Bucke's footnote to this statement is revealing (*Notes and Fragments*, p. 138 n.):
"Throughout 175 [the notes on various figures of which the Hegel discussion is a part]
as in all Whitman's writings, the hands may be the hands of Esau (Elias Hick [*sic*],
Hegel, Schelling etc., etc.) but the voice is always the voice of Jacob—Whitman himself."

[27] "Two Rivulets," pp. 485-486.

World of the real—world of the twain in one,
World of the soul, born by the world of the real alone, led to identity,
  body, by it alone. . . .[28]

But even more important is his inclusion within this poem of probably the best dialectical series in *Leaves of Grass:*

> . . . thou transcendental Union!
> By thee fact to be justified, blended with thought,
> Thought of man justified, blended with God,
> Through thy idea, lo, the immortal reality!
> Through thy reality, lo, the immortal idea![29]

To explain in dialectical terms, if we assume that fact is all of
reality, we must qualify this by admitting the antithesis: that the
concrete is perceived and defined only by thought. Man is the
"blend" of thought and fact; but we must qualify our postulation of
him as the whole of reality by admitting the existence of higher
things than man in the universe: God. All of reality is therefore
an Idea which blends God with man and both with man's world
of fact and thought. (By God is meant an immanent world-soul.)
The foregoing is partially paraphrased elsewhere, in the words
placed in the mouth of "Santa Spirita":

> Including all life on earth, touching, including God, including Saviour
>   and Satan,
> Ethereal, pervading all, (for without me what were all? what were
>   God?)
> Essence of forms, life of the real identities, permanent, positive,
>   (namely the unseen,)
> Life of the great round world, the sun and stars, and of man, I, the
>   general soul. . . .[30]

In another poem Whitman pictures a procession led by one great
figure who is followed by three groups of lesser figures. It does
not seem to be too farfetched to speculate that the poet is picturing,
in reverse, the dialectic:

> One sweeps by, attended by an immense train,
> All emblematic of peace—not a soldier or menial among them.

[28] "Thou Mother with Thy Equal Brood," p. 381.
[29] *Ibid.*, p. 380.
[30] "Chanting the Square Deific," pp. 371-372.

One sweeps by, old, with black eyes, and profuse white hair,
He has the simple magnificence of health and strength,
His face strikes as with flashes of lightning whoever it turns toward.

Three old men slowly pass, followed by three others, and they by three
  others,
They are beautiful—the one in the middle of each group holds his
  companions by the hand,
As they walk, they give out perfume wherever they walk.[31]

Thus, not only is Whitman's universe triadic, its ultimate nature
is manifested by a triadic process in time. It is not difficult to dis-
cern why Whitman might feel that the triadic poet best represented
this type of universe. As he called him in preliminary drafts of the
"Song of the Answerer," the poet is:

The Three of the Three—
There is on the one part—
Between this beautiful but dumb earth, with all its manifold eloquent
  but inarticulate shows and objects,
And on the other part the being Man, curious, questioning and at
  fault,
Now between the two comes the poet the Answerer.[32]

Thus, after the poet has established contact with the other side of
his universe, his "beautiful but dumb earth," it is his task to show
others how to accomplish this. Such is the mission of the aesthetic:

Great constituent elements of my poetry—Two, viz.: Materialism—
Spirituality—The Intellect, the Esthetic is what is to be the medium of
these and to beautify and make serviceable there.[33]

For the poet has the vision to see beyond the conflicts which irk his
fellow-men: "One part does not counteract another part, he is the
joiner, he sees how they join."[34]

The pages of *Leaves of Grass* are filled with the evidences of
Whitman's program, in accordance with which he would attempt
to be "the arbiter of the diverse"[35] who would "indicate the path

[31] "Debris," p. 482. (This portion of the rejected poem, "Debris," was used to make
up the entire poem, "One Sweeps By," which appeared in the editions published by
McKay.)
[32] *Notes and Fragments*, p. 52.   [33] *Ibid.*, p. 55.
[34] "Song of the Answerer," p. 141.   [35] "1855 Preface," p. 491.

between reality and . . . [men's] souls."[36] But few expressions of
the program are so clear as the following poem:

When the full-grown poet came,
Out spake pleased Nature (the round impassive globe, with all its
　shows of day and night,) saying, *He is mine*;
But out spake the Soul of man, proud, jealous and unreconciled, *Nay,
　he is mine alone*;

—Then the full-grown poet stood between the two, and took each by
　the hand;
And to-day and ever so stands, as blender, uniter, tightly holding
　hands,
Which he will never release until he reconciles the two,
And wholly and joyously blends them.[37]

Whitman's use of the dialectical triad in his poetry is therefore
marked by several characteristics. First, he seems to consider paired
contradictories not as representing a group two in number but as
comprising a group of three. The third member is the unity which
resolves the contradictions of the other two. Second, he alludes very
frequently to contradiction, to unity, and to a unity which contains
contradiction. In this connection, he seems deliberately to cultivate
the attainment of both poles simultaneously in order to mediate
dramatically between the extremes. Third, the Poet-self which he
created for himself was designed both to contain the extremes and
to unify them. Fourth, Whitman's universe is to be seen at any
point in time as a great sphere holding in unity two hemispheres.
The real, the physical, masculinity, the body, the earth, etc., are to
be found in one hemisphere. The ideal, the spiritual, femininity, the
soul, the sea, etc., are to be found in the other hemisphere. The
synthesis of any concept in one hemisphere with its opposite number in the other hemisphere is a symbolic representation of the
central truth of the system, or unity in diversity. Fifth, during any
interval, Whitman's universe is to be seen as manifested in time in
a series of unifications and separations:

Ever the dim beginning,
Ever the growth, the rounding of the circle,
Ever the summit and the merge at last, (to surely start again,). . . .[38]

---

[36] *Ibid.*, p. 493.
[37] "When the Full-Grown Poet Came," p. 451.
[38] "Eidolons," p. 4.

There are several hundred examples of triadic imagery in *Leaves of Grass*, represented in at least four different types. There is, first, the static triad, in which thesis and antithesis are pictured, with the binding unity either stated:

> My right and left arms around the sides of two friends, and I in the middle. . . .[39]

or implied:

> . . . the crescent child that carries its own full mother in its belly. . . .[40]

Then there is the dramatized triad, which presents thesis, antithesis, and synthesis in progressive succession:

> Reckoning ahead O soul, when thou, the time achiev'd,
> The seas all cross'd, weather'd the capes, the voyage done,
> Surrounded, copest, frontest God, yieldest, the aim attain'd,
> As fill'd with friendship, love complete, the Elder Brother found,
> The Younger melts in fondness in his arms.[41]

Third, there is the triadic series:

> Out of the dimness opposite equals advance, always substance and increase, always sex,
> Always a knit of identity, always distinction, always a breed of life.[42]

Fourth is the nuclear triad, represented twice in the early part of "Out of the Cradle Endlessly Rocking." This triad synthesizes all the contradictions around it, as the "Two together" of the mockingbird's song:

> *Two together!*
> *Winds blow south, or winds blow north,*
> *Day come white, or night come black,*
> *Home, or rivers and mountains from home,*
> *Singing all time, minding no time,*
> *While we two keep together.*[43]

and the poet's reference to himself, fusing boyhood and manhood, sand and waves, pains and joys, here and hereafter, and his experience and its suggestions:

[39] "Song of Myself," p. 54.
[40] *Ibid.*
[41] "Passage to India," p. 350.
[42] "Song of Myself," pp. 25-26.
[43] "Out of the Cradle Endlessly Rocking," p. 211.

A man, yet by these tears a little boy again,
Throwing myself on the sand, confronting the waves,
I, chanter of pains and joys, uniter of here and hereafter,
Taking all hints to use them, but swiftly leaping beyond them,
A reminiscence sing.[44]

Many of the poems in *Leaves of Grass* depend greatly upon the triadic technique for their structure. "Song of Myself" dwells from beginning to end on the double, or triple, nature of the poet's self: the "centripetal" self of the "influx" and the "centrifugal" self of the "efflux." "Starting from Paumanok" is one long dramatized triad, showing first the poet, then his comrade, then the two united. "Passage to India" depends for its most obvious content upon the triad of the East and West fused in and by the United States. "When Lilacs Last in the Dooryard Bloom'd" depicts chiefly the triad of life, death, and consolation. In fact, the question of the validity of Whitman's claims concerning the organic unity of *Leaves of Grass* can only be solved, in fairness to the poet, by reference to its triadic nature. For, as Whitman implies below, the work is dependent on the triad of unity-and-variety (note the references to variety and unity, the capitalized "Both" and "One," the parenthetical reference to contradiction). In other words, Whitman's work is as great a unity-in-variety as was his world. Each tendency is counteracted by a contrary tendency. All the poems flower from the central seed of the poet. Finally, in 1876 the two books, one representing unity, "pursuing a central idea with greater closeness," the other variety, "extremely varied in theme," are fused in "interpenetrating, composite, inseparable Unity":

The varieties and phases, (doubtless often paradoxical, contradictory,) of the two Volumes, of LEAVES, and of these RIVULETS, are ultimately to be considered as One in structure, and as mutually explanatory of each other—as the multiplex results, like a tree, of series of successive growths, (yet from one central or seed-purport)—there having been five or six such cumulative issues, editions, commencing back in 1855 and thence progressing through twenty years down to date, (1875-76)—some things added or re-shaped from time to time, as they were found wanted, and other things represt. Of the former Book, more vehement, and perhaps pursuing a central idea with greater closeness—join'd with the present

[44] *Ibid.*, p. 210.

One, extremely varied in theme—I can only briefly reiterate here, that all my pieces, alternated through Both, are only of use and value, if any, as such an interpenetrating, composite, inseparable Unity.[45]

I

The single poem perhaps most strikingly dependent on the triadic method is "Chanting the Square Deific." The four sections of the poem represent, at first glance, Jehovah, or Law; Christ, or Love; Satan, or Pride; and "Santa Spirita," or Spirit. A strict dialectical reading taking the elements in order of their appearance would result in the abstract progressive pattern: Law (thesis), Love (antithesis), Law-Love (synthesis); Law-Love (thesis), Pride (antithesis), Law-Love-Pride (synthesis); Law-Love-Pride (thesis), Spirit (antithesis), Law-Love-Pride-Spirit (synthesis). This is slightly more comprehensible if it is pictured allegorically as, first, the softening of Jehovah's law by Christ's loving kindness, after which the Pride which is Satan in man is conciliated and given an equal place in the Godhead, until finally all three combine with spirit in a great quaternity. The entire process is originated and culminated by Spirit, yet Spirit must necessarily create and be benefited by the others. Therefore, according to Whitman's reasoning, "all the sides [are] needed."

The "Square," as represented by Law, Love, Pride, and Spirit, is helpfully illuminated by Whitman's use of it in *Democratic Vistas:*

. . . in one sense, and a very grand one, good theology, good art, or good literature, has certain features shared in common. The combination fraternizes, ties the races—is, in many particulars, under laws applicable indifferently to all, irrespective of climate or date, and, from whatever source, appeals to emotions, pride, love, spirituality, common to humankind.[46]

This quotation is important because it suggests, if it does not authorize, the separation of the poem into two segments, one of which represents Law or Nature ("applicable indifferently to all"), while the other represents the other side of Whitman's familiar dualism, the human soul, with its emotions of pride and love and spirituality. One sees, then, that the first section of the poem defies the laws which govern human activity, while the second, third, and fourth

[45] "Preface to 1876 Edition," p. 516.
[46] *Complete Poetry and Prose,* II, 247.

sections show the human traits which, if properly developed under law, bring about the deification of the human who heeds the poet's instructions:

> Under the rule of God . . . be a rule unto thyself.[47]

This human being posseses the triad of pride and love:

> Encircling all, vast-darting up and wide, the American Soul, with equal hemispheres, one Love, one Dilation or Pride. . . .[48]

And he will, in time, possess the spiritual:

> Thou mental, moral orb—thou New, indeed new, Spiritual World!
> The Present holds thee not—for such vast growth as thine,
> For such unparallel'd flight as thine, such brood as thine,
> The FUTURE alone holds thee and can hold thee.[49]

The successive sections of the poem thus may be seen to be chronologically arranged, with the total embracing all of time.[50] The first section (employing the word "old" two times in the versions published before 1870, and, in one of the two changes made in this remarkably stable poem, three times in subsequent versions) represents the Past, while the second and third sections represent the present constituents of humanity, and the fourth section the Future. "Chanting the Square Deific" may thus be seen as complemented by the following poem:

> For him I sing,
> I raise the present on the past,
> (As some perennial tree out of its roots, the present on the past,)
> With time and space I him dilate and fuse the immortal laws,
> To make himself by them the law unto himself.[51]

And, much more strikingly, by the following quotations from *Democratic Vistas*, which alters the triad of pride and love to that

---

[47] "Thou Mother with Thy Equal Brood," p. 382.
[48] "Our Old Feuillage," p. 146.
[49] "Thou Mother with Thy Equal Brood," p. 384.
[50] This interpretation is supported by another use of the "Square" in *Democratic Vistas:* "To take expression, to incarnate, to endow a literature with grand and archetypal models—to fill with pride and love the utmost capacity, and to achieve spiritual meanings, and suggest the future—these, and these only, satisfy the soul" (*Complete Poetry and Prose*, II, 241).
[51] "For Him I Sing," p. 7.

of individualism and adhesiveness and shows how Democracy fosters, under law and religions old and new, the filling out of the "Square" with the final side, the Spiritual:

Democracy too is law, and of the strictest, amplest kind. . . . Would you have in yourself the divine, vast, general law? Then merge yourself in it.

And, topping democracy, this most alluring record, that it alone can bind, and ever seeks to bind, all nations, all men, of however various and distant lands, into a brotherhood, a family. It is the old, yet ever-modern dream of earth, out of her eldest and her youngest, her fond philosophers and poets. Not that half only, individualism, which isolates. There is another half, which is adhesiveness or love, that fuses, ties and aggregates, making the races comrades, and fraternizing all. Both are to be vitalized by religion, (sole worthiest elevator of man or State,) breathing into the proud, material tissues, the breath of life. For I say at the core of democracy, finally, is the religious element. All the religions, old and new, are there. Nor may the scheme step forth, clothed in resplendent beauty and command, till these, bearing the best, the latest fruit, the spiritual, shall fully appear.[52]

The "Christ," as representing that which levels and binds in a democracy, is delineated very clearly here:

What Christ appear'd for in the moral-spiritual field for human-kind, namely, that in respect to the absolute soul, there is in the possession of such by each single individual, something so transcendent, so incapable of gradations, (like life,) that, to that extent, it places all beings on a common level, utterly regardless of the distinctions of intellect, virtue, station, or any height or lowliness whatever—is tallied in like manner, in this other field, by democracy's rule that men, the nation, as a common aggregate of living identities, affording in each a separate and complete subject for freedom, worldly thrift and happiness, and for a fair chance for growth, and for protection in citizenship, &c., must, to the political extent of the suffrage or vote, if no further, be placed, in each and the whole, on one broad, primary, universal, common platform.[53]

And the place of this concept and its opposite tendencies in a Democracy is set forth further in *Democratic Vistas:*

First, let us see what we can make out of a brief, general, sentimental

[52] *Complete Poetry and Prose*, II, 223.   [53] *Ibid.*, p. 222.

consideration of political democracy, and whence it has arisen, with regard to some of its current features, as an aggregate, and as the basic structure of our future literature and authorship. We shall, it is true, quickly and continually find the origin-idea of the singleness of man, individualism, asserting itself, and cropping forth, even from the opposite ideas. But the mass, or lump character, for imperative reasons, is to be ever carefully weigh'd, borne in mind, and provided for. Only from it, and from its proper regulation and potency, comes the other, comes the chance of individualism. The two are contradictory, but our task is to reconcile them.[54]

Thus, the following paragraph, addressed to Culture, and stating how triadic Democracy will "tally" the laws behind Culture and reach a great fulfilment in the realm of spirit, is strictly in accordance with the ethic Whitman lays down in "Chanting the Square Deific." In fact, he offers the "Square" as "perhaps a deeper" principle than culture:

And now, for fear of mistake, we may not intermit to beg our absolution from all that genuinely is, or goes along with, even Culture. Pardon us, venerable shade! if we have seem'd to speak lightly of your office. The whole civilization of the earth, we know, is yours, with all the glory and the light thereof. It is indeed, in your own spirit, and seeking to tally the loftiest teachings of it, that we aim these poor utterances. For you, too, mighty minister! know that there is something greater than you, namely, the fresh, eternal qualities of Being. From them, and by them, as you, at your best, we too evoke the last, the needed help to vitalize our country and our days. Thus we pronounce not so much against the principle of Culture; we only supervise it, and pro-

[54] *Ibid.*, pp. 216-217. Whitman's footnote to this discussion shows an exact knowledge of the use of Hegelian dialectic as defined here by McTaggart:

". . . The examination of a certain category leads us to the conclusion that, if we predicate it of any subject, we are compelled by consistency to predicate of the same subject the logical contrary of that category. This brings us to an absurdity, since the predication of two contrary attributes of the same thing at the same time violates the law of contradiction. On examining the two contrary predicates further, they are seen to be capable of reconciliation in a higher category, which combines the contents of both of them, not merely placed side by side, but absorbed into a wider idea, as moments or aspects of which they can exist without contradiction" (John McTaggart Ellis McTaggart, *Studies in Hegelian Dialectic*, Cambridge, England, 1896, p. 1). Whitman's footnote reads in part: "Must not the virtue of modern Individualism, continually enlarging, usurping all, seriously affect, perhaps keep down entirely, in America, the like of the ancient virtue of Patriotism, the fervid and absorbing love of general country? I have no doubt that the two will merge, and will mutually profit and brace each other, and that from them a greater product, a third, will arise" (*Complete Poetry and Prose*, II, 261).

mulge along with it, as deep, perhaps a deeper, principle. As we have shown the New World including in itself the all-leveling aggregate of democracy, we show it also including the all-varied, all-permitting, all-free theorem of individuality, and erecting therefor a lofty and hitherto unoccupied framework or platform, broad enough for all, eligible to every farmer and mechanic—to the female equally with the male—a towering selfhood, not physically perfect only—not satisfied with the mere mind's and learning's stores, but religious, possessing the idea of the infinite, (rudder and compass sure amid this troublous voyage, o'er darkest, wildest wave, through stormiest wind, of man's or nation's progress)— realizing, above the rest, that known humanity, in deepest sense, is fair adhesion to itself, for purposes beyond—and that, finally the personality of mortal life is most important with reference to the immortal, the unknown, the spiritual, the only permanently real, which as the ocean waits for and receives the rivers, waits for us each and all.[55]

The "idea of the infinite" is an important prerequisite to the understanding of Whitman's "Santa Spirita":

> Beyond the light, lighter than light,
> Beyond the flames of hell, joyous, leaping easily above hell,
> Beyond Paradise. . . .

In "Plato," Emerson perhaps explains the "Beyond Paradise" idea: "That which the soul seeks is resolution into being above form, out of Tartarus and out of heaven,—liberation from nature."[56]

At this point, another splitting of the poem into two segments may be noted. In the division of the poem into Nature and the human, the first section alone represented Nature and the other three sections comprised the human, or self. In this instance, on the other hand, the first three sections are seen to make up the mortal, that which is within, or coextensive with, time and space; while the fourth section is immortal, infinite: beyond time and space or expression within human terms. The flexibility of the grouping here is brought about by the central triad of pride and love, or the peculiarly human qualities. The human is part of Nature by virtue of his body and his existence. On the other hand, he is part of the realm of spirit by virtue of his soul. Whitman frequently has

---

[55] *Complete Poetry and Prose*, II, 240-241.
[56] *Op. cit.*, IV, 51.

his Man belong first to one part of the dualism and again to the other in *Leaves of Grass:*

> When the full-grown poet came,
> Out spake pleased Nature . . . saying, *He is mine*;
> But out spake too the Soul of man . . . *Nay, he is mine alone. . . .*[57]

Of course, he belongs to both simultaneously, although at different times he may appear to belong principally to one or the other.

Thus Whitman's intention in "Chanting the Square Deific" begins to become clear. The first side, "Jehovah," signifies Nature, the natural, the material. The fourth side is its polar opposite: Soul, the supernatural, the Spiritual. Between these two extremes, and claimed by both, stands Man who, ideally, is part of the group by virtue of his Christ-like qualities, yet is a staunch individualist by virtue of a Satan-like pride. Nature has nurtured him: "after meteorological, vegetable, and animal cycles, man at last arises, born through them, to prove them, concentrate them, to turn upon them with wonder and love—to command them, adorn them, and carry them upward into superior realms. . . ."[58] The "superior realms," of course, are spiritual. Not until these reaches are attained is the square complete or are the other sides, particularly the second and third, divine. This may be diagrammed as: Law (thesis), Pride-Love, the human (antithesis), Law-Pride-Love, or the self-reliant Democratic human (synthesis); Law-Pride-Love (thesis), Spirit (antithesis), Law-Pride-Love-Spirit (synthesis).

There are undoubtedly other ways to read the "Square" dialectically. A particularly plausible method would begin with the lowliest side, that of Pride, and ascend through Love and Law to the pinnacle of Spirit. Spirit is the ultimate objective and it is also the aggregate, but this does not imply that it is greater than any of the other three sides. Nor, although in this particular poem they are represented as the complete Godhead, can these four be understood as exclusive of anything one might want to represent as one of Whitman's Gods. The poet has his answer to that:

> Have you thought there could be but a single supreme?
> There can be any number of supremes—one does not countervail an-

---

[57] "When the Full-Grown Poet Came," p. 451.
[58] *Complete Poetry and Prose*, II, 259.

other any more than one eyesight countervails another, or one life
countervails another.

All is eligible to all,
All is for individuals, all is for you,
No condition is prohibited, not God's or any.[59]

"Triadic Imagery" is, therefore, demonstrable throughout *Leaves
of Grass*. The extremely complex forms it takes seem to indicate
that Whitman early understood some type of dialectic, possibly
based on Emerson's essays, and after 1872 (the year of "Thou
Mother with Thy Equal Brood") probably derived from Whitman's
notions of Hegel. Much of Whitman's poetry can be interpreted
by reference to his use of this method. It provides certainly not
the only method of interpreting Whitman, but one which may often
lend new depths of clarity to readings of his poetry.

II

It is not entirely fair to Whitman's triadic method, however, to
examine it only for intellectual values. "Chanting the Square
Deific" is a powerful and unique poem; it represents as complete
and complex a poetic statement of a philosophy as one may easily
find. But the poem does not represent Whitman's great abilities
in handling drama, mood, natural imagery, and word music, abilities which may be shown to derive a great deal of their power from
the triadic method. From "Out of the Cradle Endlessly Rocking,"
the truth of this statement may perhaps best be verified.

The most important triadic theme in "Out of the Cradle Endlessly Rocking" is that of rebirth, a theme discussed above in connection with the triadic manifestation of the universe in time.
References to metempsychosis, or rebirth, abound in *Leaves of
Grass*. Whitman conceived this process as operative within both
human life and cosmic evolution. In the realm of the human, he
often equates death with the mother, both representing media of
birth. The "Dark mother" image of death in "When Lilacs Last
in the Dooryard Bloom'd" scarcely needs mentioning:

Dark mother always gliding near with soft feet. . . .

[59] "By Blue Ontario's Shores," p. 287.

The poet enunciated this doctrine clearly in the 1855 version of "The Sleepers," in addressing the night as death:

> I will duly pass the day O my mother and duly return to you;
> Not you will yield forth the dawn again more surely than you will
> yield forth me again,
> Not the womb yields the babe in its time more surely than I shall be
> yielded from you in my time.[60]

In a particularly striking image in "Song of Myself," Whitman elaborated on this theme, picturing the moment of death in terms which could only be used by one who knew well the process of human birth:

> And as to you Death, and you bitter hug of mortality, it is idle to try
> to alarm me.
>
> To his work without flinching the accoucheur comes,
> I see the elder-hand pressing receiving supporting,
> I recline by the sills of the exquisite flexible doors,
> And mark the outlet, and mark the relief and escape.[61]

In "Eidolons" he pictures the cosmic effect made by this eternally repetitive process in long periods of time:

> Ever the dim beginning,
> Ever the growth, the rounding of the circle,
> Ever the summit and the merge at last, (to surely start again,)
> Eidolons! eidolons![62]

When Whitman says, therefore, "the universe is a procession with measured and perfect motion,"[63] he is referring to the process by which the universe ameliorates toward an ever-remote ideal through many spiraling, almost identical cycles:

> In spiral routes by long detours,
> (As a much-tacking ship upon the sea,)

---

[60] *Leaves of Grass, 1855 Edition* (Facsimile Reproduction, New York, 1939), p. 77.
[61] *Inclusive Edition*, p. 74. This thought was phrased in a greatly similar manner by John Donne two hundred and fifty years earlier:
> ". . . our body's as the Wombe,
> And, as a Mid-wife, death directs it home"
("The First Anniversary," *The Poems of John Donne*, London, 1949, p. 220).
[62] *Ibid.*, p. 4.
[63] "I Sing the Body Electric," p. 83.

> For it the partial to the permanent flowing,
> For it the real to the ideal tends.[64]

And when he says, "The revolving cycles in their wide sweep having brought me again,"[65] he is depicting the rebirth functions of the cycles and showing how they have affected his own origin. But the cyclical movement is not something which affects him entirely from without. He finds that the incessant rising and falling of tides occurs in his consciousness:

> Does the tide hurry, seeking something, and never give up? Oh I
> the same. . . .[66]

So man is carried into the world by the cycles, in a way which makes their effect comparable to the rocking of a cradle:

> Cycles ferried my cradle, rowing and rowing like cheerful boat-
> men. . . .[67]

But when he is born, even discharged from the actual cradle of his childhood, the rocking continues within him, under the impetus of his desires, the vicissitudes of the world, and many other factors. And when he dies he is born into a new cycle; he will be rocked eternally by this cycle and those that succeed it. It was with these circumstances in mind that Whitman conceived the title "Out of the Cradle Endlessly Rocking."

In "Out of the Cradle Endlessly Rocking" at least two rebirths are dramatized in full and two or more others implied. The poem, to recapitulate, is based upon a reminiscence by the poet of an incident in his boyhood when he saw enacted on successive nights the drama of the happy connubial relations of two mockingbirds followed by their sad separation upon the disappearance of the female bird. In the poem the boy watches the male bird as he alternately pines and searches frantically for his mate along the seashore. The child is caught up by the pathos of the events and discovers that he too is longing for something. Finally both boy and bird come to realize, with the aid of the sea, that only in death will they find what they seek.

[64] "Song of the Universal," p. 192.
[65] "To the Garden the World," p. 77.
[66] "Not Heat Flames Up and Consumes," p. 104.
[67] "Song of Myself," p. 69.

The bird's experience, which represents the core of the fable of the poem, illustrates Whitman's idea of love as a medium of rebirth, an idea so pervasive in *Leaves of Grass* that the images of woman as lover and woman as mother are often identified:

> Unfolded out of the folds of the woman man comes unfolded, and is
>   always to come unfolded . . .
> Unfolded by brawny embraces from the well-muscled woman I love,
>   only thence come the brawny embraces of the man . . .
> First the man is shaped in the woman, he can then be shaped in
>   himself.[68]

The lover is seen by Whitman as one with his mistress in the same way as an unborn child is one with its mother. Both birth and love are important to the individual, according to Whitman, because of the great participation in synthesis: one's union with the other half of his universe. But separation is inevitable; in fact, it is part of the nature of things.

At the beginning of the poem, the emphasis is on the fusion of the boy with whatever great forces assist in the joy of childhood. The dark regions of the womb are to be seen implied in much of the imagery. In the early editions of the poem this meaning was made quite explicit:

> Out of the rocked cradle.
> Out of the mocking-bird's throat, the musical shuttle,
> Out of the boy's mother's womb, and from the nipples of her breasts.[69]

This context leaves little room for doubt that in the next line, "Out of the Ninth Month midnight,"[70] the poet is using the Quaker designation of September to imply the end of the human gestation period.

This meaning is not fully lost in the first three lines as printed in their final form:

> Out of the cradle endlessly rocking,
> Out of the mocking-bird's throat, the musical shuttle,
> Out of the Ninth-month midnight. . . .

And in the fourth line:

[68] "Unfolded Out of the Folds," pp. 327-328.
[69] "Variorum Readings," p. 636.
[70] *Leaves of Grass*, 1860 Edition, "A Word Out of the Sea."

> Over the sterile sands and the fields beyond, where the child leaving
>   his bed wander'd alone, bareheaded, barefoot,

it is reinforced by the contrast drawn by the adjective "sterile" and
the words "bareheaded, barefoot," implying the nudity of birth. The
next lines:

> Down from the shower'd halo,
> Up from the mystic play of shadows twining and twisting as if they
>   were alive,

carry the connotations into a new kind of birth imagery, the kind
used by Wordsworth in "Ode: Intimations of Immortality," depicting the holy, mystical nature of birth.

   This is not the only poetic context in which Whitman voices
this originally Platonic idea popularized by Wordsworth. W. L.
Werner,[71] in a stimulating interpretation of "The Mystic Trumpeter," sees the successive portions of that poem, each preceded by
the phrase "Blow . . . trumpeter," as depicting the consecutive periods in the poet's life. Werner does not attempt to interpret the lines
the poet writes on hearing the first notes of the trumpet. Yet, if
his interpretation of the remainder of the poem is correct (and
there seems to be little room for doubt that it is), this passage must
refer to the first significant period of Whitman's life, his childhood:

> Blow trumpeter free and clear, I follow thee,
> While at thy liquid prelude, glad, serene,
> The fretting world, the streets, the noisy hours of day withdraw,
> A holy calm descends like dew upon me,
> I walk in cool refreshing night the walks of Paradise,
> I scent the grass, the moist air and the roses;
> Thy song expands my numb'd imbonded spirit, thou freest, launchest
>   me,
> Floating and basking upon heaven's lake.[72]

   As the boy watches the bird with his mate, therefore, he is able
to share in the experience of the bird because this period of his life,
his early childhood, is analogous in intensity to the young-love period
of the bird.

[71] "Whitman's 'The Mystic Trumpeter' as Autobiography," *American Literature*, VII,
455-458 (Jan., 1936).
[72] "The Mystic Trumpeter," p. 390.

The "Two together" refrain of the bird's song is a terse symbol of Whitman's universe-in-synthesis. The use of this phrase as a nuclear triad in the passage was explained earlier:

Shine! Shine! Shine!
Pour down your warmth, great sun!
While we bask, we two together.

Two together!
Winds blow south or winds blow north,
Day come white, or night come black,
Home, or rivers and mountains from home,
Singing all time, minding no time,
While we two keep together.

The bird in "Out of the Cradle Endlessly Rocking," therefore, is seen to participate in one cycle, with a second implied. When he has his love, he is at the crest of the first cycle, and during this ecstatic period, as expressed in his song, all contradictions and conflicts and longings disappear. But with the loss of his mate the bird descends into the trough between cycles. The inference that only in death, the next cycle, will the bird reascend to the heights which he occupied before the loss of his mate is part of the great discovery of the poem.

The remainder of that discovery is the inference that the boy, too, will find what he seeks in death. Since he cannot be seeking a lost mate, the most likely inference is that he is seeking his mother —dead, or simply unable to keep the years from alienating her growing child from her.

"Out of the Cradle Endlessly Rocking" deals, therefore, with what Whitman felt to be the three pinnacles of human life: birth, love, and death. Man progresses from one height to the next only by descent into a valley of loss and despair. The boy is placed in the birth cycle and participates in the analogous experiences of the bird in the love cycle. Both boy and bird, as well as the reminiscing poet in the background, take part in the portion of the death cycle which is foreshadowed in the poem. This fusion is fostered by the magical intermediation of the shore, which he calls elsewhere "that suggesting, dividing line, contact, junction, the solid marrying the liquid—that curious, lurking something . . . which means far more

than its first sight. . . ."[73] When the boy searches for the answer
to his quest,

> O give me the clew! (it lurks in the night here somewhere,)
> Or if I am to have so much, let me have more!
>
> A word then, (for I will conquer it,)
> The word final, superior to all,
> Subtle, sent up—what is it?—I listen;

he looks to the sea and the sands,

> Are you whispering it, and have been all the time, you sea waves?
> Is that it from your liquid rims and wet sands?

And, as if he had spoken the "Open Sesame" of the spiritual universe,

> . . . the sea
> Delaying not, hurrying not,
> Whisper'd me . . .
> Death, death, death, death, death.

Then, the great fusion of the song of the bird, the songs of
Whitman man and boy, and the word "death" comes about.

> But fuse the song of my dusky demon and brother,
> That he sang to me in the moonlight on Paumanok's gray beach,
> With the thousand responsive songs at random,
> My own songs awaked from that hour,
> And with them the key, the word up from the waves,
> The word of that sweetest song and all songs,
> That strong and delicious word which, creeping to my feet. . . .

And death is then shown as identical with birth in the image of an
"old crone," rocking the cradle which is death:

> (Or like some old crone rocking the cradle, swathed in sweet gar-
>   ments, bending aside,)
> The sea whisper'd me.

The use of the cradle image carries the additional implication that
even death is not at all the last cycle in which a human being participates. As the poet says elsewhere:

> . . . When we become the enfolders of these orbs, and the pleasure and

---

[73] *Supra*, pp. 103-104.

*knowledge of every thing in them, shall we be fill'd and satisfied then?
. . . No, we but level that lift to pass and continue beyond.*[74]

Whitman's treatment of the cycles in "Out of the Cradle Endlessly Rocking" is, however, not marked solely by its use of the
high, the ecstatic, moments. In fact, the mood of despair into which
each cycle descends and from which each subsequent cycle must
ascend is the predominant mood of the poem. Whitman never
forgot that man must periodically know despair. When he por-
trays these moments in his poetry, no memory of happier moods
avails to do more than deepen his depression:

> . . . before all my arrogant poems the real Me stands yet untouch'd,
>   untold, altogether unreach'd,
> Withdrawn far, mocking me with mock-congratulatory signs and
>   bows,
> With peals of distant ironical laughter at every word I have written . . .
> Because I have dared to open my mouth to sing at all.[75]

Such was the mood of Whitman in his moments of doubt,
moments whose experiencing he called, "wend[ing] to the shores
I know not."[76] Its opposite mood he calls in the same poem
"wend[ing] . . . the shores I know. . . ."[77] These are the moods
which Whitman's triadic technique reconciles in "As I Ebb'd with
the Ocean of Life," with the line: "You oceans both, I close with
you. . . ."

In "Out of the Cradle Endlessly Rocking," the mood of longing
gives way to a mood which is, in great measure, a fusion of man's
longing for life with his fear of death, his doubt with his faith.
The revolution is accomplished by Whitman's treatment of death
as analogous to love and the things which man seeks in life. This
theme is motivated by the same preconceptions which led the poet
to write in 1855:

Has Life much purport?—Ah, Death has the greatest purport.[78]

[74] "Song of Myself," p. 71.
[75] "As I Ebb'd with the Ocean of Life," p. 217.
[76] *Ibid.*, p. 216.
[77] *Ibid.*
[78] "Variorum Readings," p. 467

And in 1892:

> And I myself for long, O Death, have breath'd my every breath
> Amid the nearness and the silent thought of thee.[79]

This is the "thought of death" which he speaks of in "When Lilacs Last in the Dooryard Bloom'd." It is the fusion of death with life. And, finally, this synthesis is the height which man must scale after youthful love is gone and before death comes to take its place.

Whitman has much to say about this "thought of death," in his prose as well as his poetry. In fact, if one is to see the mature poet Whitman as participating in "Out of the Cradle Endlessly Rocking," and is to search, as was done above with the child, for the analogous experience in the life of the poet at that time to which he was relating the experiences of the boy and the bird, the only cycle in which he might be placed would be that cycle within which this consciousness of death gave the principal published meaning to his life. This must be true, because it is the principal message of the poem. To Whitman at this stage, life only has purport as "Death has the greatest purport."

This is the final fusion in "Out of the Cradle Endlessly Rocking," the poem in which the techniques of fusion and cyclical movement see their greatest development. Whitman's use of natural imagery (the rising and falling of the water, the ascent of the moon, the play of the shadows, the "shuttle" of the bird's song) serves to heighten the effect of these techniques while concealing the relatively simple logic which lies behind them.

Triadic imagery yields, in "Out of the Cradle Endlessly Rocking," therefore, poetic forms as dramatic and musical as those in "Chanting the Square Deific" are terse and logical. The technique is simple, but it yields a theme upon which Whitman can and does play with endless variation. In tracing its ramifications one may determine the meaning, to the poet and his poetry, of some of Whitman's seemingly most abstruse and complicated ideas.

[79] "Death's Valley," p. 462.

Whitman Pursued
Emory Holloway

Writers interested in Walt Whitman's psychology have had much to say about his response, or lack of response, to the attractions of the opposite sex. Less has been said about his attraction for that sex. Yet the latter influence would seem to be one measure of the former. The importance of determining beyond question whether Whitman did, or could, enter into a normal heterosexual relation with at least one woman lies in the effect such determination would have upon the interpretation of not a few of his poems. Were a single such relationship established in a way none could question, he might perhaps be classified as bisexual and his poems interpreted accordingly, but he could never be treated as a simple homosexual. In that event the paradox of his poems need no longer tempt critics and biographers to slight inconvenient facts in their straining for a simple and consistent interpretation of his verse.

It has been generally known that some women have been so strongly attracted by his poetry that they have been personally drawn to the man who so ambiguously identified himself with his book. Anne Gilchrist is a case in point, as perhaps is Mrs. James Parton ("Fanny Fern"). The recent Bradley edition of the fourth volume of Horace Traubel's *With Walt Whitman in Camden* adds another instance.[1] It prints a letter, preserved by Whitman for more than a quarter of a century, written by one Susan Garnet Smith, of Hartford, Connecticut, in 1860, inviting him to become the father of a child by her, though she had never met him except in the pages of his book—presumably the third edition. Whitman's first reaction to the peculiar letter was to question Miss Smith's sanity, as Burroughs was to think Anne Gilchrist "neurotic."[2] Nothing further is known of Miss Smith.

There is evidence that he was attractive to women who *had* met him personally. I do not here refer to the person who inspired

[1] Philadelphia, 1953, pp. 312-313.
[2] Clara Barrus, *Whitman and Burroughs, Comrades* (Boston, 1931), p. 157.

"Once I Pass'd through a Populous City" (if we are to disregard Whitman's expressed wish that it be taken only as a poetic idea poetically expressed and not as having reference to a personal experience of the author) for it is possible this person may have been either a woman or a man.[3] Nor do I refer to Mrs. Nellie Eyster, who in 1870, inspired not only by his poems but also by frequent sights of Walt on a Washington street car, wrote him a reverential letter, which is preserved by Traubel.[4] But this lady author has never met him, is about to leave for her home in Harrisburg, and thus far, at least, seeks no more intimate acquaintance.

[3] To complete the record it may be well to give a version of this poem published in the *American Magazine* in December, 1887 (N.S. II, 217-222). There Cyrus Field Willard, in an article entitled "A Chat with the Good Gray Poet," describes a visit paid Whitman by him and a friend named Patterson, bearing introductions from Thomas Donaldson. After Whitman had declined to recite any of his own poems for them, Patterson said, " 'The other night my friend here recited a poem of yours, Mr. Whitman, to a party of ladies who were very much charmed with it.' 'Ah, what one was that?' said the ancient poet, with a purr of pleasure in his vast voice. Whereupon," continues Willard, "I repeated these lines of tremendous flattery:

> Once in the days of my youth,
>   I roamed through a beautiful city,
> Noting the houses, the stores, the
>   churches, theatres,
> Markets: acquiring the architecture,
>   customs
> Looks and lingo of the people;
>   hiving them
> All up for future reference.
> But now all that I remember
>   of that
> City is a Woman who detained me
> There for the Love of me. Houses, stores,
> Customs, costumes, churches,
>   theatres, looks
> And lingoes all are vanished, are
> Gone, are played out. But the
> Woman—She remains.

" 'Yes, I believe I wrote some lines like those,' said Walt in low, slow tones, as if his mind, while he spoke, had travelled back years, many years, and was now operating his voice from a great grim distance. Then, with a touch of pardonable vanity in his utterance: 'So they liked it, did they?' 'Yes,' said I, 'they were highly pleased with it.' "

At first this version appears to be the result of very poor memorizing and still worse comprehension of Whitman's verse; yet in the same article is a perfect quotation of "O Captain! My Captain!" If the latter had been checked by Whitman's text, why not the present poem? If, on the other hand, it be deliberate parody, it more or less harmonizes with the concluding poem, "America's Greeting to Walt" by "one of his admirers," in which eulogy is mixed with conscious or unconscious caricature. For our present purpose, the significant fact is that a version which emphasizes the femininity of the lover proved pleasing to women, and apparently Whitman was satisfied to have it so.

[4] *With Walt Whitman in Camden* (Boston, 1906), I, 34-35.

But one day in 1888 Mrs. Davis, Whitman's devoted housekeeper, speaking of a portrait on the poet's mantelpiece, said:

"Mr. Whitman, what a charming, winning face this lady has. I take a look at her every time I come into the room."

"Ah, do you think that?"

"Yes."

"Some day when I feel more like it than I do now I will tell you about her. She was an old sweetheart of mine—a sweetheart, many, many years ago."

"Is she living yet?" The question seemed to stir Whitman profoundly [Traubel says]. He closed his eyes, shook his head.

"I'd rather not say anything more about that just now."[5]

This was probably the same portrait that Whitman himself referred to in an autobiographical sketch which, over a pseudonym, he had written for the *Critic* in 1885. Describing his room, he had said, "Hung or tacked up on the walls are pictures, those of his father, mother and sisters holding the places of honor, a portrait of a sweetheart of long ago, etc."[6] The picture was apparently still there when Dr. Theodore F. Wolfe called on Whitman in his last years. In listing the pictures he saw, he includes "portraits of his parents (his father's face is a good one) and sisters, and of another—not a sister."[7] It is quite possible that the picture is also the one referred to by Henry Bryan Binns in a letter to Edward Carpenter: "J. H. Johnston [showed me] a photo of a young N. Y. actress who had been 'one of Walt's sweethearts.'"[8] This could hardly have been Christine Nilsson, the Swedish concert and operatic star, although it is known that Whitman did have a photograph of her.[9] She was twenty-seven when she came to America in 1870; Whitman fifty-one. Even if she met him soon after her arrival, the date would hardly have seemed "long ago" in 1885. Her first appearance was at Steinway Hall in New York, with Brignoli, one of Whitman's favorite singers. Walt was personally acquainted with him.[10] Possibly Whit-

[5] *Ibid.,* I, 389.

[6] Emory Holloway, ed., *The Uncollected Poetry and Prose of Walt Whitman* (Garden City, 1921), II, 60.

[7] *Literary Shrines* (Philadelphia, 1897), p. 206.

[8] This letter, dated Sept. 28, 1904, was printed by Edward Naumberg, Jr., in the *Princeton University Library Chronicle*, III, 12-13 (Nov., 1941), in an interesting article, "A Collector Looks at Whitman."

[9] This picture is now in the possession of Mr. John Clopton Farley of Los Angeles. It is not a picture, it need hardly be said, of the same person as that in the 1859 Whitman notebook (reproduced in *Uncollected Poetry and Prose,* II, facing p. 70).

[10] *With Walt Whitman in Camden,* IV (Bradley ed.), 250.

man met her through Brignoli and at some time was given a photo-graph of her.

The "sweetheart" photograph, then, remains unidentified, but its amply established existence tends to support Whitman's claim to have had a love affair. He reacted with emotion when shown an un-signed article about himself in the New York *Herald* of September 23, 1888. Though Whitman was himself sending many contribu-tions to the *Herald* at the time, he said he was unable to identify the writer. His adverse criticism was limited to one paragraph. "There's that last paragraph—the bad taste of it; I 'never had a love affair,' he says, 'Taint true—Taint true!'"[11]

Two bits of evidence that Whitman had had intimate relations with one or more women (if any reader of the "Children of Adam" poems feels the need of such evidence) may here be introduced. A letter to Whitman from Pete Doyle in the Pierpont Morgan Library, dated September 27, 1868, contains the following:

Jim Sorrill sends his love & best respects & says he is alive & kicking but

---

[11] *With Walt Whitman in Camden* (New York, 1908), II, 425. The author says that he had met Whitman in 1885 and had seen him frequently since. He quotes Whitman on a number of subjects and declares the direct quotations (of which the passage Whitman objected to is one) were checked by the poet himself. All the others agree with Whitman's views as elsewhere expressed, and even with his idiom, but the passage in question certainly does not sound like Whitman, nor is it corroborated by any other such statement about himself. The exact words are: "I am an old bachelor who never had a love affair. Nature supplied the place of a bride, with suffering to be nursed and scenes to be poetically clothed." It is true that in repudiating the quotation Whitman gave as evidence of its inaccuracy his unsupported statement that one of his descendants had recently desired to visit him but had been discouraged by Whitman because to do so would mean sacrificing a fortune of $30,000 or $40,000 "for a sentiment." A week before he had found the same article amusing (*ibid.*, p. 383), but in the meantime he appears from Traubel's account to have denied checking the quotations in it, and now he has become very serious and emotional. The explanation may be that his biographer Bucke has written Traubel that he is highly pleased with the *Herald* article, especially the disputed passage. At this very time Whitman had begun to hint to Traubel that there was a big secret in his life, and to let this article go unchallenged, it might be argued, would destroy the consistency of any story he had to tell. (Later he wrote to Bucke about it also. Barrus, *op. cit.*, p. 338 n.) Such an argument would be equally sound whether the story of his illegitimate fatherhood were true or, as Charles W. Eldridge believed, the result of hallucination (Barrus, *op. cit.*, p. 336; Naum-berg, *op. cit.*, p. 13). Eldridge gives no facts to support his assumption. If Whitman was *compos mentis* at this time, the only way to attack his story is to attack the moral character or the memory of the witness. That others have done so, supplying him with adequate motives for lying, I am well aware. But this is not the place to argue the matter. Three years before, he had declared over a pseudonym that he had had a love affair and in 1888 he repeats the declaration in the presence of Traubel and Mrs. Davis, and categorically denies a published statement to the contrary. We can hardly use the word of an anonymous journalist to prove that he is not telling the truth. The burden still rests on those who impeach his veracity or his sanity.

the most thing that he don't understand is that young Lady that said you make such a good bed fellow.

This seems to contradict the report of Whitman given in the interview which prefaces the *Calamus* letters, where Doyle is quoted as saying:

I never knew a case of Walt's being bothered up by a woman. In fact, he had nothing special to do with any woman except Mrs. O'Connor and Mrs. Burroughs. His disposition was different. Woman in that sense never came into his head. Walt was too clean. No trace of any kind of dissipation in him. I ought to know about him those years—we were awful close together.[12]

It is true he limits his testimony to the years of his close association with Whitman, but in the letter from Binns to Carpenter already quoted the author declares, "Maynard[13] says that Doyle admitted he knew a woman in Washington with whom Whitman had sex relations." This woman and the one mentioned in the Jim Sorrill quotation above need not be the same one, but, taken together, the two remarks make perfectly clear Doyle's meaning, and they weaken the testimony of the *Calamus* preface as it has been commonly interpreted.

In his biography of Whitman, in referring to Whitman's often quoted assertion to Symonds that he was himself an unmarried father, H. B. Binns prints what information he had picked up pertinent to the matter. "There is a love-letter extant, signed with a pseudonym, dated from New York in 1862, evidently written by a cultivated woman."[14] But he does not tell quite all that he knows, for in the letter to Carpenter to which two references have already been made he is more explicit: "Traubel showed me a love-letter from Ellen Eyre (? of New York) in 1860. . . ." This "Ellen Eyre" letter may still exist; in any case, there are copies of it, one of which was presented to me by Mrs. F. R. Garrett of Freeport, New York, and another has recently been turned over to the New York Public Library with the Lion Collection.[15] The primary purpose of the

[12] Walt Whitman, *Complete Writings* (New York, 1902), VIII, 7.

[13] Laurens Maynard, who published *Calamus* in Boston in 1897, the volume in which Doyle's somewhat unclear statement about Walt's not having been "bothered up" occurs. The volume was edited by Dr. R. M. Bucke. Cf. footnote 12 *supra*.

[14] *A Life of Walt Whitman* (New York, 1905), p. 350.

[15] The present article was accepted for publication before the author knew of the forth-

present article is to ascertain, if possible, whether the original can be found or information obtained concerning the identity of "Ellen Eyre." Though my own copy is a photostat, it is useless for comparing handwritings since it, like the Lion copy, is not made from the original, but from a copy once given by Horace Traubel to Dr. G. P. Wicksell, and by him given to Mr. John Clopton Farley. It appears not to be in Traubel's handwriting, but may be in Wicksell's. Mrs. Traubel told Mr. Farley she could not find the original letter among her husband's manuscripts.

Tuesday Mar 25 1862

MY DEAR MR WHITMAN:

I fear you took me last night for a female privateer.

It is true I was sailing under *false colors.*—but the flag I assure you covered nothing piratical though I would joyfully have made your heart a captive.

Women have an unequal chance in this world. Men are its monarchs and "Full many a rose is born to blush

unseen and waste its sweetness
on the desert air."

Such I was resolved would not be the fate of the fancy I had long vouchsafed for you.[16]

A gold mine may be found by the Divining Rod but there is no such instrument for detecting in the crowded streets of a great city the unknown mine of latent affection a man may have unconsciously inspired in a woman's heart. I make these explanations in extenuation not by way of apology. My social position enjoins precaution and mystery and perhaps the enjoyment of my friends society is heightened [if] while yielding to its fascination I preserve my incognito. Yet mystery lends an ineffable charm to love and when a woman is bent upon the gratification of her inclination she is pardonable if she still spreads the veil of decorum over her actions. Hypocrisy is said to be the homage sin pays to virtue, and yet I can see no vice in that generous sympathy in which we share our caprices with those who have inspired us with tenderness. I trust you will think well enoug[h] of me soon to renew the pleasure you afforded me last P. M. and I therefore write to remind you that there is a sensible head as well as a sympathetic heart, both of which would glad-

coming publication of the Lion copy of the "Ellen Eyre" letter in Professor Gay W. Allen's biography of Whitman.—*Editor's note.*

[16] There are evidences of hasty copying, so that it may well be that the original letter contained only two long paragraphs, for some indentations are slight and irregular. I have, however, reproduced them as they appear in my copy.

ly evolve with warmth for your diversion and comfort [.] You have already my whereabouts and my house. It shall only depend upon you to make them yours and me the happiest of women.

I am always yours sincerely

ELLEN EYRE

No address is given in the heading, but Binns is probably right in suggesting New York. Not only does the letter itself refer to "the crowded streets of a great city," but Whitman was in the Brooklyn-New York region at the time. His "Brooklyniana" sketches in the Brooklyn *Standard* did not end until November 1, 1862, having begun in the preceding year. Furthermore his New York *Leader* articles began on March 15, 1862, ten days before the "Ellen Eyre" letter was written.[17] There is ample evidence that Whitman remained at home until he went to the battlefields of Virginia on December 16, 1862.

That something more than a meeting and a letter may have come from the encounter is indicated by a brief entry in a Whitman notebook, one of many he used to keep track of his chance acquaintances.

Frank Sweeney (july 8th '62) 5th Ave. Brown face, large features, black moustache (is the one I told the whole story to about Ellen Eyre)— talks very little.[18]

The phrase "whole story" suggests that there may have been more than a mere incident, and, since the notebook entry was made more than three months after the receipt of the letter, there was, of course, time for the development of intimacy. Who Sweeney was can only be conjectured. His name does not appear in either New York or Brooklyn directories for this period, nor does any other Sweeney with a Fifth Avenue address. The indefinite "5th Ave." may therefore have referred to the Fifth Avenue line of buses, which Whitman says he frequented, fraternizing with the drivers.[19] Obviously one reason for picking him, and only him, for a confidant was that he "talks very little." And if he belonged to the unsophisticated race of bus drivers he would be far removed from the Bohemian group of

---

[17] Charles I. Glicksberg, *Walt Whitman and the Civil War* (Philadelphia, 1933), p. 18.
[18] In the Harned Collection of the Library of Congress; quoted, in part, in Charles I. Glicksberg, "Walt Whitman in 1862," *American Literature*, VI, 276 (Nov., 1934); printed in full in Louis Untermeyer, *The Poetry and Prose of Walt Whitman* (New York, 1949), p. 53.
[19] *Complete Prose* (New York, 1914), p. 12.

actresses and literati that Whitman regularly met at Pfaff's beer
cellar, of whom "Ellen Eyre" may well have been one.

I have a letter addressed to Whitman the following April in
which he is saluted as the "Prince of Bohemians."[20]   Henry Clapp
was "King of Bohemia" and the acknowledged "Queen of Bohemia"
was the author and actress Ada Clare.   "Ellen Eyre" had said that
Whitman knew where her house was (which fact, taken with her
precaution, accounts for the absence of her address from the letter),
and the address of Ada Clare's house, 86 West 42 Street, appears
twice in Whitman's memoranda.   The pseudonym in the letter was
obviously used for anonymity, not for identification, since the writer
had been with Whitman the preceding evening; yet it may be mentioned that Ada Clare had once acted a minor part in *Jane Eyre*.[21]

Ada Clare, born Jane McElhinney, was a cousin of Paul Hamilton Hayne, the poet, and grandniece of Senator Robert Hayne, to
whom Webster made his famous reply.   If we may trust the description of Charles Warren Stoddard, one of her ardent admirers, she
was a beautiful blonde, with blue eyes and golden, naturally wavy
hair.   At nineteen she left her Southern home with the well known
musician, Louis M. Gottschalk, who, though she bore him a child,
abandoned her without marrying her.   She went to Paris, but was
soon in New York publishing poetry in the New York *Atlas,* in the
same year that Whitman issued *Leaves of Grass.*   She was about
twenty-six[22] when the "Ellen Eyre" letter was written.   By this time
she was not only a journalist but an actress of beauty and charm.
Her code of morals was unconventional and she is said to have been
accustomed to sign hotel registers "Miss Ada Clare and son."   James
Brownlee Brown said, "Ada Clare is virtuous after the French fashion, namely, has but one lover at a time."[23]   When she died of
hydrophobia in 1874, Whitman wrote to Mrs. O'Connor: "Poor,
poor Ada Clare—I have been inexpressibly shocked by the horrible
& sudden close of her gay, easy, sunny, free, loose, but *not ungood*
life."[24]   However unconventional Whitman's own conduct may

[20] Printed by Roger M. Asselineau in "Walt Whitman, Child of Adam?," *Modern
Language Quarterly*, X, 91-95 (March, 1949).

[21] George C. Odell, *Annals of the New York Stage* (New York, 1927-1939), VI, 493.

[22] If a newspaper account of her death (New York *Herald*, March 6, 1874) is accurate,
she would have been thirty in 1862.

[23] Barrus, *op. cit.,* p. 3.

[24] *Ibid.,* p. 4. ALS in the Berg Collection of the New York Public Library.

have been at this time, and the frequently quoted passage from the *Notes* he helped John Burroughs to write in 1867 certainly suggests that it was far from Puritan, he did not approve of all Ada Clare did. Clara Barrus tells the story of his having rebuked her when she advised a young would-be suitor to first seduce his fiancee and then return to her.[25] Still, Albert Parry may be right when he says, "Whitman admired Ada Clare because of her great charm, but also because he saw in her a New Woman born too soon."[26]

Yet there is reason to question whether Ada was the author of the "Ellen Eyre" letter. It seems rather out of character for her to be so respectful of conventions and so fearful of losing her position in society. The probability that Whitman had met her before March, 1862, the date of the letter, is less significant, for "Ellen" writes of "the fancy I had long vouchsafed for you." That Ada knew of and admired Walt's poetry as early as December, 1859, is shown by the warm praise in her review of "Out of the Cradle Endlessly Rocking" which she published when it came out. Like Whitman she wrote for the New York *Leader* in 1862.[27] The address of Ada's house found in Whitman's notebook appears in the New York Directory for 1861 but not in that for 1862. Moreover, the Whitman memoranda appear in a notebook which also contains the date November 26, 1860, though it may well have covered more than one year. That Whitman had been at her house there is little doubt. Speaking to Traubel of his meeting Ned Wilkins, he said, "I think it was at Ada Clare's: and by the way, it is very curious that the girls have been my sturdiest defenders, upholders. Some would say they were girls little to my credit, but I disagree with them there."[28] She was in the habit of holding court with her Bohemian friends in her home, and the context of Whitman's reference suggests that he had attended a soiree there. The address in his notebook may accordingly mean no more than this. Yet some woman, not likely "Ellen Eyre," had inspired Whitman, by October 12, 1861, to write "I Heard You Solemn-Sweet Pipes of the Organ," for it was

[25] *Ibid.*, p. 3.
[26] *Garrets and Pretenders* (New York, 1933), p. 14. To this book I am indebted for several of the details given about Ada Clare. Others will be found in Holloway and Adimari, *New York Dissected* (New York, 1936), pp. 232-233.
[27] Barrus, *op. cit.*, p. 2.
[28] *With Walt Whitman in Camden*, III, 117.

published on that date in a form which, to me, makes it clearly a romantic rather than a patriotic poem.[29]

If Ada Clare, whatever the degree of her intimacy with Whitman, was not the author of the "Ellen Eyre" letter, then who was? Dismissing as altogether unlikely Mrs. James Parton, who, nearly seven years earlier had written an enthusiastic review of *Leaves of Grass,* the first by a woman, there is one other possibility which I have thus far been unable to trace. It is Mrs. Juliette H. Beach, of Albion, New York. She was another admirer of Whitman mentioned by Clara Barrus; she wrote Whitman many beautiful letters. These Burroughs was unable to persuade her to have published. Miss Barrus affirms that "Out of the Rolling Ocean the Crowd" was inspired by her.[30] Presumably in the early days of their association in Washington Whitman was less reserved concerning his personal life than he later became, and Burroughs confided in Miss Barrus. Mrs. William Douglas O'Connor (later Mrs. Calder) also thought that this poem had been inspired by a married woman, but she fixed the date tentatively as 1864.[31] So far as the date of publication is concerned, it could fit either Mrs. Beach or some woman whom Whitman had known in Washington, possibly the one to whom Pete Doyle refers.

That Whitman, on his part, would not be deterred from any sort of personal relationship that seemed to him desirable is suggested not only by poems like "Native Moments" but also by one of the injunctions he directed to himself when composing *Leaves of Grass.* This one Dr. Bucke says was written "about 1856," though I have sometimes found Bucke to be very inaccurate in such guesses.

Boldness—*Nonchalant ease and indifference.* To encourage me or any one continually to strike out alone.—So it seems good *to me*—This is *my* way, *my* pleasure, *my* choice, *my* costume, friendship, amour, or what not.[32]

This agrees with the not-to-be-forgotten passage from Burroughs's *Notes on Walt Whitman as Poet and Person* to which reference

[29] The original version, quoted from the New York *Leader,* is given in the present writer's *Walt Whitman, Complete Poetry and Selected Prose and Letters* (London, 1938), p. 1066.

[30] *Life and Letters of John Burroughs* (Boston, 1925), I, 120 n. In the index the author says Mrs. Beach wrote "verses" as well as letters to Whitman.

[31] *Uncollected Poetry and Prose of Walt Whitman,* I, lviii n. 15.

[32] *Complete Writings,* VI, 7.

has already been made. The little book appeared only about five years after the "Ellen Eyre" letter.

Through this period (1840-55), without entering into particulars, it is enough to say that he sounded all experiences of life, with all their passions, pleasures and abandonments. He was young, in perfect bodily condition, and had the city of New York and its ample opportunities around him. I trace this period in some of the poems of "Children of Adam" and occasionally in other parts of the book, including "Calamus."[33]

If the little information presented in this article should elicit more, until we have factual proof of just what was Whitman's emotional make-up, much biographical and critical attention that has been devoted to the subject could turn to the understanding of the poetry itself. That would be something devoutly to be wished.

[33] New York, 1867, p. 81.

Transcendentalist Catalogue Rhetoric:
Vision Versus Form
Lawrence Buell

WHITMAN'S CATALOGUES are a most salient feature of his poetry, and certainly the most neglected. It is tempting to skip over them as we read. "The pure contralto sings in the organ loft," etc.—why bother with the rest? After all, we can predict what the next sixty lines will say. And so we pass quickly by the redundant images to follow the "movement" of the poem, whatever that is, so as to be able to come up with a theory of structure which will satisfy our struggling students, and our own rage for order. Dawdling among the catalogues only slows us down.

Still, when we allow ourselves to "loafe" awhile, we may be struck by Whitman's art in such passages, which at first seem the very antithesis of art. Sensitive discussions of Whitman, like Randall Jarrell's, show that other readers have felt the same way;[1] and the impact of catalogue rhetoric upon poets is certainly attested to by the tradition in American poetry which, following Whitman, employs it, not to mention the long antecedent tradition of prophetic

---

[1] See Jarrell's essay, "Some Lines from Whitman," in *Poetry and the Age* (New York, 1955), pp. 101-120. Several more scholarly though less sensitive studies of Whitman's catalogues have been made. Mattie Swayne, "Whitman's Catalogue Rhetoric," *University of Texas Studies in English*, XXI, 162-178 (July, 1941), is illuminating on the underlying purpose of the catalogue but confines its discussion of the style itself mainly to the characteristic grammatical patterns used by Whitman. Detlev W. Schumann, "Enumerative Style and Its Significance in Whitman, Rilke, Werfel," *Modern Language Quarterly*, III, 171-204 (June, 1942), is chiefly valuable for general comparisons and contrasts among the three writers. Stanley K. Coffman, Jr., "'Crossing Brooklyn Ferry': A Note on the Catalogue Technique in Whitman's Poetry," *Modern Philology*, LI, 225-232 (May, 1954), defends the artfulness of the catalogue as a structural device in terms of a particular example, as I attempt to do in the first section of this paper. Especially stimulating is Coffman's discussion of the progression of tone and idea within and between the two principal catalogues in "Brooklyn Ferry." Harry R. Warfel, "Whitman's Structural Principles in 'Spontaneous Me,'" *College English*, XVIII, 190-195 (Jan., 1957), detects unity and movement in the apparent randomness of another catalogue. All four scholars relate Whitman's use of the catalogue to transcendentalist idealism, and their observations—though quite brief, except in Miss Swayne's case—should be compared with mine below, as should Roger Asselineau's interpretation of catalogues as "spiritual exercises" in *The Evolution of Walt Whitman: The Creation of a Book* (Cambridge, Mass., 1962), pp. 102-103.

poetry from the Bible to Blake. But not only can Whitman's catalogues be regarded as prominent examples of a pedigreed technique; in his case the device has special significance because it is the exact stylistic counterpart of an important article of transcedentalist philosophy, as advanced by himself, Thoreau, and especially Emerson, whose essays make use of the catalogue almost as frequently as Whitman's verse, and for similar reasons. In reading Emerson, indeed, we are apt to experience just the same sort of alternation of impatience and fascination as our mental mood switches from analysis to receptivity and back again. Such responses to Emerson may be less keen than to Whitman, because Emerson is writing in prose and his appeal is intellectual rather than sensuous; but by the same token, he writes oftener and more articulately about the aesthetic theory behind the catalogue, and it is to him we must frequently turn in order to understand Whitman's use of the technique.

In this essay, then, I shall want to consider the catalogue, in Whitman's verse and Emerson's essays, both as an aesthetic device and as the expression of transcendentalist thought, relying on Whitman for most of the examples and Emerson for most of the theory. In particular, I hope to defend the catalogue against the charge of formlessness which has frequently been made against it.

I

To see how a good Whitman catalogue works, let us examine the following lyric from "Calamus":[2]

> Roots and leaves themselves alone are these,
> Scents brought to me[n] and women from the wild woods
>   and pond-side,[3]
> Breast-sorrel and pinks of love, fingers that wind around
>   tighter than vines,
> Gushes from the throats of birds hid in the foliage of trees as
>   the sun is risen,
> Breezes of land and love sent from living shores to you on the
>   living sea, to you O sailors!

[2] The following and all subsequent quotations from Whitman are from *Leaves of Grass, Comprehensive Reader's Edition,* ed. Harold W. Blodgett and Sculley Bradley (New York, 1967).

[3] I cannot believe that "me" in this line is correct. It makes no sense, and it is not to be found in any previous printings of the 1892 or 1860 editions which I have consulted.

> Frost-mellow'd berries and Third-month twigs offer'd fresh
>   to young persons wandering out in the fields when the
>   winter breaks up,
> Love-buds put before you and within you whoever you are,
> Buds to be unfolded on the old terms,
> If you bring the warmth of the sun to them they will open
>   and bring form, color, perfume, to you,
> If you become the aliment and the wet they will become
>   flowers, fruits, tall branches and trees.

Upon first reading, the poem appears to be little more than it says it is: a cluster of images, placed in loose apposition, with a bit of moralizing at the end. The casual bouquet is presented to the reader as if unsorted and not yet even in bloom. "Roots and leaves themselves alone are *these*"—these lines, in other words, which are to the finished poem what buds are to flowers. These buds of language are "to be unfolded on the old terms": we must "bring the warmth of the sun to them" and supply the nourishment ourselves if the cluster is to blossom for us. In plain language, Whitman seems to be saying that his poem, more than most, depends for its meaningfulness upon our participation. This is true, and not merely of this one lyric, but of all of Whitman's poetry. It requires us to take part in two main ways.

First, the reader must respond sensuously: smell the scents; feel the fingers tighter than vines, and the breezes; hear the gushes from the throats of birds; taste the frost-mellowed berries; and behold all. This is not as easy to do as it may seem. The sensuous appeal of poetry is made via the intellect and is too often weakened in the process; it is one thing to recognize the technique of synesthesia used here, another thing to participate in it. The odors in the poem, for instance, are much more apt to come across as "perfume" in the abstract than as the particular scents of "breast-sorrel and pinks of love." After all, most readers do not know what sorrel and pinks smell like, and the mixture of floral and human odors here implied may seem droll or repulsive (though only to the mind, not to the lover actually experiencing the sensation), so that the degree to which even the most sensitive reader can unfold such buds as these is bound to be limited. Nevertheless, a greater opening of the senses than is usually made in reading poetry is possible here, and if we can so respond, the buds *will* open and bring color and perfume to us. And in the same manner, all of Whitman's good catalogues will be felt as far richer than most poems.

But, one might argue, not only must the buds blossom; they must also be arranged, in order to be fully satisfying as art. As will soon become evident, I think this proposition is debatable, but since Whitman does promise that his buds can take "form" for us, we may assume that a second demand a Whitman catalogue makes upon us is the perception of some sort of design. So, too, does most poetry; but in Whitman's case, the demand is more difficult, because it is made so faintly. To find structure in Whitman's catalogues, beyond the obvious and rudimentary prosodic controls, is much harder than responding to them sensuously. In the "Calamus" poem quoted above, one immediately feels that some of the images could be repositioned with almost equal effect; that in places words, phrases, and even lines could be excised or added without doing great violence to the poem. Still, like a surprising number of Whitman's catalogues and catalogue poems, it has a definite organization, as subtle in its own way as a good lyric by that modern master of plethora, Dylan Thomas.

To begin with, the very miscellaneousness of the poem is a kind of unity. "A great disorder is an order," as Stevens's Connoisseur of Chaos says. Roots, leaves, scents, vine-like fingers, breast-sorrel, pinks, and all the rest come tumbling out of Whitman's horn of plenty, creating the impression of all nature (here a metaphor for the poet's words) burgeoning to unfold itself to the lover-reader. Through the piling up of images in every line Whitman conveys the sense of plentitude which is also his message.

Indeed throughout Whitman a main purpose of the catalogue seems to be to express the boundless fecundity of nature and human life, and thereby his own "leaves" also. The tone varies, of course. In "Roots and Leaves" it is loving and intimate. Elsewhere the poet may be filled with a religious awe, as in "limitless are leaves stiff or drooping in the fields. . . ." And sometimes the catalogue has a comic aspect:

> I find I incorporate gneiss, coal, long-threaded moss, fruits,
>   grains, esculent roots,
> And am stucco'd with quadrupeds and birds all over . . . .
>
> ("Song of Myself," ll. 670-671)

These lines are of special interest, because they show in miniature
how, in the midst of apparent randomness, Whitman may structure
his lists in a second and more subtle way, so as to express something
more than mere plenitude. At first, we probably feel a kind of
bemused amazement: gneiss, coal, long-threaded moss, fruits, grains,
esculent roots—how in the world did all these diverse things get
thrown together in one package? The speaker seems just as sur-
prised as the reader: "I find I incorporate" so many different things,
he exclaims. The heterogeneity of the list is positively droll, especially the zoological collage in the second line. But despite this
initial response, and the fact that it depends partly upon the sense
that the items in the passage are as unrelated as the items in a
garbage can, we can find a careful and significant arrangement of
parts. Word sounds help to paste them together, subliminally, as
it were. Gneiss–moss, fruits–roots, stucco–quadrupeds—these are
some examples of coherence by means of alliteration and assonance.
But in addition to this, Whitman has listed the items in an almost-
evolutionary order, beginning with gneiss, which is inanimate, and
moving up the scale of being to quadrupeds and birds. The lines
which follow give the key to the progression:

> And have distanced what is behind me for good reasons,
> But call any thing back again when I desire it. (ll. 672-673)

The "I" of the passage, that is, personifies the evolutionary process,
which has just unscrolled itself in the previous catalogue.

   In "Roots and Leaves" as well, the sheer proliferation of images
is like an ornate screen which hides as much of Whitman's artistry
as it exhibits. Other devices lie behind it, implicit. One, already
noted, is the appeal to *all five* senses. Parallelism, too, shapes and
gives emphasis: in lines 7-8, which point to the moral, and 9-10,
which draw the conclusion, for example. More subtle is the
alternation earlier in the poem of lines which merely list (1, 3, 4)
with lines that connect the images to a subject (2, 5, 6) and are
constructed around the pattern noun-past-participle-to-subject-(from-

place). One wonders if this pattern was consciously formulated, but
its existence shows, in any case, a sense of order on Whitman's part.
There is even a visual pattern in the lines, a little like the floral
arrangement of Thoreau's *"Sic Vita."* The first six lines are pro-
gressively longer; then two short lines make the assertion which ties
together what precedes, while the implications dangle like the stems
in a bouquet in the two longer lines at the end of the poem.

In order to show that Whitman's catalogues *can* be as rich in
unity as they are in diversity, I have deliberately chosen good examples. Often, it is true, the structure of his catalogues consists
almost wholly in their plenitude, in the parallelism of piled-up, end-
stopped lines, producing, at its worst, rudimentary paeans or chants
like litanies from the *Book of Common Prayer*. But often enough
both tone and structure are more complex, creating tapestries of
imagery and rhetoric which are fine by any standard, like the
eighth section of "Song of Myself," section three of "Brooklyn
Ferry," and the two shorter examples analyzed here. We tend not
to acknowledge the art of such passages, partly because we read
Whitman's good catalogues with his bad ones in mind, but partly
because Whitman's art is so implicit. His verbal pyrotechnics are
meant to seem spontaneous, but that does not mean they are.

And yet because Whitman's art *is* so implicit it is dangerous to
analyze it too persistently in the way I have just done, stressing the
instances of sophisticated design in his catalogues. It is necessary
to realize that such design can be found, but wrong to attach too
much significance to it. In so doing we are liable to rest in a too
simple evaluation of Whitman's poetry: to divide his catalogues
into a small group which have design and are therefore "good," and
a large group which are relatively amorphous and therefore "flawed."
Such a polarization ignores the fact that the element of structure in
a Whitman catalogue—indeed in any Whitman poem—even where
refined, is relatively unstressed. The order of importance is the
order in which we have proceeded: the individual sensuous and
emotional responses are paramount, then the sense of plenitude, and
lastly, when it exists, the design. Nor is this order of priority mainly
the result of sloppiness or incapacity on Whitman's part, though
these doubtless contributed. Rather it reflects Whitman's conscious
aesthetic purpose, which will become more clear as we define, in

the next section, the sense of values which underlies the catalogue technique.

II

It has been noted that among his contemporaries Whitman was by no means the sole maker of literary catalogues. Emerson, Thoreau, and even Melville also used the device; indeed, the paratactic and reiterative qualities of Emerson's and Thoreau's prose are so strong that in places they are indistinguishable from Whitman's verse.

What was responsible for this affinity? Partly, no doubt, the stylistic influence of Emerson and/or Carlyle. But a more basic reason is that the catalogue expresses a particular way of looking at the world, one which has its roots in transcendentalist idealism but was shared with Emerson and Thoreau by Whitman and, to a lesser extent, Melville.

A look at a representative Emerson catalogue, from "Compensation," will help show the connection:

The world globes itself in a drop of dew. The microscope cannot find the animalcule which is less perfect for being little. Eyes, ears, taste, smell, motion, resistance, appetite, and organs of reproduction that take hold on eternity,—all find room to consist in the small creature. So do we put our life into every act. The true doctrine of omnipresence is that God reappears with all his parts in every moss and cobweb. The value of the universe contrives to throw itself into every point. If the good is there, so is the evil; if the affinity, so the repulsion; if the force, so the limitation.[4]

Stylistically, this paragraph differs from Whitman's catalogues only in the irregular length of its items and their predominantly intellectual appeal. In Whitmanian fashion, each sentence repeats the first assertion in a fresh context. The doctrine of the microcosm is justified in turn by microbiology, human action, theology, metaphysics, and the laws of morality and physics. Like the separate lines of Whitman's catalogues, Emerson's sentences give the appearance of being self-contained and interchangeable; transitions are at a minimum; and it seems as if sentences could be added or deleted

[4] *The Complete Works of Ralph Waldo Emerson,* ed. Edward Waldo Emerson (Boston, 1903-1904), II, 101-102.

without cost. But again like Whitman, closer inspection shows that rhythm and Emerson's tactic of moving from the elementary (dew-drop, animalcule) to the more significant (human action, doctrine of omnipresence) do give the order of the paragraph a certain amount of inevitability. And again, this twofold impression the passage makes is well suited to what seems to be Emerson's purpose—to overwhelm us with the multiplicity of instances but at the same time impress us with the design inherent in these. The sentences are the dewdrops, and the paragraph is the world.

But more noteworthy than the parallels between Emerson's lists and Whitman's is the fact that this paragraph reveals the basis for those affinities, the principle of microcosm itself. In both writers, this principle underlies and, to a great extent, determines the use of the catalogue. Elsewhere Emerson's criticism makes this quite plain. Because every particular nature is a symbol of spirit, all natures, he argues, are related to each other by analogy: "each creature is only a modification of the other" (I, 44). And just as symbol and analogy are the bases of natural law, so they are the chief methods of literary style, for a work of art is properly "an abstract or epitome of the world . . . . the result or expression of nature, in miniature" (I, 23). In the process of composition (an-other term which Emerson characteristically uses with double refer-ence to rhetoric and nature, to denote the arrangement of parts both in a landscape and in a discourse), analogy is of special importance. For the order of nature is a unity of endless variety, in a constant state of flux, with all objects blending together on the one hand, and melting into spirit on the other—"as the bird alights on the bough, then plunges into the air again, so the thoughts of God pause but for a moment in any form" (VIII, 15). Therefore "the quality of the imagination" must likewise be "to flow, and not to freeze" (III, 34). The "essential mark" of good poetry "is that it betrays in every word instant activity of mind, shown in new uses of every fact and image, in preternatural quickness or perception of relations" (VIII, 17).[5]

---

[5] The foregoing analysis gives Emerson's essential view of the subject, but there is, we should note, one important inconsistency, due to Emerson's ambivalent and changing philosophy of nature. In *Nature* a rigid conception of nature as a closed system of 1:1 correspondences is adumbrated in "Language," side by side with the more flexible view just analyzed, which is expressed in "Discipline" and "Idealism." The former notion,

The rapidity of metamorphosis which Emerson perceives in nature and demands of literature is precisely the outstanding feature of his own dazzling batteries of aphorisms in such passages as the one from "Compensation" quoted above. For many readers, this quality has seemed the hallmark of his style and thought, as distinctive to him as the verse catalogue is to Whitman. "The whole fascination of life" for Emerson, O. W. Firkins once wrote, without much exaggeration, "lay in the disclosure of identity in variety, that is in the concurrence, the *running together,* of several distinct images or ideas."[6]

A similar sense of nature's unity in diversity, we have seen, underlies the plenitude of images in the Whitman catalogues discussed earlier. But Whitman, less concerned with man's relation to nature than with his relation to other men, characteristically expressed the principle in a way slightly different from Emerson. He accentuated its democratic side, so to speak. Whitman's fundamental purpose in *Leaves of Grass,* as he often said, was "to articulate and faithfully express in literary or poetic form, and uncompromisingly, my own physical, emotional, moral, intellectual, and aesthetic Personality, in the midst of, and tallying, the momentous spirit and facts of its immediate days, and of current America."[7] This plan, however, had much the same implications for style as Emerson's theory of nature, because Whitman shared Emerson's basic assumption of divine immanence. For this reason, the persona—the "I"—in Whitman's poetry is, like the "self" described in "Self-Reliance," not merely individual but cosmic, and as such can participate in the experiences of all men in the same way that Emerson's Oversoul inheres in all men and all parts of nature. For rendering this collective conception of the self poetically, the catalogue is a most appro-

---

derived mainly from Swedenborg and his disciples, Emerson never quite outgrew; it comforted him, perhaps, to go on believing that natural objects "are really parts of a symmetrical universe, like words of a sentence; and if their true order is found, the poet can read their divine significance orderly as in a Bible" (VIII, 8). But for the most part, the idea of a symbolic universe was a liberating, rather than a restricting conception for Emerson, and he liked to stress the versatility of the symbol both in nature and in the poet's hands. In "The Poet" he specifically repudiated the point of view of the "mystic," who "nails a symbol to one sense, which was a true sense for a moment, but soon becomes old and false" (III, 34).

[6] *Ralph Waldo Emerson* (Cambridge, Mass., 1915), p. 237.
[7] "A Backward Glance o'er Travel'd Roads," p. 563.

priate technique. Through it, the self can be sung in such a way as
to incorporate, or seem to incorporate, all particular selves. "Of
these one and all I weave the song of myself," Whitman says at the
end of one long catalogue. "These" are the disparate images of
human life which the poet has just listed, to the end of showing how,
"one and all," they are united in "myself." The method of the
song mirrors the complex unity of the singer.

We must be careful, of course, not to apply the principle of unity
in diversity to the analysis of catalogue rhetoric in a too mechanical
way, to reduce every catalogue to an illustration of the principle.
Nobody writes great poetry on principle, at least not very often.
On the contrary, it is likely that the flatness of Whitman's later
poetry, for example, was caused at least in part by writing from
principle, by imitating himself, as it were. And yet the connection
between paratactic style and microcosmic universe was undeniably
felt by him and by Emerson; it was not merely a matter of principle
but of perception. Thoreau's sensitivity to it was equally keen (see
the conclusion to his description of the thawing Walden hillside in
"Spring") and so, almost, was Melville's. Melville is an especially
interesting case because he was writing out of doubt instead of
affirmation and yet adapted the catalogue brilliantly to those ends
in the rhetoric of such passages as "The Whiteness of the Whale."
Unlike the other three writers, he exploited the ironic possibilities
of the technique: the variety of instances Ishmael cites may or may
not have unity; the appearances may or may not be significant.
But the habit of conveying ideas by means of a barrage of linked
analogies is distinctively transcendental. It is the end product of
transcendentalism's cardinal tenet: that the Oversoul is immanent
in all persons and things, which are all thereby symbols of spirit
and conjoined by analogy in an organic universe.

III

The fact that the transcendental catalogue is based upon the sense
of the universe's spiritual unity in diversity makes it unique in
Western literature. Though the catalogue as a literary device is as
old as Homer, and the principle of plenitude is almost as hoary, in
no other period, so far as I know, are the technique and the

Weltanschauung fused so closely as they are in the American renaissance.

This fusion, to my mind, accounts for a good deal of the richness and fascination of transcendentalist literature. It has not, however, tended to arouse much enthusiasm in other readers. An important reason for this seems to be that it also goes far in explaining why, in the style of the catalogue, structure plays a subordinate role and why, in general, transcendentalist literature is often rather formless. For Emerson, Whitman, and Thoreau all regarded art pragmatically, that is, as properly the expression of something beyond itself—call it vision, truth, or what you will; they were, in short, not trying to write poems but nature; and they were therefore convinced that the secret of design in art rested rather in the ability to perceive the natural order than in imposing an aesthetic order upon their perceptions. Thus Thoreau structured his major works around the days of the week or the course of the seasons or the sequence of a journey; Whitman, for his controlling motifs in "Lilacs" to "Passage to India," relied on personal experience and contemporary history; and Emerson arranged his first book and many subsequent essays in what he considered were natural orders, hierarchical and dialectical patterns chiefly. Clearly all three believed that there was design in nature and likewise valued design in art; but they did not believe in making the latter an end in itself. And so we find Emerson exclaiming in one place: "It is much to write sentences; it is more to add method, and write out the spirit of your life symmetrically . . . to arrange many general reflections in their natural order so that I shall have one homogeneous piece"—but affirming elsewhere that "the truthspeaker may dismiss all solicitude as to the proportion and congruency of the aggregate of his thoughts, so long as he is a faithful reporter of particular impressions."[8]

Recent criticism, setting a high valuation upon structure, has often been nettled by this second attitude and blamed transcendentalist art for insufficient attention to form and transcendentalist criticism for making art the handmaiden of its nebulous doctrines. Such criticisms invariably hold up the catalogue as the epitome of these deficiencies. Charles Feidelson, for example, has argued in the case

[8] *Journals of Ralph Waldo Emerson,* ed. Edward Waldo Emerson (Boston, 1909-1914), VI, 47-48, and V, 327.

of Emerson that the principle of unity in diversity inhibits him as
a symbolist because when applied as a concept of structure it provides
"no brake on the transmutation of form" and thus easily degenerates
into a mere multiplication of instances.[9]

Up to a point, this line of reasoning is persuasive. Plenitude,
both as a theory of nature and as a theory of structure is, in itself, a
quite elementary conception. In fact, from remarks like Emerson's
last, one suspects that the transcendentalists used it partly just as a
substitute for something better: that they seized upon it as a formula
for order partly because it was such a convenient way of accounting
for the prevailing *dis*order. The principle was specific enough to
give them a sense of design, yet vague enough to relieve them of
the need to order their thoughts more rigorously—a difficult problem to begin with for diarists like Emerson and Thoreau or an
imagist like Whitman. As a result, their catalogues, like the
thought which produced them, seem fitted as structures for the
short run only. In the more elementary units of composition—the
short lyric, the paragraph, the passage: in other words, the kinds
of examples analyzed above—they were able to do impressive things
with plenitude as an ordering principle, but when they extended
themselves further they lapsed into sheer itemization. Perhaps
Whitman had this problem in mind when he made the decision to
divide his longer poems into sections or when, in his old age, he
stated his agreement with Poe's dictum that there is no such thing
as a long poem.[10]

But is "Roots and Leaves" really a better poem than "Song of
Myself," or even a better catalogue than the longest section of the
"Song," section 33, which is much less tightly knit than many of
Whitman's shorter lists? State the issue this way and at once we
sense that it is risky to disparage the catalogue for formlessness, even
where it is clearly amorphous, and riskier still to chastise the transcendentalist world view, however simple, for cramping its style.

[9] *Symbolism and American Literature* (Chicago, 1953), p. 150. See also René Wellek's
section on Emerson in *A History of Modern Criticism* (New Haven, Conn., 1965), III, 163-
176. "For both scholars, the catalogue and the principle of plenitude behind it seem to
represent what is weakest in Emerson's art and criticism." Both discussions, especially
Feidelson's, are very provocative, and it will be obvious to the reader that I have been
influenced by them even while reacting against them.

[10] "A Backward Glance," *op. cit.*, p. 569.

Where the lines are good, who cares about the structure? Where the philosophy makes good poetry, why cut off the stream at its source?

The passage just referred to begins with a beautiful eighty-line list of places visited by the singer, now "afoot with my vision" more ecstatically than at any other place in the poem. The voyager sees, for example:

> Where herds of buffalo make a crawling spread of the square
>   miles far and near,
> Where the humming-bird shimmers, where the neck of the
>   long-lived swan is curving, and winding,
> Where the laughing-gull scoots by the shore, where she laughs
>   her near-human laugh,
> Where bee-hives range on a gray bench in the garden half hid
>   by the high weeds,
> Where band-neck'd partridges roost in a ring on the ground
>   with their heads out . . . . (ll. 761-765)

The list could be, and is meant to seem, endless. It is the longest and loosest catalogue in a long, loose poem. Even in these five lines, the connection among the images is tenuous. All are pictures of wildlife, and one could say something about interplay between motion and rest or near and distant perspective, but the true impact of these lines does not really depend upon such relations, any more than it depends elsewhere in Whitman upon almost-evolutionary orders or the tailoring of a poem's shape to look like a bouquet of flowers. The contribution of rhythm excepted, it consists in the language ("crawling spread of the square miles," "humming-bird shimmers," "scoots by the shore," "range on a gray bench in the garden half hid," "roost in a ring on the ground with their heads out," etc.) and the tremendous sense of vitality conveyed by running these and many more epiphanies together—a vitality made more intense by those phrases within individual lines whose sounds slide and bounce into one another, as in the five phrases just quoted. Texture and vision: these, in short, are what make the passage beautiful. We cannot share as doctrine the Emersonian idea that every creature is only a modification of every other, but we can experience it by allowing ourselves to drift with the speaker through these images.

Indeed we have to experience it, even accept it, if we are to read the passage, since the visionary element is inextricable from the best "poetic" qualities of these and other Whitman catalogues. In its ascendency, this element forces structure and aesthetic considerations generally to play second fiddle, but at the same time produces great poetry. Our recognition of this fact needs to be less grudging. We tend to separate inspiration from craftsmanship as naïvely as the transcendentalists confused them, and so are deprived of the critical habits and terminology needed to appreciate works which are committed to the use of style as a vehicle for vision. The distinction, to be sure, is important, but when taken as inherent rather than provisional it prevents us from reading a catalogue for anything more than the pictures. The poet and the prophet are not so easily divorced; and we may even find that it is the second which makes the first worthwhile, if we will permit ourselves to think like Old Critics for a moment. In much good literature, I should venture to say, and certainly in literature so vatic as the transcendentalists', the literary expression is only the beginning, albeit an indispensable beginning, of its appeal, just as it was only the result or end product of the forces which produced it.

Such, at any rate, was the opinion of the transcendentalists. The basic message they had to offer, if one may generalize so sweepingly about a field so wide and hazy, was power. Books, as Emerson wrote in "The American Scholar," "are for nothing but to inspire" (I, 89). This purpose finds impetus and justification in the principle of plenitude, the idea of microcosm underlying it, and the belief in divine immanence which is at the heart of both. All of these are essentially doctrines of open-endedness, promising limitless possibilities for adumbration, refinement, and growth. To the end of expressing these conceptions, and above all the sense of power from which they spring, the catalogue is ideally suited. Even where formless—indeed, we could say, *especially* where formless—the catalogue has the potential for power. Its very rawness makes it all the more vigorous and striking.

The structural limitations of the catalogue, then, are finally irrelevant. It is meant to be wild; the inspired poet, as Emerson put it, "knows that he speaks adequately . . . only when he speaks somewhat wildly" (III, 27). If there is a limit to the length a catalogue can be sustained, it is not so much in the number as the quality of the items. We could easily dispense with a "Salut au Monde," but that does not mean that another catalogue poem of the same length cannot succeed. Naturally, just as the mixture of short and long sentences in a paragraph makes for a pleasing variety, so in a poem of sizable proportions or a prose work as long as an Emerson essay, discursive passages are most effective if punctuated by terse ones. The same rule of variety applies in miniature to rhythm and line-length, as Emerson's less inspired efforts in iambic tetrameter couplets attest. But both expansion and concentration can be equally effective; and so long as there are freshness and variety in the images, and a minimum amount of modulation from one item to the next in addition to mere juxtaposing, the catalogue can be prolonged almost indefinitely.

What the reader most needs to bring to the catalogue, perhaps, is a sense of abandonment. This does not mean the complete denial of the critical faculty, but only its suspension, for as long as it takes to get caught up, or at least to give the piece a fair trial. One feels that whatever intricate design a catalogue may later be seen to have, it is essentially an outpouring, intended to stir up, not to settle. Maybe this is partly why Whitman, in so many poems like "Roots and Leaves," explicitly beckons to the reader and invites him to participate. An Emerson paragraph makes the same demand, in its own way. It is not merely a bag of duckshot, as Carlyle suggested, speaking like a structural critic;[1] it is a bag of snakes. And the fact that so often critics, even as they deplore the lack of discipline in Emerson's prose, line their own paragraphs with his aphorisms, shows that they are still hissing.

[1] *The Correspondence of Emerson and Carlyle,* ed. Joseph Slater (New York and London, 1964), p. 371.

The Quaker Influence on Walt Whitman
Lawrence Templin

ON NOVEMBER 20, 1855, *Leaves of Grass* was the main topic of conversation at a meeting of Quaker abolitionists in Philadelphia. One of the members of the group had purchased a copy for his seventeen-year-old daughter and was himself delighted by it and its Emersonian style.[1] It was not by accident that there were at least a few Quakers able to appreciate Whitman's poetic message, for Whitman was at his core a religious man, and the core of his religion was his belief in what the Quakers call the Inner Light.

In order to place Whitman into relationship with Quakerism it is perhaps valuable to begin with the simple fact that early Quakerism was simultaneously an extension of fundamental Puritan ideas and a revolt against the Puritan tendency to solidify ideas into authoritarian theology. Thus, "whereas the Puritans had 'purified' the church of prayer-books, vestments and music, the Quakers wished to go one step further and purify the church of clergy."[2] They wished to maintain an openness to the source of religious illumination. They firmly believed that God did speak directly *to individuals* and that a community of believers was possible without the intervention of ecclesiastic authority. Just as the Quakers went beyond Puritanism, however, Whitman went beyond Quakerism, recognizing both his differences and his likenesses to the followers of the Inner Light.

The purpose of this article is to summarize the facts of Whitman's relationship to Quakerism and to define at least three basic kinds of indebtedness: for what Whitman calls his Quaker intui-

[1] Frederick B. Tolles, "A Quaker Reaction to *Leaves of Grass*," *American Literature*, XIX (May, 1947), 170–171.

[2] Frederick B. Tolles, "Emerson and Quakerism," *American Literature*, X (May, 1938), 144. Mr. Tolles describes the kinship between Emerson and Quakerism in terms of this extension of Puritan ideas and revolt against Puritanism. According to F. O. Matthiessen, "the sympathetic kinship that Emerson felt with Quakerism in his liberated maturity had belonged to Whitman as his birthright" (*American Renaissance*, New York, 1941, p. 538). Thus Whitman may be thought of as an individual who did not merely revolt against Puritanism, but who in some ways carried on the tradition through his connection with Quakerism.

tion; for the inspirational effect on Whitman of the Quaker leader, Elias Hicks; and for the implications of Quakerism to Whitman. The relationship has not, I think, been fully summarized and explored for the light it sheds on Whitman's work as a creative artist.

I

I have a sense of things that seems to precede all judgments.
. . . It's the Quaker in me—in me strong here and there.[3]

There are relatively few biographical facts concerning Whitman's Quaker background and its possible influence on him. This is revealed in the fact that some critical biographers, John Burroughs[4] and Gay Wilson Allen,[5] for example, have almost nothing to say about the Quaker influence. Others—notably Henry Seidel Canby,[6] Emory Holloway,[7] Clifton Furness,[8] and F. O. Matthiessen[9] —do rather generally credit Whitman's mysticism, religious outlook, and humanitarian principles to Quakerism.

It was from his mother that Whitman was supposed to have acquired his Quaker tendencies. Louisa Van Velsor was part Quaker in the sense that her mother, Naomi Williams, came from Quaker stock and maintained Quaker ways and sympathies. It is probable that Whitman's maternal grandmother, or her parents, were barred from Quaker membership for marrying outside the society.[10] Thus, as far as formal membership is concerned, Whitman was two or three generations removed from Quaker circles, and certainly the Whitmans were not Quaker in any formal or active sense. Yet in later life Whitman seems to have been increasingly absorbed with the desire to pick up threads of influence, and Quakerism was important to him as one of these threads.

Another connection with Quakerism mentioned by Whitman was the association of his grandfather with the Quaker leader, Elias Hicks. Hicks was well known on Long Island. In his youth he had

[3] Horace Traubel, *With Walt Whitman in Camden*, 4 vols. (I, Boston, 1906; II, III, New York, 1908, 1914; IV, Philadelphia, 1953), II, 207.
[4] *Whitman, A Study* (Boston, 1896).
[5] *The Solitary Singer: A Critical Biography of Walt Whitman* (New York, 1955).
[6] *Walt Whitman, An American* (Boston, 1943), pp. 33–36; and *Classic Americans* (New York, 1931), pp. 312–313, 322–323.
[7] *The Uncollected Poetry and Prose of Walt Whitman*, 2 vols. (Garden City, N.Y., 1921), I, xxiv.
[8] *Walt Whitman's Workshop* (Cambridge, Mass., 1928), pp. 192, 212–213.
[9] *American Renaissance* (New York, 1941), pp. 536–540.
[10] Henry Bryan Binns, *A Life of Walt Whitman* (London, 1905), pp. 347–348.

been a sociable fellow who liked to dance, go hunting and fishing, and join in the general merrymaking of young people his age. He happened at this time to be in a group with which Whitman's grandfather was also associated.[11] Later, when Hicks became well known on Long Island as a relatively prosperous farmer, a Quaker leader, and a preacher attracting large crowds, Whitman's parents attended some of his public meetings. Whitman made much in later years of the influence of Hicks on his family and himself. He said once, "It was through my mother that I learned of Hicks: when she found I liked to hear of him she seemed to like to speak."[12]

Though the formal connections with Quakerism were few, Whitman picked out the Quaker influence, slender as it may have been, to explain the humanitarian and intuitive characteristics in his own nature. His "Quaker" mother is thus made a source of style and inspiration: "Leaves of Grass is the flower of her temperament active in me."[13] His father's antislavery attitude is explained as a result of his being a follower of Hicks; and all Quakers, Whitman said, were opposed to slavery.[14] It is interesting to note, however, that even as an old man, mellowed by this reminiscing, Whitman was forced to admit the discontinuity and the vagueness of the Quaker influence in his own general makeup. He knew he was not, could not be, in fact, a real Quaker, as he told Horace Traubel.

[Whitman:] "When I was a young fellow up on the Long Island shore I seriously debated whether I was not by spiritual bent a Quaker?— whether if not one I should not become one? But the question went its way again: I put it aside as impossible: I was never made to live inside a fence." [Traubel:] "If you had turned a Quaker would Leaves of Grass ever have been written?" [Whitman:] "It is more than likely not—quite probably not—almost certainly not."[15]

If Whitman had become a Quaker at the age of twenty, by Quaker discipline he would have had to give up going to stage plays and concerts, to avoid reading "pernicious" books, to give up any inclination toward accepting a governmental office, and generally to live simply and not in "conformity to the vain and changeable

---

[11] Bliss Forbush, *Elias Hicks, Quaker Liberal* (New York, 1956), p. 9.
[12] Traubel, II, 114.
[13] Ibid., p. 113.
[14] Ibid., III, 109.
[15] Ibid., II, 19.

fashions of the world."[16] Instead of adopting any such quietistic creed, Whitman went to work as a printer, joined debating societies, became an editor, and enjoyed plays, concerts, and operas, preparing himself for the affirmations of the activities of the world in the early *Leaves of Grass*. In an editorial for the *Daily Crescent* in 1848 the young Whitman explicitly rejected the Quaker refusal to bear arms in these words: "Quakerism can never become the creed of the race; and you might as well expect all men to adopt the straight-cut coat and plain phraseology of the followers of Fox, as to hope that the principles of peace will ever become the law of men's opinions and actions."[17]

Even in later life, when Whitman could speak fondly of his "Quaker" mother, and of his own Quaker intuition, he was well aware of the narrowness of the sect in custom and discipline and could speak with some feeling of their "damnable unreason" for being "fiercely opposed to pictures, music in their houses." He wanted to flaunt the picture of Elias Hicks in the faces of the Quakers who would buy *November Boughs*.[18] In the same year, 1888, Whitman received a short friendly note from the Quaker poet Whittier. Traubel asked Whitman whether Whittier had finally committed himself to *Leaves of Grass*. "Good heavens no!" said Whitman. "He has too much respect for himself, for his puritan conscience, to take such a leap."[19]

Walt Whitman was well aware of the real gap that separated him from the Puritan conscience of the Quaker. There was too much of the love of the world in Whitman to set up the typical Quaker hedge against outside influences. Yet Whitman could feel the effect of the root similarities between his own mystical experiences and the experiences of the Quaker in silent meeting "centering down" and waiting for illumination. He correctly labeled this root similarity his "Quaker intuition." Through it he shared the Quaker concern for unity and humanitarian equality that lies beneath the surface of apparent religious formlessness and unworld-liness in Quakerism. One could perhaps better phrase this as the paradox of the individual and the *en masse*, or of the community

---

[16] *Discipline of the Yearly Meeting of Friends Held in New York* (New York, 1839), p. 54 et passim.
[17] *The Uncollected Poetry and Prose of Walt Whitman*, I, 197.
[18] Traubel, II, 125.
[19] Ibid., p. 7.

achieved through individual intuition of the Inner Light, that works itself out in many ways in both Whitman and Quakerism. It was largely through Elias Hicks that Whitman seems to have got the sense of this paradoxical conception.

II

The fullness of the Godhead rests in man and in every blade of grass.[20]

—ELIAS HICKS

In his early days Whitman had learned much about Elias Hicks, who was admired by the boy's parents and by his grandfather Whitman. In November 1829 Whitman heard Hicks preach his last sermon before a large audience in a second-floor ballroom of Morrison's Hotel in Brooklyn. Hicks was eighty-one and died a few months later. The unity of the Quakers was already shattered by the Separation into Orthodox and Hicksite meetings. Yet according to Whitman's vivid account, written years later, Hicks did not mention the Separation. In contrast to the well-dressed dignitaries, including officers from the nearby Navy Yard, and to the gay decorations of the ballroom, a row of grim-looking Quakers in simple dress and broadbrimmed hats sat on the stage in complete silence. Years later Whitman recalled the voice of Hicks, but not his words. Speaking of the sermon he said: "A pleading, tender, nearly agonizing conviction, and magnetic stream of natural eloquence, before which all minds and natures, all emotions, high or low, gentle or simple, yielded entirely without exception, was its cause, method and effect."[21]

One would like to know what Hicks actually said in this sermon which so impressed the ten-year-old boy. Hicks describes his last meetings in the New York area as leading into "the openings of

[20] Forbush, p. 224. This statement is not a direct quotation but was attributed to Hicks by the English Quakeress Anne Braithwaite, who was "laboring" with Hicks prior to the Separation of Orthodox and Hicksite Quakers in 1827–1828. The Separation divided Quakers who accepted the Bible as an authority for Christian doctrine, the so-called Orthodox, from the Hicksites, who maintained that the Inner Light in each man was the ultimate source of all religious truth. On the Separation see Rufus M. Jones, *The Later Periods of Quakerism*, 2 vols. (London, 1921), I, 435–487. On Elias Hicks, his relationship to the Separation, and some suggestions of his relationship to Whitman, see D. Elton Trueblood, "The Career of Elias Hicks," in *Byways in Quaker History*, ed. Howard Brinton (Wallingford, Pa., 1944), pp. 77–93.

[21] *The Complete Writings of Walt Whitman*, ed. R. M. Bucke, Thomas B. Harned, Horace Traubel, and Oscar Lovell Triggs, 10 vols. (New York, 1902), VI, 259.

truth" about the Kingdom of God and way of admittance into it.[22]
His first words were these: "*What is the chief end of man?* I was
told in my early youth, it was to *glorify God, and seek and enjoy
him forever*." And as Whitman remembered, he said much about
"the light within."[23] It is not difficult to reconstruct what Hicks
might have said; he was a man with a single, consistent message,
which can be found repeated in all of his sermons. He might have
said something like this on the Inner Light:

"In him was life, and the life was the light of man; and this is the true
light, which enlighteneth every man that cometh into the world." [John
1 : 4, 9.] This light is in us, and we know it to be so, and it reproveth
the world of sin. It will lead and guide us into all truth, and, consequently, out of all error. It will teach us all things, and bring all things
to our remembrance. And this is what I would recommend to you; for
nothing is required on our part but obedience.[24]

Or this, speaking on unity through the Inner Light:

Now in this light, this seed of God, there is unity; but out of it there is
no unity in heaven or in earth. Everything that stands out of this light,
is in that contentiousness which is calculated to spoil society; to break
the bonds of union: for you know that the strength of social beings depends upon their unity. What else is there to bind them, but the light
and love of God in their souls; that love that is stronger than death?
When a soul has this love he would rather die than wound another:
yea, he would rather give up his life than to offend.[25]

The chief end of man, then, is to glorify God by obedience to
the inward truth received directly by each individual from God.
Whitman describes this central message of Elias Hicks in these
words: "Always E. H. gives the service of pointing to the fountain
of all naked theology, all religion, all worship, all the truth to
which you are possibly eligible—namely in *yourself* and your inherent relations."[26] Though Whitman's belief in the reality of religious intuition was reinforced by Emerson and other transcendentalist influences, there is little doubt that, directly or indirectly,

[22] *Journal of the Life and Religious Labours of Elias Hicks, Written by Himself*, 3rd
ed. (New York, 1832), p. 438.
[23] *Complete Writings*, III, 258.
[24] *The Quaker, Being a Series of Sermons by Members of the Society of Friends*, 4
vols. (Philadelphia, 1827), IV, 275-276.
[25] *A Series of Extemporaneous Discourses* (Philadelphia, 1825), p. 73.
[26] *Complete Writings*, VI, 242.

the primary influence was the Quaker preacher, Elias Hicks. Whitman is too conscious of his debt to forget this. He tried hard to
write a book on Elias Hicks in his later years but failed, as he said,
because of ill health. He felt he owed it to his parents and to the
Quakers of Long Island,[27] and he felt peculiarly qualified to write
such a book because of his Long Island background and his sympathetic perspective.[28]

During the Camden period recorded by Horace Traubel, Whitman often spoke of his projected book on Elias Hicks. He had been
intending to write it, he said, for anywhere from thirty to fifty
years (I, 398; II, 19, 36). In his room in the Camden house he had
both a bust and a portrait of Hicks to inspire him. There was much
material: a bundle of notes, clippings, Hicks's *Journal*, and some
eighty pages of manuscript (I, 154). Whitman had been asked for
the book by Lippincott (I, 155). Yet from all this Whitman was
able to produce but an essay of some 9,000 words bearing the cautious title "Notes (such as they are) founded on Elias Hicks,"
hurriedly put together to finish out *November Boughs*. He described it as a "broken memorandum of [Hicks's] formation, his
earlier life," like the "cross-notch that rude wanderers make in the
woods, to remind them afterwards of some matter of first-rate importance and full investigation."[29] In it he quotes almost excessively
from Hicks's *Journal* and from his letters and sermons on the Inner
Light, purity, charity, toleration, and the inadequacies of the outer
forms of religion. There is no doubt that Whitman had the material
for a full-scale interpretation of Elias Hicks, and there is no doubt
that he knew what it meant to him and what he ought to do with
it. But it was more than sickness that prevented him from writing
on Hicks. The key is in the essay itself: Whitman could dwell on
the inspiration that he remembered as a boy, and on the greatness
of the central message, the "over-arching thought," but he could not
feel at home with the bareness of Hicks's quietism and his somber
ministry. "One must not be dominated by the man's almost absurd
saturation in cut and dried biblical phraseology, and in ways, talk,
and standard, regardful mainly of the one need he dwelt on, above

[27] Ibid., p. 241.
[28] Traubel, III, 191.
[29] *Complete Writings*, VI, 242–243.

all the rest."[30] And this one need was, of course, the Inner Light, or to Whitman the religion within man's nature.

III

Ah more than any priest O soul we too believe in God.
But with the mystery of God we dare not dally.
                                              ("Passage to India")

It was typical of Walt Whitman that when someone told him Hicks had shown too much personal ambition and pride of leadership, and hoped perhaps to establish a sect bearing his name, Whitman had reacted with a shrug of the shoulders: "Very likely. Such indeed seems the means, all through progress and civilization, by which strong men and strong convictions achieve anything definite."[31] Whitman was apparently incapable of appreciating the self-negating background out of which Hicks's testimony had come. Hicks himself would have been horrified, indeed, if he had been seriously accused of personal ambition and pride of leadership by someone whose judgment he respected. Whitman could understand the central message of Hicks, but he gives no evidence of being able to understand or to appreciate the self-denying discipline out of which that message grew.

It is quite clear from his biography, his journal, his sermons, and his letters that Hicks was first and foremost a mystic of the quietist variety. This is well summarized by Rufus Jones:

He leaned strongly—no Friend of his time more strongly—in the direction of Quietism. He declares again and again that it will not do to have any confidence in the "creature," or in "reasoning" as it operates in man's "fallen nature." He builds no hopes at all on man in his "natural" condition. He shows himself in this particular a product of the past rather than a prophet of the future. There must be, he continually insists, a withdrawal from the "world," a relaxing of all dependence on outward props and helps of every sort, "a sequestration from everything of an outward or external nature," a return into the holy place within, a patient travail of soul, through inward poverty and death to "own-will," until the soul finds itself merged in union of will with the will of the Highest.[32]

---

[30] Ibid., p. 242.
[31] Ibid., pp. 267–268.
[32] Jones, I, 442. Jones has abstracted Elias Hicks's beliefs from the *Journal*, pp. 131, 165, 175, 180, 383 et passim. In a footnote he adds, "In fact it was his excessive op-

This quietism involved a number of assumptions that were obviously unacceptable to an optimist like Walt Whitman. Hicks believed that man is depraved, but not because of original sin. He abhorred the idea of original sin, considering it a blasphemy against a merciful God, just as much as he abhorred the idea of an elect, for the same reason. But sin and depravity resulted from the free choice of the natural way in opposition to God's way, and there was the possibility of salvation for every man only through the grace of God. It was through the seed of the divine, or the Inner Light in each man, Christian or non-Christian, that grace could come. The only conditions of grace and salvation were complete passivity and obedience; man had to wait for the light to shine, or for the voice of God to speak, and then to obey it. All decisions prior to, or contrary to, instructions from God led to the disunity and destruction that was obvious and inevitable in the natural, physical world.[33] From this naturally followed the Quaker customs: silence in worship while waiting on the spirit, the great distrust of the purely rational mind, the refusal to take part in obviously divisive and destructive practices and customs of society, and the simplicity and purity of behavior distinguishing the Quaker from the worldly man.

The fundamental assumption behind all this is a dualism of natural mind and Inner Light. There is a similar dualism in Whitman; but always he seems to be trying to eliminate the dualism, to bridge what for the Quakers was unbridgeable, or at the very least to set up a sort of comradeship between his soul and body.

> O I say these are not the parts and poems of the body only,
>   but of the soul,
> O I say now these are the soul!
>   (Children of Adam, "I sing the Body Electric," sec. 9)

> O soul, repressless, I with thee and thou with me,
> Thy circumnavigation of the world begin,
> Of man, the voyage of his mind's return,
> To reason's early paradise,

position to everything external and 'creaturely' that led him to undervalue those aspects of historical Christianity which the orthodox party insisted upon."

[33] During the period of the Quaker Separation Hicks was often questioned on Christian doctrine. The best expression of his theology is therefore found in his answers to queries during this period. See, for example, in *Letters of Elias Hicks* (Philadelphia, 1861), pp. 213–214.

> Back, back to wisdom's birth, to innocent intuitions,
> Again with fair creation.
>
>   ("Passage to India," sec. 7)

Whatever Whitman's own theology, whatever the inconsistencies of his persona in the poetry, certainly he went beyond the Quakers in his attempt to retrieve the physical self from damnation by linking it to the spiritual soul. He sought to save the physical world by interfusing it with spirit.

As to the significance of the Inner Light, or the spiritual side of the equation, there was no essential disagreement between Elias Hicks and Walt Whitman. It was for this that Whitman could venerate Hicks, comparing him to a little stream of pure water which had come down from an unpolluted source, to point to the true source of all truth and all religion—*in man*.[34] This Inner Light meant several things to the Quakers. It was preeminently, of course, the spirit of God in each man, which could be cultivated by quietism, and which accounted for three forms of the insight or light: conscience, intuition of religious truth, and occult prophecy. Quakers were not at all strong on occult prophecy after George Fox, according to Brand Blanshard.[35] Conscience, like man's law, was largely negative. It was God's law written into the spirit in man. Elias Hicks called it "true knowledge," connecting it with the second form, the intuition of religious truth. It is evident that for Hicks the latter is the more basic of the two, "true knowledge" being merely the obvious manifestation and proof of intuition or Inner Light. He said, for example,

We learn it from a consciousness within us, of having done right or wrong; because whenever we do amiss, and turn aside from the path of rectitude, we find something in us, that impeaches us, that brings guilt and remorse upon us. Now what is this, my friends? It certainly is something invisible to the outward senses of animal man; yet we know it to exist in us. There is nothing more self-evident to us than this fact; and here it is, then, through this medium, that we are to get right knowledge, right ideas, and right views of the divine character.[36]

It is clear from all this that the Inner Light was conceived as an instrument something like a divine radio set tuned to the right channel to receive messages from God. But there is also an element

---

[34] *Complete Writings*, VI, 242.
[35] "The Inner Light," in *Byways*, pp. 158–159.
[36] *Extemporaneous Discourses*, pp. 185–186.

of retention involved, insofar as one is able to learn from experience and develop a growing awareness and sensitivity to what is right and wrong. The Inner Light seems to be not only a receiver but a recorder of true knowledge. At this point difficulties enter. It may be argued that a good recording is better than bad reception. Thus Scripture and ecclesiastic authority enter into the picture to give permanent form and discipline to religious life. Hicks was especially sensitive at this point. It was his particular concern as a Quaker to give witness to the primacy of the Inner Light as instrument.

There is a paradox in all this which brings Hicks and Whitman close together. The essence of this paradox is the idea, put into secular terms, that democratic unity can be achieved only through true individualism. Whitman, as poet, begins with these words:

> One's self I sing, a simple separate person,
> Yet utter the word Democratic, the word En-Masse.

Hicks everywhere speaks of the unity that is in the Light. It was an irony that Hicks could hardly have expected or wished for that his own insistence on the central tenet of the Quakers would lead to disunity among Quakers. He deplored this disunity, he did everything in his power to avoid being in the seceding group in his own New York Yearly Meeting. He was probably not primarily responsible for the seceding of the liberal group from the Philadelphia meeting. The Quaker meetings split both ways, sometimes the liberal Hicksites and sometimes the Orthodox retaining the legal and formal control after Separation. Both sides claimed to be the true Quakers. Hicks's belief in unity through the Light was in a sense vindicated by the fact that the Orthodox Quakers continued to split into smaller groups. It was bound to happen, as it had happened in all Protestant denominations, because wherever unity depended on scriptural interpretation it was a shaky and temporary kind of unity at best.

Both Hicks and Whitman were aware of the evils of Christ worship which left out of account the Christ *in* man. Whitman tried to quote Hicks from memory on this point: " 'When I put on the one side the good that this worship has done, on the other the bad, I am at a loss whether the bad does not outweigh the good'— words meaning that, perhaps like them." [37] Hicks said of the Bible:

[37] Traubel, IV, 289.

What dreadful work has it made among the children of men! It proves itself what it is; that it is nothing but a history of passing events, which occurred eighteen hundred years ago, a great portion of which may be true. . . . [Christendom] has divided into hundreds of sects, all fixing their foundation upon this literal book, as though it were a sufficient rule. . . . There never was any thing made more a nose of wax of, than the Bible: and it is the most mischievous thing, when held up above what it is.[38]

And of Christ worship:

Now, if we make an image in our minds;—if we offer up prayers to some image;—if remembering that Christ without, who did these mighty miracles—that Jesus Christ of Nazareth, who did these miracles, we make an image of that man, and bow down to him; we worship an image, as much as if we worshipped a golden image like Nebuchadnezzar's.[39]

Whitman, looking around him at religion in America, put the negative part of his belief in the religion *in* man very eloquently:

Really what has America to do with all this mummery of prayer and rituals and the rant of the exhorters and priests? We are not at all deceived by this great show that confronts us of churches, priests and rituals—for piercing beneath, we find there is no life, no faith, no reality of belief, but that all is essentially a pretense, a sham.[40]

Whitman undoubtedly received from Quakerism, through Elias Hicks, not only his belief in the validity of religious individualism, but also the paradoxical affirmation that out of such individualism would come democratic union and social consciousness. *All* testimony was valid and proper in Quaker "group mysticism," even the testimony of the least articulate member of the group. Quakers as a whole, in spite of their quietism, were welded together by their unity in concern over such worldly matters as freeing slaves, refusing to bear arms, leading a simple and industrious life, and practicing mutual aid and brotherly love. "Man is made for society," said Hicks, in the sense that man is part of a natural order of beings designed by God to live together in peace and harmony, but in freedom.[41] Whitman sums this all up very well.

[38] *Extemporaneous Discourses*, pp. 315–316.
[39] *The Quaker*, II, 267–268.
[40] Furness, p. 41.
[41] *Extemporaneous Discourses*, pp. 63f.

I wanted to write of Hicks as a democrat—the only real democrat among all religious teachers: the democrat in religion as Jefferson was a democrat in politics. . . . Hicks was a greater hero than any man Carlyle celebrated in his book. But it does not surprise me that nobody has written him up: he was not sensational—he was too commonplace—too much like the rest of the people in his bravery to be taken for an official hero. I would have had a lot to say about his democracy. There were features in his mysticism with which I had little sympathy but the purport of his message had my entire approval. Hicks was in the last degree a simple character. . . . He kept a house over his head and a little money in the bank. He was not irresponsible—he did not default in his obligations: he lived the plainest life and he paid his bills.[42]

IV

And it was not long before I felt an impressive concern to utter a few words, which I yielded to in great fear and dread; but O the joy and sweet consolation that my soul experienced, as a reward for this act of faithfulness.[43]

—ELIAS HICKS

Various parallels have been noted by scholars between Elias Hicks and Walt Whitman: their early life on Long Island, love of nature, tendency toward mystical experiences, belief in the validity of individualistic religion, identification with the democratic spirit of America, and even a certain kind of cadence in their use of language.[44] It is important also to notice the differences. Hicks was a recorded minister who lived strictly under Quaker discipline. He led a quiet and industrious family life as a farmer on Long Island, yet he attracted large audiences during the period of his public ministry toward the end of his life. It is significant that Elias Hicks's message grew out of a long life of discipline and experience. He spoke only when he felt an "impressive concern," and he spoke from depth of experience. In contrast, it is perhaps the weakness of Whitman as a man—accountable for his failure as an orator, a political leader, a religious leader, or even as an editor—that he lacked and had rejected precisely the kind of disciplined life that gave Hicks his great strength and power with words. Yet somehow Whit-

[42] Traubel, II, 36–37.
[43] *Journal*, p. 16.
[44] These parallels have been noted particularly by F. O. Matthiessen, Clifton Furness, Henry Seidel Canby, D. Elton Trueblood, as cited earlier, and briefly by Janna Burgess, "Walt Whitman and Elias Hicks," *Friends Intelligencer*, CI (1944), 54–55.

man managed to translate this feeling for the power of inspired words into poetry, secularized and interfused with all that the world had to offer and that Whitman had voraciously absorbed. Whitman was, in a sense, the exact opposite of Hicks. Hicks shut out worldly experience and disciplined himself to sensitivity to the Inner Life; Whitman absorbed experience like a sponge and found his discipline in bardic utterance.

The important influence of Hicks on Whitman was through his power of words, through oratory. Whitman frequently ranked Hicks along with great opera singers, actors, and orators like the famous Methodist preacher Father Taylor of Boston, who was the model for Father Mapple in *Moby-Dick*. These men had vocal power, something that "touches the soul, the abysm." Whitman described Father Taylor and Hicks as essentially perfect orators. "Both had the same inner, apparently inexhaustible, fund of latent volcanic passion—the same tenderness, blended with a curious remorseless firmness, as of some surgeon operating on a belov'd patient."[45] The secret of this oratorical power, if Whitman could not command it himself, was at least translatable into an organic theory of poetry. Thus, "from the opening of the Oration [or the Poem] & on through, the great thing is to be inspired as one divinely possessed, blind to all subordinate affairs and given up entirely to the surgings and utterances of the mighty tempestuous demon."[46] It is important to realize, however, that for Hicks the words and even the inspiration were only a means to an end. In the sermon that Whitman had remembered for such a long time, Hicks had said that the end of man is "to glorify God, and seek and enjoy him forever." For Whitman the words and the inspiration in themselves became the end and justification of his life. He became, in short, a poet.

Whitman had wanted to write something about Hicks for a long while—thirty to fifty years, he said in 1888. This puts the original idea squarely into the period of Whitman's beginning as a serious poet. During this same period Whitman was absorbed with the idea of being an orator, and he jotted down ideas for lectures or "lessons." One of the first notes under the heading of "Notes for Lectures on Religion"[47] in *Walt Whitman's Workshop* reads,

[45] *Complete Writings*, VI, 113.
[46] Furness, p. 37.
[47] Ibid., pp. 39–53.

"Change the name from Elias Hicks / make no allusion to him at all." It is implied in this that the original conception had been a lecture on Elias Hicks. Whatever may have entered into Whitman's mind to change it, his ideas on religion were originally, and no doubt fundamentally, associated with his memory of Elias Hicks. The notes show the fundamental relationship between the two men and the way in which Whitman secularized and went beyond the insight of the Inner Light.

The "spinal cord" of the lecture was to be the idea that investigation of religion should be released from all authority, it should be scientific, and each age should study religion for itself. Underneath all religious form (churches, scriptures, ritual, authority) is the "deep, silent, mysterious"—this is the real essence of religion. Whitman then introduces, probably for the first time, the image that later developed into "a noiseless Patient Spider": the little worm on an isolated promontory sending its filaments out into space, like the soul trying to make connections in the immensity of the spiritual and unknown. There is much of the negative corollary of the Inner Light in the notes. Beware of priests, churches, ritual, prayer, says Whitman—all this stands in the way of real religion. "There is nothing in the universe more divine than man." Whitman makes no claim to settle religious questions, he can only stimulate thought by asserting that all religions serve their purpose in their time, all are equally valid.

> Taking them all for what they are worth and not a cent more,
> Admitting they were alive and did the work of their days. . . .
> ("Song of Myself," sec. 41)

The basic concepts of Whitman's ideas on religion can be found in Elias Hicks. He was well aware of this in later life when he wrote on Hicks and George Fox. The difference lay in the fact that Whitman's ideas were uprooted from religious form, even from Quaker form, which, with its discipline of silence and purity, is in a way the most binding of all forms of discipline. Through some miracle of sublimation he managed to translate the inspiration of the Inner Light into poetry. It may well have been a kind of spiritual defeat for the man, but it was an immeasurable gain for the poet and for literary culture.

It is interesting now to look back from the modern point of

view at the doctrine of the Inner Light. Brand Blanshard has noted four ways in which elements of truth in the Quaker doctrine have persisted into modern language and ways of thinking:

The doctrine of the Inner Light was . . . an insistence, and a justified insistence, on firsthandedness and genuineness in religious and moral experience. . . .

As against the whole tribe of relativists and subjectivists, the early Friends were thoroughly right in maintaining that we had knowledge, as certain as knowledge can be, about good and evil, right and wrong and duty.

They were correct, once more, in holding that the Inner Light does not apply merely to the moral and narrowly religious spheres. . . . The Light gives guidance on matters that we should now call metaphysical. . . .

They were sowing seed whose natural flowering was in a religious cosmopolitanism and a theological charity which were far wider than they knew.[48]

The chief difficulty from the modern point of view, according to Brand Blandshard, lies in the Quaker dualism: the tendency to keep up the partition between the natural and the supernatural, the human and the divine. It is precisely from the modern point of view that we can understand both the likenesses and the differences between Elias Hicks and Walt Whitman. Whitman was modern in his tendency to break down the partition and to escape from the obscurantism that resulted from the otherworldly emphasis. Yet he maintained from his childhood a sense of the divinity and genuineness of individual experience which could lead to a democratic unity and brotherhood. Whitman's poetry is to a large extent an attempt to synthesize the natural and the supernatural, and it is not too much to say that he received his impetus in this direction both negatively and positively, from Quakerism and Elias Hicks.

[48] "The Inner Light," pp. 163–167.

'Chants Democratic and Native American':
A Neglected Sequence in the Growth of
Leaves of Grass
Robin P. Hoople

"O Present! I return while yet I may to you!"
(*Leaves of Grass*, 1860)

I

IN THE BROODING AND FATEFUL DAYS of the spring of 1860 Walt Whitman issued the third edition of *Leaves of Grass*. While the political crisis swirled through the nation's cities, Walt Whitman read galley proofs of this new edition in the office of Thayer and Eldridge, his new publishers, in Boston. Though it might seem that the erstwhile Democratic party ward worker was committing an act of gross indifference by sitting back and watching his party crumble and his nation divide into two hostile ideological camps, the truth is that Whitman was now finally working to achieve the goal of a "Poet of Democracy," to write his "evangel poem of comrades." If tempers flared around him, he would, in his new volume, answer tempers with his own combination of gentle persuasion, anger and superideological reconstruction of the American experience. He referred to this revised and greatly augmented edition of *Leaves of Grass* as the "New Bible."[1] The revelation of its "scriptures" was the ordained Union of States, in themselves a new type of answer to the eternal cry of mankind for the messiah and for the millennium.[2] Far from being the work of an aimless and disillusioned village-democrat-turned-sour, *Leaves of Grass* 1860 was

[1] Fredson T. Bowers, ed., *Whitman's Manuscripts: Leaves of Grass 1860* (Chicago, 1954), pp. xxxiv–xxxv. Bowers cites documents from the Feinberg collection of Whitman manuscripts.

[2] Internal evidence that Whitman conceived of the founding of the republic as the millennium comes from "Chants Democratic and Native American" no. 1, in which Whitman speaks of "the haughty defiance of the Year 1—war, peace, the formation of the Constitution" (*Leaves of Grass*, Boston, 1860, p. 113). In dating the third edition on the title page Whitman uses this "Year One" technique in addition to Christian calendar designations: "Year 85 of the States./ (1860–1861)" (ibid., title page).

nothing short of a nineteenth-century poet-priest's attempt to bring about an evangelical conversion of the heretics of democracy.

Critics differ in assigning the place of honor among the new poems and poem sequences of the 1860 *Leaves of Grass*.[3] They seem almost unanimous, however, in refusing to assign that place to "Chants Democratic and Native American,"[4] the second major poetic cycle of the book, preceded only by "Proto-Leaf," the prologue, and "Walt Whitman" (later, in revised form, "Song of Myself"). Many critics of the third edition give only passing recognition to "Chants Democratic," treating important poems within the sequence instead of evaluating the sequence as a whole.[5] Yet in this neglect, these critics miss the point of the third edition. For in it, "Calamus" and "Enfans d'Adam" and even the miraculous "Walt Whitman" are subordinate to and dependent upon "Chants Democratic": in that year of national crisis the Poet of Democracy was most directly concerned with the crisis of politics. He made "Chants Democratic" the political handbook for the cosmic democracy of the future. Even at that dismal juncture Whitman thought this hypothetical future possible.

To point out that in covering ninety pages, "Chants Democratic" consumes virtually one-fifth of the book is less important than to demonstrate that "Chants Democratic" has the richest and most carefully wrought internal structure of all the poem clusters in the 1860 *Leaves of Grass*. To say that "Chants Democratic" is longer than "Calamus" and "Enfans d'Adam" combined is less important than to note that after the third edition "Chants Democratic" as a

[3] There is a fairly clear consensus that the trio "A Word Out of the Sea," "Enfans d'Adam," and "Calamus" share the honor. From the vantage point of the authorized version of *Leaves of Grass* (1891–1892), there is no question that they should.

[4] This section covers pp. 105–194 in the third edition of *Leaves of Grass*. No poem except the prologue, "Apostroph," has a title. In referring to the whole section I shall hereafter shorten to "Chants Democratic." Individual poems will be referred to by number. References to the third edition of *Leaves of Grass* will be given in parentheses in the text.

[5] Frederik Schyberg, *Walt Whitman*, trans. Evie Allison Allen (New York, 1951), is characteristic of this approach. After extensive treatment of the 1860 edition, pp. 151–170, covering "Calamus" and "Enfans d'Adam," Schyberg comments separately on several poems of the "Chants Democratic" sequence without comment on the sequence as a whole. Gay Wilson Allen, *The Solitary Singer* (New York, 1955), treats "Chants Democratic" with contempt as "perhaps the weakest group in the book" (p. 241). In the introduction to the facsimile of the 1860 edition of *Leaves of Grass*, Roy Harvey Pearce devotes only a scant half-paragraph to the sequence (pp. xxviii–xxix). Pearce does find more value in the sequence than does Allen, since the sequence "successfully establishes the dialectical tension between the poet and his world" (ibid., p. xxix).

title and as a construct never again appeared in *Leaves of Grass*.[6] Most important of all, "Chants Democratic" was the only sequence dedicated principally to the theme of the nation-state, a theme that is treated only fragmentarily in the authorized edition of *Leaves of Grass*. It is by now virtually a truism to say that Whitman intended the third edition of the work to be the authorized and final form.[7] The relationship of "Chants Democratic" to this edition is crucial.

II

The poem cycle divides into subordinate sequences. The first, numbers 1–3, opens a view on virgin land, fills it with pioneers, founds an economy—occupations that elicit Pythagorean harmonies —and evolves a poetic consciousness responsive to the sounds of the landscape in each successive stage of becoming. The sequence etches an outline and gives generic terms of reference. The second sequence, numbers 4–7, crystallizes the abstractions indispensable to political life: "compacts," "the past," "non-conformity," "greatnesses." The terms for the abstractions are peculiarly Whitman's own—he makes them his own even if he has borrowed them from elsewhere. They are the laws (ancient, dating from the year one) of the democratic state and simultaneously the metaphors of the poet of democracy. The third sequence, numbers 8–11, utters a dithyramb on organic growth. It superimposes the growth of civilization on the growth of things in nature. It makes all growth relevant to the vibrating organism of sovereign states matrixed by consent and organically symbolized by a spinal river. The fourth sequence, numbers 12–14, turns prophetic, idolizes a future that will yield a race of poet-priests and poet-priestesses. The fifth sequence, numbers 15–18, confronts the present, filled with danger as well as with opportunity. All politics, Whitman suggests, are pure, because all positions have become polarized. Opportunity exists precisely because all ambiguity has vanished from the available choices. The final sequence is a coda, summarizing prior themes, re-

[6] It is only fair to point out that two other sequences also made swan-song first appearances in the 1860 *Leaves of Grass*. These were "Leaves of Grass," which followed "Chants Democratic," and "Messenger Leaves," the last sequence of the book. The ambiguity of the internal title "Leaves of Grass" was alone enough to warrant its dismissal. "Messenger Leaves" was a series of poems delivered in a broad pattern over the actual and mythical landscapes of the nation.

[7] Schyberg has made this suggestion. His evidence appears on pp. 177–179. Pearce calls the 1860 *Leaves of Grass* "Whitman's Greatest" (p. i).

affirming the optative mood and insisting on the validity and urgency of choice. The last poem concludes by harmonizing democracy and vision.

"Apostroph," the prologue to "Chants Democratic," voices the poet's sense of crisis:

> O, as I walk'd the beach, I heard the mournful notes foreboding
>   a tempest—the low, oft-repeated shriek of the diver, the long-
>   lived loon;
> O I heard, and yet hear, angry thunder;—O you sailors! O ships!
>   make quick preparation!
> O from his masterful sweep, the warning cry of the eagle!
> (Give way there, all! It is useless! Give up your spoils)
>
>   (pp. 105–106)

The eagle sounds the "barbaric yawp" of American experience—wilderness against consciousness, the martial fact of national birth, territorial expansion by violence. The eagle symbolizes the fusion of races into ultrarace. Whitman reifies the integral nation in the symbol of the avenging eagle, an assimilation of unspecific masses into monolithic force. The eagle's voice is the transcendent voice of man unified, crying down his enemies—profiteers and disseverers of union.

The nation-inchoate landscape in the first sequence of "Chants Democratic" draws broad boundaries and rough-sketches the history of the inhabitants. The sequence includes number 1 (later "By Blue Ontario's Shores"), number 2 (later "Song of the Broad Axe"), and number 3 (later "Song for Occupations"). As the figures of the landscape take form, the poet takes character—not in the form of nature- and self-consciousness alone, as we had seen in "Walt Whitman," but additionally in the form of collective conscience: "[one] who goes through the streets with a barbed tongue [Diogenes-like], questioning everyone I meet [Socrates-like]" (p. 110). The cynical questioner transforms (temporarily; he will return in number 5) into the lover of the race. He is the bard merging with the race, then rising from it to sing its praises; he becomes the type of its perfect citizen.

The poet in the creative act is, like the nation, constructive: "O America, because you build for mankind, I build for you" (p. 114). Whitman's passionate affirmation is his giving hand; but like most visionary poets, he had a retracting hand as well. He affirms the truths of his vision as though they had no contraries and bathes consciousness in a succoring ambience. But he often swiftly follows such affirmations with a second voice, a critical voice, that dispels the cloud of ambience and states a contrary disjunctively: "if you want to crystallize this vision into experience, you must be prepared to work, to sacrifice for it." The American that builds for mankind requires a high quality of commitment and understanding from the poet's countrymen: "Have you learned the physiology, phrenology, politics, geography, pride, freedom, friendship of my land?" (p. 117). They must be prepared to leave an establishment dead behind them. Whitman's revolution is gentle, however, and proposes to subject only institutions to the firing squad; men can be reformed. The institutional church, for example, will vanish: "There will shortly be no more priests—I say their work is done" (p. 120). As formal institutions die, new noninstitutions will spring up to take their place: "friendship, self-esteem, justice" (p. 121). The contractual basis of democracy becomes a "compact . . . altogether with individuals" (p. 122). The new compact promotes the willing marriage of the multitude, a marriage that demands the preservation of personal equality and personal freedom. The nation is a loose compact of individuals which fosters the freedom and self-realization of each separately. Such harmonious unity must precede the complex landscape of love that the poet will explore later in the book in "Enfans d'Adam" and "Calamus."

Whitman must confront an infinite number of paradoxes if he is to make any kind of case for democracy. Earlier political forms might well have been unjust, but some rudimentary internal logic— such as the logic of man as brute, requiring careful and unending control—could be observed in them. Democracy begins with a principle—that society shall be just, or that men shall be equal—and casts logic, or at least experience, to the winds. Whitman has announced his intention to treat the paradox of the one and the many early in the sequence. In number 2, Whitman treats the paradox of power. The symbol of power in his democracy is the broadax. Whitman manipulates it in several directions: he opposes it to the headsman's ax, the ancient European symbol of political repression; he anatomizes its essential or natural forms—iron and wood—for the sake of symbolic transformation; he analogizes the broadax, by which the pioneer shaped his wilderness, to the creative natural force necessary to hew out of men the shapes fit for participation in a wholly voluntary society. He concludes by praising power harnessed to serve man and intensified to promote the creative thrust of nature.

The broadax is thus friendly and familiar rather than oppressive:

> I see the headsman withdraw and become useless,
> I see the scaffold untrodden and mouldy—I see no longer any axe
>   upon it,
> I see the mighty and friendly emblem of the power of my own
>   race, the newest largest race.
> . . . .
> The axe leaps!
> The solid forest gives fluid utterances,
> They tumble forth, they rise and form. . . .   (pp. 136–137)

Yet the broad ax is essentially the same tool as the headsman's ax. Its metamorphosis into a creative instrument corresponds to the metamorphosis of the man from serf or subject to possessor—of himself, of his liberty, of his universe.

Whitman moves in several directions after anatomizing the broadax into prime substances. Wood becomes rifle butt; iron becomes rifle-barrel. As the ax was the hewer and creator to the pioneer, the rifle was the provisioner and protector. Whitman is talking not only about primary materials but about essential relationships, essential harmonies. But he allows the idyllic past to lapse in order to raise questions about the troubled present. Both society and politics have lost focus on the spirit of frontier democracy. The ax has become both symbol of and creator of modern corruption. Its more modern creations are the formal seats in courtrooms, the liquor bar, the gambling board, the whore's bed, and, ominously, the scaffold once again. The rifle has found its way into the hands of militants, has become the instrument of the oppression of slaves and the symbol of impending fraternal war in the hostile camps of the disintegrating union (p. 139).

Whitman resurrects the ax by analogizing the pioneer civilization with a broad creative base in nature—and in man because he belongs to nature. "The shapes arise," cries Whitman, the prophetic fury on him once again: the shape of a strong man, of a strong woman, "the main shapes" of democracy. Though it is spontaneous sensitivity to the growing-power of nature that nurtures the new pioneers, the broadax remains its principal symbol. Number 2, in prophesying a redeemed future, raises more practical than theoretical problems. The redeeming spirit exists and the necessary equipment is at hand. The question that lingers is how shall these be joined to produce the new society? Whitman attempts to answer in number 3.

That poem, the "Song for Occupations," pictures a world of laborers and skilled artisans, all happily engaged in their routine occupations because work itself is a part of the magnificence of modern America. Work is holy because it is full and abundant, because it is an expression of the union of impulse. There is no serfdom or working for the glory and emolument of the liege lord; the liege lord is the self. The happy worker gives substance to the dream. Work creates the product that supports life; the worker creates civilization itself: "All doctrines, all politics and civilization, exurge from you" (p. 149). The contemporary conflict of values draws the battle line between "the apparent custodians" and "the real custodians, standing, menacing, silent. . . ."[8] In these real custodians rests the hope for a redeemed republic. Whitman anticipates the time when the order of things will be appropriate to the democracy:

> When the psalm sings instead of the singer,
> When the script preaches instead of the preacher,
> When the pulpit descends and goes instead of the carver that carved the supporting-desk,
> When I can touch the body of books, by night or by day, and when they touch my body back again,
> When the holy vessels, or the bits of the eucharist, or the lath and plast, procreate as effectually as the young silver-smiths or bakers, or the masons in their over-alls,

[8] Ibid., p. 119. It is the ghost of the magnificent Daniel Webster that we hear in Whitman's lines. Webster had spoken clearly for the power of the people in founding the Union as early as the 1830 secession crisis. In his briefs for a Supreme Court argument, Webster had set down as the first of his "American Principles" the following: "1.—The People are the source of all political power; Govt is instituted for their good; and its members are their agents and servants. The people exercise their power by regulated suffrage" (quoted in S. P. Lyman, *The Public and Private Life of Daniel Webster*, Philadelphia, 1852, p. 291).

When a university course convinces like a slumbering woman and
   child convince, `

· ·

I intend to reach them my hand, and make as much of them as I
   do of men and women like you.   (p. 158)

The first three poems of "Chants Democratic" thus reaffirm
America's creative spirit. In the common will and the common
effort; in the very heterogeneity of enlightened democratic men
this spirit still exists and propels the nation toward a brilliant future.
The new society has its enemies, however, in the exploiters and institutions. The exploiters plot to create a new form of serfdom; the
institutions, fixed abstractions, protect vested interest.[9] Presidents,
courts, congressmen are only servants of the people, but such servants have a way of turning the tables. If we remember that by
1860 America had been awaiting the arrival of a decisive president
for at least twelve years and that the power of industry had begun
to hold the reins of American economic life, we can understand
Whitman's distrust of the power accumulations that excluded the
people at large.

The second subordinate sequence of "Chants Democratic" includes number 4 (later "Our Old Feuillage"), number 5 (later
"Transpositions"; ultimately rejected), number 6 (later "Think of
the Soul"; ultimately rejected), number 7 (later "With Antecedents"). This sequence progresses from Whitman's statement of
contempt for the "paper contracts" of These States through an in-
temperate catharsis in revolution to a historical description of the
meaning of "our moment" in history. In place of paper contracts,
Whitman proposes "Organic compacts," natural metaphors for
emotional and political ties that transcend imperfect human laws.
The tone of the four poems is expository as well as revolutionary,
and the poet intends, especially in the poem "Think of the Soul,"
to describe to the young the mysteries and beauties of citizenship
in the republic. In the process, Whitman works to crystallize the
abstractions of the purified democratic community.

Number 4 insists that Americans adopt spiritual and symbolic

---

[9] In "Calamus" number 24 Whitman says, "I hear it is charged against me that I
seek to destroy institutions, but I am neither for nor against institutions" (p. 367). In
"Chants Democratic" number 2, however, he speaks of "the American contempt for
statutes and ceremonies, the boundless impatience for restraint" (p. 128).

alternatives to the mere political organization of states as evidence that they are "inseparably bound" and that they achieve "ONE IDENTITY" (p. 165). Whitman compares, for example, East and West with sunrise and sunset. Between these two ultimate compass points, there are "compact lands" (p. 160), inseparably allied by the diurnal metaphor. More elaborate, however, is the metaphor of the birds of passage, birds which inhabit both North and South, and find each part suitable to its season, each part no less essential than the other. These natural metaphors "organically unify" North and South, East and West, in antithesis to traditional sectional rivalries. The metaphors have the effect of unifying in broad strokes, of cementing the outer boundaries. Whitman adopts a further organic metaphor to represent the unity of the internal substance of the republic.

The grass metaphor of "Walt Whitman"—"A child said *What is the Grass*" and so on—becomes the foliage metaphor of this poem. Whereas in "Walt Whitman" the poet speaks of the grass "sprouting alike in broad zones and in narrow zones, / Growing among black folks as among white, / Kanuck, Tuckahoe, Congressman, Cuff" (p. 29), in "Our Old Feuillage" the growing power of America affords "endless feuillage to me and to America." Whitman asks, "how can I do less than pass the clew of the Union of them, to afford the like to you?" (p. 166). The reader is invited to "collect bouquets of the incomparable feuillage of These States" (p. 166). In this manner Whitman suggests that the garden image of America, the "New Eden," is a further symbol of unity and the natural or organic contract binding the people. To make the merely legal pacts of the Union seem totally redundant, Whitman develops a comparison between his own anatomy and the anatomy of the Union: "my body no more inevitably united, part to part, and made one identity, any more than my lands are inevitably united, and made ONE IDENTITY" (p. 165). Whitman insists through these metaphors that not man but nature has engendered the republic. If the republic springs from natural process—the result of immutable laws—then the critic is just in disregarding the political basis of union if this basis should allow opportunists and profiteers in high places to traduce writs, codes, and laws for selfish gain.

Number 5 was later called "Transpositions," though in the authorized version only a few lines survive. The poem declares war on the republic of the spirit that Whitman has been at such pains thus far in the sequence to promote. It belongs in "Chants Democratic" as devil's advocacy and exploits two principal ironies: that the poet, who knows more directly, more intuitively than any other man the contours of the experience of the republic, is for his expert knowledge a more incisive critic of it; and that the anguish of present conditions makes the sort of reversal that he pictures an unpleasant but very real possibility. Elsewhere in the 1860 *Leaves of Grass* Whitman offers a capsule version of these same ironies, this time in relation to the slave: "A man's body at auction! I help the auctioneer—the sloven does not half know his business" ("Enfans d'Adam," no. 3, p. 297). The salient thrust of "Transpositions" is its attack upon the three "greatnesses" or noninstitutions of the New Bible: religion, love, and democracy. In the whole welter of what Whitman must ordinarily consider immoral behavior for an enlightened democratic man, three ironic reversals stand out. He counters religion by calling out, "Let none but infidels be countenanced" (p. 168). He attacks the holiness of free love by saying, "Let men among themselves talk and think obscenely of women! and let women among themselves talk and think obscenely of men!" (p. 168). Against the "institution" that most strongly characterizes his idea of democracy, equality, Whitman says, "Let the slaves be masters! Let the masters become slaves!" (p. 169). "Transpositions" fits Whitman's plan for "Chants Democratic" as pure anguish.

In number 6, the tender song of initiation of the young, Whitman divides his statement between a prudential imperative: remember the evils of the European past and the high principles of our founding fathers; and an inspirational imperative: "Anticipate your own life" (p. 172); the future will demand a stern self-sacrifice from the young and the sanguine of today.[10] To inspire the young with their mission to preserve the enduring values and their duty to promote "eternal progress" Whitman recalls to them, "the everwelcome defiers," the "savans" [*sic*] of the past who have rejected self-interest for the sake of mankind: "Recall," says Whitman, "the sages, poets, saviours, inventors, lawgivers of the earth. / Recall Christ, brother of rejected persons—brother of slaves, felons, idiots,

---

[10] It is puzzling to understand Whitman's omission of this lovely poem from the authorized edition of *Leaves of Grass*, since it has qualities that suggest Bryant's "Inscription for the Entrance to a Wood" and qualities that ally it in temperament with Emerson's "Waldeinsamkeit."

and of the insane and diseased persons" (p. 173). Manhood and womanhood, into which these "just-maturing youth" are about to enter, are estates worth upholding in a democracy (pp. 173-174).

In number 7, Whitman completes his address to the young. In spite of all our antecedents, he says, modern America transcends the past. He offers respect to that past, but he is preoccupied with the beauty of present existence, the sense of having arrived to perform a magnificent duty. This duty he foresees as the condition of an almost posthistorical world. America is not merely a stage between past and future empires but the empire of the present as well. All times are joined in the moment, but the concern is how to extend the present into an indefinite future:

O but it is not the years—it is I—it is You,
We touch all laws, and tally all antecedents,
We are the skald, the oracle, the monk and the knight—
     we easily include them, and more,
We stand amid time, beginningless and endless. . . .   (p. 175)

The next sequence is at once dithyrambic and mystically passive. It includes number 8 (later "Song at Sunset"), numbers 9 and 11 (later "Thoughts" numbers 1 and 2) and number 10 (later "To a Historian"). In this new mood, Whitman comments on some of the virtues of being alive. He continues to explore past and present, returns to the metaphor of the foliage, and celebrates the sun as the source of light. He challenges the reader to seek the most significant records of the past. He chides the historians for having busied themselves with political and other public documents; an intelligent historian, he tells us, will search for the wisdom of the past in the human heart. With his poems in the historical mood he has illuminated "feelings, faults, yearnings, hopes, . . . character of personality." He has projected "the ideal man, the American of the future" (p. 181). But in number 11, Whitman returns to the great theme, the organic unity of the United States. He repeats the image of the Mississippi River, this time as lifegiver of the garden and again as the "Spinal River" that holds the nation together and translates all its impulses into united action. "What is gain," Whitman asks concluding with a thrust at selfish dissension, "to savageness and freedom?" (p. 183).

The next sequence moves from the dithyrambic to the prophetic.

Number 12 (later "Vocalism") prophesies bards who will be "oratists"—"orators and oratresses" as Whitman explains—giving the law again, preaching the new and ultimate morality:

> Of a great vocalism, when you hear it, the merciless light shall
>   pour, and the storm rage around,
> Every flash shall be a revelation, an insult,
> The glaring flame turned on depths, on heights, on suns, on stars,
> On the interior and exterior of man or woman,
> On the laws of Nature—on passive materials,
> On what you called death—and what to you therefore was death,
> As far as there can be death.   (pp. 184–185)

Whitman's juxtaposition of an oratory of fire and conviction with an enunciation of the ideal ultimate knowledge reflects the rending tensions of his culture in a rhetoric that recalls the antislavery Protestant ministers of the era—Henry Ward Beecher, George B. Cheever, and Fales Henry Newhall. Whitman's faith in the wisdom of man persists, nonetheless, even when his vision of violence has reached its apocalyptic climax. He tells us of his belief that death is not a sorrow; and yet he reflects the apprehension of his culture by dwelling upon death.

Number 13 (later "Laws for Creations") rephrases the law of Amos by suggesting that the soul will receive its satisfaction from "walk[ing] free and own[ing] no superior" (p. 186). Number 14 (later "Poets to Come") proposes that Whitman's value will be "realized" in the hands of the Americans who follow him. He pronounces his faith in the ability of the coming American to penetrate his disguise of assumed nonchalance and to grasp his message fully: "I am a man who, sauntering along, without fully stopping, turns a casual look upon you, and then averts his face,/Leaving it to you to prove and define it, / Expecting the main things from you" (p. 187). Number 16 (later "Mediums") suggests that the orators of the future will become like Spiritualist mediums. Their understanding of the material world as commodity will give them the perspective from which to create a new and continually expanding gospel which will comprehend the entire spiritual world.

But the affirmative mood fades with the balancing rhythm of a pessimistic countercurrent. In number 15 (later "Excelsior") Whitman returns to a hyperbole reminiscent of "Transpositions." He betrays an anguished consciousness of the mechanism of disunity in his culture which erodes his belief in the indestructible nation. The poem develops his own symbolic aspiration for better things. Whitman queries, "Who has projected beautiful words through the longest time?" He answers, "By God I will outvie him! I will say such words, they shall stretch through longer time" (p. 188). His final hyperbole, however, suggests—despite the pose of good will and affirmation—a covert participation in the "devouring" demonic spirit of the age:

> And who has made hymns fit for the earth? For I am mad with a devouring exstacy [sic] to make joyous hymns for the whole earth!   (p. 189)

In number 17, Whitman returns to the subject of the separation of states: "We confer on equal terms with each of The States, / We make trial of ourselves" (p. 190). This trial is the test of democratic faith, and Whitman's "horde" of the common man passes the test. But brooding over the scene is Whitman's awareness of sectional hostility: "We say to ourselves, Remember, fear not, be candid," Whitman warns; "Promulge real things—never forget the equality of humankind, and never forget immortality" (p. 190). Number 18 (later "Me Imperturbe") begins by showing the poet to be at ease with nature. The rumbling sense of foreboding emerges when the poet concludes with the painful "O to confront night, storms, hunger, ridicule, accidents, rebuffs, as the trees and animals do" (p. 191). Since Whitman's whole case for organic compacts and the natural image of union has been based on the kinship between democratic man and benevolent nature, this sudden loss of touch with nature suggests that the organic oneness of the States is in jeopardy.

In two very brief poems, number 19 (later "I Was Looking a Long While") and number 20 (later "I Hear America Singing"), the poet attempts to reestablish the mood of affirmation and optimism. Number 19 tells us that the history of his own past and of his "Chants" is "in Democracy—in this America" as well as in the Old World (p. 192). Like other blessings this history emerges from the "divine average." In number 20 Whitman sings again the song of happy workers creating for a better world and singing themselves into a nobler future. But the mood is temporary.

The final poem, number 21, pictures again the clash between the self-seekers and the builders. "I see ships," says Whitman, in a glance at the commercial world; but he adds that "they will last [only] a few years" in order to distinguish between the merely commercial values and enduring values of the builder. He hears "the indorsement of all and [does] not object to it" (p. 194). Whitman counters the transitory commercial values with what he calls "my realities," his term for the liberal democratic values that he has been promoting in "Chants Democratic."

These "realities" are broken into two groups: the historic values of American democracy and a strange assortment of essentially nineteenth-century values. Whitman phrases these as "Libertad, and the divine average—Freedom to every slave on the face of the earth." While they are traditional values, they are also peculiarly Whitman's own—spiced with his own phrases and enriched by the associations that Whitman has heaped upon them. The more mystical values of the second set come to Whitman from the Quakerism of Elias Hicks, the Transcendentalism of Emerson, and the Perfectionism of John Humphrey Noyes as well as from other intellectual currents of the nineteenth century. Whitman enumerates them as "the rapt promises and lumine of seers—the spiritual world—these centuries-lasting songs, / And our visions, the visions of poets, the most solid announcements" (p. 194). The inner light of seers, the vision of poet priests, the dwelling in the spiritual world, the mystical community of those who sing song-scriptures—these are the values that give substance and endurance to the more prosaic ones of traditional democracy. These are the values that Whitman believes to be typical of the common man.

No harm, Whitman suggests, can come to a society made up exclusively of the common people. The concluding statement of number 21, that the people will endure, draws again the battle line between the opposing forces. We the People, Whitman suggests, "announce solid things,"

> For we support all,
> After the rest is done and gone, we remain,
> There is no final reliance but upon us,
> Democracy rests finally upon us, (I, my brethren, begin it,)
> And our visions sweep through eternity.   (p. 194)

When we consider the nature of the opponents to the unity of the nation, whom Whitman so clearly saw, we can see cause for his pessimism, for the clenching of teeth and the setting of jaws.

There were selfish men in the business and political worlds, and by 1860 these men represented no small force in America. A mere glance at the economic history of the time shows the commercial and industrial exploitation of the South by Northerners. The Congress included many who played sectional interests off against each other for personal gain.[11] In the South, the "first families" were generally made up of people unequivocally committed to "the peculiar Southern institution." And in both North and South there were those apocalyptic figures—abolitionists and fire-eaters—who stood upon principles that must lead only to intra-national conflagration and civil war.

III

"Chants Democratic and Native American" contains Whitman's assessment of contemporary American democracy. Though the cycle is not a chronicle, it reflects the explosive tensions in Whitman's political surroundings. The whole sequence shows a sense of time present, of current reality and of profound urgency, all tempered by Whitman's unquenchable capacity to create visions. Whitman had seldom grasped such a sense of the immediate in his earlier editions of *Leaves of Grass;* he would never approach it again in his poetry. His best grasp of the gilded age is suggested in the remote and unreal celebration of the past and of American technology in "Passage to India."

"Chants Democratic" was poised equally between optimism for a brilliant future for the republic and the ominous rumblings of "inevitable conflict." There can be little doubt that the country in 1860 would have been in better condition to avoid armed conflict if the vast network of mutually contradictory vested interests had not existed. "Chants Democratic" bears witness to alternatives that the ruling power of America appeared not to see; for, inevitable or not, the armed conflict came. With it, something that had seemed good in America disappeared—something like the sensitive hope for perfection that Whitman expressed in his poem cycle. John

[11] See, e.g., Francis Butler Simkins, *A History of the South* (New York, 1958), pp. 190–191.

Brown, the harbinger of civil war, the prototype of the inharmon-
ious voice of dissent, triumphed posthumously. Whitman, the prototype of the Unionist, lived to rewrite *Leaves of Grass* so that the
hopeful "Chants Democratic" never appeared again. Though a number of criticisms might be brought against the structure of *Leaves
of Grass* 1860, "Chants Democratic" secures the essential unity of
the edition.

In his introduction to the facsimile of the 1860 edition of *Leaves
of Grass* Roy Harvey Pearce speaks of the "failure" of the 1892 or
authorized edition.[12] The validity of such a criticism cannot be
argued here, though there is certainly some prima facie support
for it. Any shortcomings of the authorized edition reflect Whitman's
rejection of "Chants Democratic" as a sequence. I have suggested
that "Chants Democratic" is an important sequence in the growth
of *Leaves of Grass*. In this sequence Whitman dared to write of his
hopes not only for salvaging the republic, not only for reasserting
the values of its founders, but also for the realization of the visionary
republic that was somehow just around the corner. Whatever else
Leaves of Grass was to become, it would never again show the
daring, the conviction, and the profound hope for political resolution represented in this sequence. "Chants Democratic" was precisely what the volume would *not* become. Perhaps this lost aspect
of hope is what Mr. Pearce senses when he speaks of the failure
of the authorized edition. Perhaps, too, after the magnitude of
Whitman's failure to convince the Americans of his day to adopt
his vision of the republic of the common man, he turned truly inward and irrevocably away from his most comfortable pose as the
poet of all Americans.

[12] Pearce, p. xvii.

Whitman and the Magazines: Some Documentary Evidence
Robert Scholnick

I

IN MARCH, 1874, *Harper's New Monthly Magazine* published Whitman's "Prayer of Columbus," a clearly autobiographical poem portraying the emotions of a prophet unrecognized in his own country. In explaining the poem's biographical significance, Harold W. Blodgett and Sculley Bradley observe, "On January 23 of the preceding year, Walt Whitman had suffered a paralytic stroke; just four months later, May 23, he had lost his mother; and during the 1870's, despite occasional placement of poems in the magazines, he was feeling the public neglect." The poem, the monologue of "A batter'd, wrecked old man . . . Venting a heavy heart,"[1] has contributed to the general impression that during his life, Whitman was a neglected writer. In view of the importance of the monthlies as "the principal voices of the genteel era,"[2] Whitman viewed his ability to publish in the magazines as a crucial indicator of his literary position. In this regard it is ironic that his "Prayer" should appear in *Harper's*, certainly the most successful middle-class magazine of the time. We might well ask just what was Whitman's standing with the important monthlies?

Less than two years later, in "Whitman's Actual American Position," an article which the poet himself wrote but had inserted in the regular columns of the *West Jersey Press* for January 26, 1876,[3] he made the following statement:

[1] Walt Whitman, *Leaves of Grass*, ed. Harold W. Blodgett and Sculley Bradley (New York, 1965), p. 421.

[2] Malcolm Cowley, *After the Genteel Tradition*, rev. ed. (Carbondale, Ill., 1964), p. 10.

[3] *Walt Whitman's Workshop*, ed. Clifton J. Furness (Cambridge, Mass., 1928), pp. 245–246. Furness, basing his case on internal evidence, has shown that Whitman himself wrote the article. A previously unpublished letter from Edmund C. Stedman to Thomas Bailey Aldrich contains the first external evidence. On June 11, 1880, Stedman wrote, "The ed. of the *West Jersey Press* tells me that all his editorials about Whitman *are written by Walt himself.*" The letter is in the Houghton Library and is quoted by permission of the

Repeated attempts to secure a small income by writing for the magazines
during his illness have been utter failures. The *Atlantic* will not touch
him. His offerings to *Scribner* are returned with insulting notes; the
Galaxy the same. *Harper's* did print a couple of his pieces two years ago,
but imperative orders from head quarters have stopped anything further.

Such treatment, he charged, is one of the factors contributing to the
"bleakness of the actual situation":

> The real truth is that with the exception of a very few readers (women
> equally with men), Whitman's poems in their public reception have
> fallen still-born in this country. They have been met, and are met today,
> with the determined denial, disgust and scorn of orthodox American
> authors, publishers and editors, and, in a pecuniary and worldly sense,
> have certainly wrecked the life of their author.

These are serious charges.

In 1880 Edmund C. Stedman asked the editor of each magazine
named by Whitman in the *West Jersey Press* to describe his magazine's relationship with the poet. Quoting Whitman's charges directly, he asked the editors to list both acceptances and rejections
and to explain the "grounds" for any rejections. The responses of the
editors, W. D. Howells of the *Atlantic*, J. G. Holland of *Scribner's*,
W. C. Church of the *Galaxy* and H. M. Alden of *Harper's*, are contained in the Edmund C. Stedman Collection at Columbia University
and previously have not been published.[4] They warrant a reconsider-
ation of Whitman's standing with these monthlies in the years
before 1880. The evidence indicates that Whitman did indeed have
just grounds for his complaint against *Scribner's* and that a harsh
rejection note from Dr. Holland may well have been the precipitating
factor for the important *West Jersey Press* article. However, Whitman
fared remarkably well as a contributor to the other magazines,
although critical understanding and appreciation of his work was
slow in coming.

Before quoting the letters from the editors to Stedman, it is
necessary to say a word about the *West Jersey Press* controversy and

Harvard College Library. Mr. William H. Bond, Librarian, and his staff provided me with
valuable assistance.

[4] These letters are owned by Columbia University and are published with the permission
of the University. I appreciate the assistance of Mr. Kenneth Lohf, Librarian for Rare Books
and Manuscripts, and his staff.

Stedman's involvement. With this article, Whitman very shrewdly launched an advertising campaign which resulted in a dramatic rise in his American reputation. He sent a copy to his friend William Michael Rossetti in England with the request that "you should have it put, if convenient, in the *Academy*, or any other literary gazette, your way, if thought proper."[5] Rossetti was able to have it printed in the London *Athenaeum* on March 11, and this prompted Robert Buchanan's furious condemnation of the American literary establishment in a letter to the London *Daily News*, published on March 13.[6] Bayard Taylor's defense of the establishment on March 28 in the New York *Daily Tribune* opened the American theater of battle, giving first John Burroughs and then William D. O'Connor the opportunity to defend Whitman in letters to the widely circulated *Tribune*.[7] Eventually, the responsible American literary monthlies were forced to consider the Whitman problem and it could not be said that this poet, like his contemporary Herman Melville, was a forgotten American author.

The culminating event in the controversy was the publication in *Scribner's* for November, 1880, of Stedman's sympathetic "Walt Whitman."[8] As Charles B. Willard has observed, this essay "marks the beginning of . . . public critical acceptance by others than the members of the Whitman circle."[9] Dr. Holland, one of Whitman's most vehement opponents, attempted to dissuade Stedman from printing the article. But, as Stedman explained, "I made it clear to him . . . that it was time such an article should appear, and second, That no review of the *American Poets* could *ignore* a man who had made himself so much talked-of at home and abroad, and had assumed a position of his own."[10] Through his skillful self-advertisements, Whitman succeeded in forcing the issue and won the battle.

While preparing his Whitman essay for *Scribner's*, Stedman

[5] Walt Whitman, *The Correspondence*, ed. Edwin Haviland Miller (New York, 1964), III, 20.

[6] Furness, pp. 247, 158. Buchanan's letter is reprinted in Clara Barrus, *Whitman and Burroughs Comrades* (Boston, 1931), pp. 116–117.

[7] A summary of these events is given in Barrus, and in Whitman, *Correspondence*, III, 39, n. 86. Burroughs' letter appeared on April 13 and is printed in Barrus, pp. 125–128. O'Connor's letter was published on April 22.

[8] *Scribner's Monthly*, XXI (Nov., 1880), 44–64.

[9] Charles B. Willard, *Whitman's American Fame* (Providence, 1950), pp. 23–24.

[10] Laura Stedman and George M. Gould, *Life and Letters of Edmund Clarence Stedman* (New York, 1910), II, 106. From a letter to W. D. Howells, dated May 8, 1880.

sent identical letters to the four editors. The Houghton Library at
Harvard contains the letter sent to Howells.[11]

Confidential

80 Broadway, New York.
New York, April 26th 1880
Dear Sir

It is my intention soon to write a critical article upon Walt Whitman.
A few years ago Mr. Whitman sent me a "slip" copy of a leader in the
West Jersey Press, which contains the following passage.[12]

"Repeated attempts to secure a small income by writing for the
magazines during his illness have been utter failures. The *Atlantic* will
not touch him. His offerings to *Scribner* are returned with insulting
notes; the *Galaxy* the same. *Harper's* did print a couple of his pieces two
years ago, but imperative orders from headquarters have stopped anything further."

I have the impression that this is overstated. Will you have the kindness
to inform me (1) whether any contributions by Whitman have ever
appeared in your magazine? (2) whether he ever offered any poems that
you rejected? (3) If so upon what grounds did you decline to use them?

This information is not desired for public use, but that I may rightly
understand Mr. Whitman's position.

Very truly yrs.,
Edmund C. Stedman

To/
    The Editor of the *Atlantic Monthly*
       Boston

While Stedman's interjection of his own opinion, that "Mr. Whitman's position" is "overstated," may disqualify this as a scientific
questionnaire, the letter is a direct and straightforward attempt to
learn the facts of the situation.

II

What is especially surprising about the *West Jersey Press* article
is that Whitman indiscriminately attacked all four magazines. The
fact is that the editors had widely different attitudes toward his

[11] The letter is quoted by permission of the Harvard College Library.

[12] Evidently Whitman hoped Stedman would publicize his plight. He also sent copies
to Rudolf Schmidt and Edward Dowden. See Whitman, *Correspondence*, III, 21–22.

work. The two letters which I will print from Dr. Holland to Stedman give vivid illustration of the sort of insults which Holland was capable of delivering to Whitman. On the other hand, the *Galaxy* paid Whitman well for almost everything which he submitted and opened its columns regularly to John Burroughs, perhaps Whitman's most articulate disciple. *Harper's* and the *Atlantic* ranged between these two poles. With all the magazines a wide variety of factors were involved in the treatment of Whitman, and in printing the letters from the editors to Stedman, I will explore the relevant factors in each instance.

Holland alone determined the policy of *Scribner's* toward Whitman, from the time of the first number in November, 1870, to his death in October, 1881. So successful was he that the magazine quickly rivaled *Harper's* for the position of the most popular literary magazine in the country. In his monthly "Topics of the Time" column, Holland preached to the nation his exalted faith in the Puritan ethic, and he became, as Edward Eggleston observed in a memorial notice, "the most popular and effective preacher of social and domestic moralities in his age; the oracle of the active and ambitious young man; of the susceptible and enthusiastic young woman; the guide, philosopher, and school-master of humanity at large, touching all questions of life and character."[13] His "influence was so strong in the post-bellum decade that one of his critics bitterly conceded that the period should be known as 'the Holland age of letters.' "[14] Whitman recognized that the magazine's strong opposition to him changed dramatically when Richard Watson Gilder assumed the editorship in 1881. As he told Traubel in May, 1888, after the magazine had changed its name:

The Century under Gilder has always accepted my pieces and paid for them. Gilder is quite a different man—noway of the Holland type. Holland is a dead man—there's hardly anything of him left today: he had his strut and is passed on: he was a man of his time, not possessed of the slightest forereach. . . . But Holland was all right: he did his deed in the Holland way: why should we ask or expect him to do more?[15]

[13]*Century Magazine*, XIII (Dec., 1881), 164.

[14] Benjamin T. Spencer, *The Quest for Nationality* (Syracuse, 1957), p. 295. Spencer does not identify Holland's critic.

[15] Horace Traubel, *With Walt Whitman in Camden* (New York, 1915), I, 184-185.

Less than a decade after Holland's death, Whitman was able to view his antagonist with remarkable objectivity.

In the seventies, however, he was deeply affected by a rejection letter from Holland.

I sent a poem, which was rejected—not rejected mildly, noncommittedly, in the customary way, but with a note of the most offensive character. I was sick and blue at the time: the note provoked me: I threw it into the fire. I was always sorry I destroyed it: had I been well I should not have done so: it was a good specimen insult for the historian. . . .[16]

Whitman dated the letter offering the poem only "12/12." If, as seems probable,[17] the year was 1875, it is likely that Holland's letter was the precipitating factor, the provocation, for the *West Jersey Press* article which appeared on January 26, 1876. Six weeks would be more than enough time for Holland to return the poem and for Whitman to compose and place the article. Receiving the letter at a time of illness and concern over lagging creativity, Whitman may very well have been led to strike out against his "opponents." Such a letter from Holland would definitely explain Whitman's statement that "His offerings to *Scribner* are returned with insulting notes."

Both of Holland's principal editorial assistants, Richard Watson Gilder and Robert Underwood Johnson, were sympathetic to Whitman, and it appears that neither objected to Stedman's plan to include an essay on Whitman in the projected series on American poets. Holland had other ideas.

[16] Ibid., p. 184.

[17] Whitman, *Correspondence*, III, 66. Miller, in footnote 5, suggests 1876, but it is unlikely that Whitman would offer Holland a poem less than a year after the appearance of the *West Jersey Press* article. Further, the poem, "Eidolons," appears in the New York *Tribune* (February 19, 1876) and in *Two Rivulets*, published early in 1876. Miller himself notes that "it is strange that W. W. submitted poems after Holland's hostile criticism in the May issue of *Scribner's Monthly*, XII (1876), 123–125." But he justfies the 1876 dating as "almost certain" because " 'Eidolons' was composed in 1876." This seems doubtful since *Two Rivulets* was "nearly ready" for distribution on December 17, 1875, as Whitman told Burroughs (*Correspondence*, III, 344).

March 22, 1879

Editorial Rooms
  of Scribner's Monthly
743 Broadway
New York

My Dear Stedman:

I was delighted to hear from Johnson that you propose to begin upon the long contemplated enterprise. You are the man for it. You will do it for the literary class as well as Lowell, and for the popular reader a great deal better.

You will do me a great kindness now, if you will tell me frankly how much you think I ought to pay you for your work. You know I am generously disposed. It is simply a question of how much I can afford to pay. I would like to get at your ideas, and then I will hold myself free to take or leave them. I do not hesitate to be frank.

The taking any notice whatever of Whitman in Scribner's Monthly will be to me, of course, a bitter pill. If he ever gets a notice here it will be solely out of respect to you. How can you touch the wretched old fraud? His personal character is disgusting. Much of his work is too nasty to be taken up into a respectable house—work that he has never repented of—and refuses to [take] out of his books—and he has not yet a single follower. Now for a man to make a new and bold departure in verse, and in a whole life fail to secure one follower or imitator, to say nothing of founding a school—is to stand self-exposed as a failure. He has been the author of a certain sort of eloquence, but I am sure the world will never agree that he is a poet.

He has offered me his stuff for publication, but it has seemed to me to be my duty to American literature to discountenance him entirely. He seems to me to be utterly a pest and an abomination.

Yours always truly,
J. G. Holland

The strategy Holland uses in attempting to dissuade Stedman reveals much about the strong impact which Whitman's poetry made upon him. As a powerful editor, he might simply have explained that Whitman was hardly an important writer and that he should be treated, if at all, in one of the chapters reserved for minor poets. But clearly, Whitman is not a "minor" poet to him and he is not capable of dealing with the question calmly. There is, after all, a "certain sort of eloquence" which he finds attractive. But Whitman, in his open treatment of sex and the "new and bold departure in verse," is a threat to everything which the "Holland age" represented. The complex of explosive emotions involved, such as attraction, threat and repulsion, could easily result in the sort of rejection slip which Whitman claimed to have received.

Holland's anger bursts to the surface again in his response to Stedman's questionnaire.

April 27, 1880

Editorial Rooms
Scribner's Magazine
743 Broadway
New York

My Dear Stedman:

Yes, Whitman sent me "Eidolons," and I returned it to him, with a frank and courteous note. You know me pretty well, and ought to know whether it is in me to be discourteous to anybody. Nobody but Whitman himself could have been responsible for the statement that I sent him an "insulting" note, and the statement is like him, and in the line of his constant policy. He plays the role of the suffering literary genius—the great unappreciated—and has so far seemed to find his account in it.

I do not expect or wish that anything I may say to you about Whitman will change your attitude toward him, but I confess to regarding him with complete antipathy. He seems to be a heathen in his morals and a barbarian in his art. His "Leaves of Grass" ought to be under the legal ban of all obscene publications; and the remarkable thing is that the old wretch, after having outlived his passions, cannot see that this book merits expurgation. I have no faith whatever in the sincerity of his method—that is, I don't believe his theory of poetry demands his style of work, and I am sure that all he does is simply to make himself notorious. He will found no school because there is nothing in his thought or art to found it upon. To me he stands in the category of curiosities, and is not a particularly interesting one at that.

Yours truly
J. G. Holland

(Last page)

There is little doubt that Holland's rejection letter was far more "frank" than "courteous." The very length and intensity of his response to Stedman, calling Whitman a "heathen," "barbarian," and an "old wretch," belies his claim that the poet was "not . . . particularly interesting."

Further, he devoted portions of three "Topics of the Times" columns to Whitman, making *Scribner's* the only one of the four magazines to attack him in the years before 1880. The increasingly bitter tone of these notices, May, 1876, October, 1878, and October, 1881, reflects a rise in Whitman's reputation and, conversely, the ending of the "Holland age." In the first of these columns, Holland responds to the *West Jersey Press* article. He is smugly confident while disposing of Whitman's claims. He assures his readers that he has "none but the kindliest feelings toward him, and the heartiest wishes for his good fame." As evidence, he remarks in concluding, "we have refrained from citing, or even alluding to, those portions of his early book which are most open to criticism, and especially those portions of which, in the subsidence of his grosser self, he must now be ashamed." No, it is simply a matter of verse technique, and Holland devotes most of the essay to proving that Whitman just is not a poet. His argument, developed by means of long excerpts, is that Whitman's verse is no more poetic than lines from Emerson and Carlyle written out as prose. But in keeping with the "friendly" tone of the article, he cites approvingly "To a Locomotive in Winter," noting that the last three lines "are good, honest decasyllabic verse."[18] He is willing to accept only the Whitman most in tune with the new era of machinery and power, the poet as celebrator of the new industrial age.

But in the next reference, the bitterness is overt. Whitman has received some favorable attention, and in an essay on "Our Garnered Names," Holland wonders

How an age that possesses a Longfellow and an appreciative ear for his melody can tolerate in the slightest degree the abominable dissonances of which Walt Whitman is the author, is one of the unsolved mysteries. There is a morbid love of the eccentric abroad in the country which, let

[18] *Scribner's Monthly*, XII (May, 1876), 123-125.

us hope, will die out as the love of nastiness has died out. At present we say but little about our immortals, and give ourselves over to the discussion of claims of which our posterity will never hear, or of which they will only hear to wonder over, or to laugh at.[19]

Poe and Thoreau joined Whitman on Holland's list of unhealthy writers, but clearly Whitman is the chief villain.

In fact, the "Whitman problem" continued to plague him until his death in October, 1881. In "Literary Eccentricity," printed in the October *Scribner's* of that year, he correctly recognizes that Whitman represents the most formidable challenge to his concept of an American literary tradition based firmly on English models, a tradition of definite "limitations, outside of which no one can go without convicting himself of eccentricity and bad taste." He had counted upon the English critics to condemn out of hand the claims of the American literary nationalists, and was baffled by their recognition of Whitman.

Our cousins on the other side of the water are a little unreasonable in expecting from us a literature cast into some new form. They threw up their hats when Walt Whitman appeared, but Walt Whitman is a more egregious blunderer than Carlyle was, with a smaller supply of brains. We believe we appreciate all the vitalities of Walt Whitman's literary performances, but his productions, in their forms, are simply abominable. They are literary eccentricities. . . . Even those who praise him and his barbarisms would scorn the use of his forms in any production whatever.[20]

The knowledge that his own magazine, in printing Stedman's "Walt Whitman," did much to further that poet's reputation, must, indeed, have been a "bitter pill."

III

The conflict between Stedman and Holland over the publication of "Walt Whitman" has a definite bearing on Whitman's standing with the *Atlantic*. For Howells, in responding to Stedman's letter, invited him to print the paper in the *Atlantic*:

[19] Ibid., XVI (Oct., 1878), 896.
[20] Ibid., XXII (Oct., 1881), 945–946.

April 29, 1880

Editorial Office of
The Atlantic Monthly
47 Franklin Street
Boston

My dear Stedman:

How extraordinary that my old friend should address me as the Editor
of the Atlantic Monthly, and not even write me in his own hand! I ought
to answer you in kind:

*The Editor of the Atlantic Monthly presents his compliments to Mr.
Stedman, and begs to note that he has no recollection of ever declining
or receiving any poems from Mr. Whitman.*

Yours ever,
W. D. Howells

P.S. Do you care to print your paper in the Atlantic?

If Holland resisted arguments on the appropriateness of an article
on Whitman, Stedman might have threatened to take the article,
as well as his other work, to the *Atlantic*. William Sloan Kennedy
touched upon this matter in the course of a *Conservator* article in
November, 1896

The significance and bravery of Stedman's article on Walt Whitman,
published in that citadel of orthodoxy, the old *Scribner's* . . . is perhaps
not fully weighed by the younger men of to-day. That black-maned
athlete, J. G. Holland, was cast in too narrow a mold to appreciate
Whitman, and Stedman told me, I remember, that he had a serious time
with him, and had to threaten him that he would altogether stop the
series he was writing if his article on Whitman was not admitted to the
columns of the magazine. The immediate results of that article and its
influence from that time on in book form have been great.[21]

If Stedman had published the article in the *Atlantic Monthly*, Whitman would have benefited from the dramatic shifting and the con-
sequent recognition by the impeccable Brahmin periodical. Of course,
Holland knew this and could not allow it. But that the *Atlantic*
went out of its way to solicit Stedman's article indicates that, at least

[21] William Sloan Kennedy, "Sursum Corda, Comrades!" *The Conservator*, VII (Nov.,
1896), 140.

in the closing years of Howells's editorship, it was not so totally opposed to Whitman as has been thought.

I will consider first Whitman's acceptance record and then the
magazine's critical treatment of his work. Howells served as J. T.
Fields's assistant editor from 1866 to 1871 and held the editorship
from 1871 to 1881. His letter to Stedman indicates that Whitman
did not submit anything during the 1870's.

In the 1860's his acceptance record with the magazine, as far as
I can determine, was good. He submitted poems on three occasions
and was accepted twice. The first editor, James Russell Lowell,
accepted "Bardic Symbols," later titled "As I Ebb'd with the Ocean
of Life." The poem occupied over two pages in the issue for April,
1860.[22] Portia Baker, whose article on the subject paints a picture
of distinct coolness on the part of the magazine toward Whitman
during his lifetime, theorizes that "this triumph was achieved during
the editorship of Lowell, as a result, one surmises, of the fact that the
third edition of the *Leaves of Grass* was being brought out by a
respected Boston House," Thayer and Eldridge.[23] This may be so,
although there is no indication that the fastidious Lowell felt it a
part of his job as editor to give a hearing to every poet published by
a reputable Boston house. The fact is that the *Atlantic* published the
poem and paid Whitman for it. The poet, as Holloway has written,
"was proud of having appeared in such a magazine."[24]

In October, 1861, Whitman submitted "1861," a poem on the War,
and two others, which have not been identified. Fields had succeeded
Lowell as editor, and it was evidently from him that Whitman received a rejection slip stating that the poems could not be used
"before their interest,—which is of the present,—would have
passed."[25] I see no reason to accept Portia Baker's claim that this
rejection "may be taken as support for a theory of hostility on the
part of the magazine." She herself notes that "Holloway does not
regard it so," and concedes that "it is easy enough to find records of
rejections sent to persons whose literary status was much more

[22] *Atlantic Monthly*, V (April, 1860), 445–447.
[23] Portia Baker, "Walt Whitman and *The Atlantic Monthly*," *American Literature*,
VI (Nov., 1935), 292.
[24] Emory Holloway, *Whitman* (New York, 1969), pp. 188–189.
[25] Horace Traubel, *With Walt Whitman in Camden* (New York, 1914), II, 213.

secure than Whitman's could have been."[26] Further, at the beginning of the Civil War there was a pervasive feeling in the North that
the rebellion would be suppressed in short order. The incident cannot in itself be read as a reflection of hostility.

In a letter of November 30, 1868, Whitman asked Emerson to
act as his agent in offering "Proud Music of the Storm" to Fields.
He specified, "If available at all, I propose it for about the February
number of the magazine. The price is $100 & 30 copies of the num-
ber in which it may be printed—and I will ask Mr. Fields to do me
the favor to send me an answer within a week from the time he
receives the piece. . . ."[27] This seems like a prescription for a rejection
slip. But on December 5, Fields accepted the poem, enclosing the
one hundred dollars which Whitman requested, even though it was
the policy of the magazine to pay only after a piece appeared in
print.[28] It was published in February, 1869.

As regards the critical attention given Whitman in the magazine
the picture is different. The *Atlantic* did not, like *Scribner's*, attack
him actively. But it was not until December, 1877, that it attempted
anything like a full critical analysis; a limited but favorable discussion appeared in the "Contributor's Club." The only review Whitman received was a brief dismissal of the minor pamphlet *After All
Not to Create Only* (1871) as "one of his curious catalogues of the
American emotions, inventions, and geographical sub-divisions."[29]
One would think that a literary magazine of the *Atlantic's* reputation
would feel bound to say something substantive about a writer of
Whitman's importance before 1877. In this sense Portia Baker is
right in concluding that "the *Atlantic* Whitman record from 1860
to 1877 gives support to the poet's statement that in the early days
respectable critics generally ignored him."[30]

The reasons for this are not entirely clear. Before the establishment of the "Contributor's Club" in 1877, there were two possible
ways for the *Atlantic* to treat Whitman critically: in a feature article

[26] Baker, p. 285.
[27] Whitman, *Correspondence*, II, 72.
[28] Fields's letter may be found in Traubel, II, 211. Howells reports on the payment
policy of the magazine in "Recollections of an Atlantic Editorship," *Atlantic Monthly*, C
(Nov., 1907), 603.
[29] *Atlantic Monthly* XXIX (Jan., 1872), 108–109.
[30] Baker, p. 293. For Whitman's statement, see Traubel, I, 127.

or through reviewing his books. There were distinct problems with each. Since all but two of his works during the period were privately printed, it is not at all certain that the magazine actually received review copies. The Boston firm of Roberts Brothers brought out the previously mentioned *After All Not to Create Only*. The 1861 Thayer and Eldridge *Leaves* was listed in "Recent American Publications" for July, 1860, but evidently Lowell chose not to review it. However, if the *Atlantic* editors had wished to review the privately printed books, a way could have been found to obtain copies.

On the question of a feature article, it must be remembered that the *Atlantic*, despite its literary prestige, was not financially successful. One of the "obstacles" which its editors had to face was the "moral censorship required by certain segments of the reading public. Especially explosive, of course, were references to religious unorthodoxy and suggestions of sensuality."[31] In this climate, an article on Whitman would be extremely risky. In September, 1869, during Fields's absence, Howells published Mrs. Stowe's "The True Story of Lady Byron's Life," which vaguely suggested that Byron had an incestuous relationship with his half-sister. The article created such a sensation that circulation dropped from 50,000 to 35,000.[32] Certainly, the editors had to be especially careful in considering any feature or "stated" article.

Nevertheless, there is evidence that the *Atlantic* considered running such an article on Whitman in 1866. John Burroughs recalled

a letter from the *Atlantic*, in answer to one of mine, in which they stated they were quite ready to *see* an article on W. W., though their editors were not prepared to champion him in so unqualified a manner as Mr. Emerson had, led me to prepare an article on "Drum Taps." Hearing that Howells was going there on the editorial staff, I hurried it off, but not in time—"Willie, dear" was there ahead of me, and of course it was not accepted.[33]

This shows the interest of the *Atlantic* under Fields in addressing itself to the "Whitman problem." It is difficult to say exactly why

[31] James C. Austin, *Fields of the Atlantic Monthly* (San Marino, 1953), p. 45.

[32] Frank Luther Mott, *A History of American Magazines* (Cambridge, Mass., 1938), II, 505.

[33] Clara Barrus, *The Life and Letters of John Burroughs* (Cambridge, Mass., 1925), II, 116.

this article, which Burroughs published in the *Galaxy* for December, 1866, was rejected.

Of course, Howells may have exerted a veto. Shortly before joining the *Atlantic* staff, he had treated *Drum Taps* unfavorably in a review for the *Round Table*, published on November 11, 1865. His argument was directed against Whitman's "artistic method," which he felt was "mistaken." But clearly he had not closed his mind.

There are such rich possibilities in the man that it is lamentable to contemplate his error of theory. He has truly and thoroughly absorbed the idea of our American life, and we say to him as he says to himself, "You've got enough in you, Walt; why don't you get it out?" A man's greatness is good for nothing folded up in him, and if emitted in barbaric yawps, it is not more filling than Ossian or the east wind.[34]

Perhaps the sensitive Whitman did not submit anything to the *Atlantic* during the seventies because he was aware of Howells's critical opinion. But there was a clear need for a technical article on Whitman's verse technique, one demonstrating the legitimacy of his metrical principles. I can hardly think that Howells would be biased against such a paper. Burroughs's article, however, is neither technical nor critical, but eulogistic. Whitman is presented as a nearly flawless human being, and the article concludes by asserting that "Walt Whitman possesses almost in excess, a quality in which every current poet is lacking. We mean the faculty of being in entire sympathy with nature, and the objects and shows of nature . . . ."[35] Though he protested that in making this statement "we mean discredit to none," the *Atlantic*'s readers could interpret it only as a criticism of such writers as Emerson, Lowell and Longfellow. Whitman's position with the magazine's readership was already delicate. A case for him could not be made at the expense of other writers. Whatever the predilection of the editors, the *Atlantic* could not risk committing its prestige by featuring such an article.

It was not until the founding of the "Contributor's Club" in January, 1877, that the magazine had the flexibility which made it possible for informal essays to be tucked away unobtrusively. Within a year of its founding, the "Club" contained a sympathetic article on

[34] William Dean Howells, "Drum Taps," *Round Table*, II (Nov. 11, 1865), 147–148.
[35] John Burroughs, "Walt Whitman and His 'Drum Taps,'" *Galaxy*, II (Dec. 1, 1866), 615.

Whitman. Clearly, the effects of the *West Jersey Press* campaign
are evident as the author uses a "lull in the Walt Whitman controversy" to take "a dispassionate view of his work." He agrees with
the accepted judgment that portions of the poet's early work are
"nasty" and that the cataloguing is "tedious and prosaic," but defends
the verse technique enthusiastically. However, like Holland, he
singles out for specific praise "To a Locomotive in Winter" and
concludes that "the poetization of modern machinery" is "the department of art for which Whitman is best fitted by nature."[36]
Clearly, this is a limited view. But by 1880, as Howells's letter to
Stedman shows, the *Atlantic* was willing to publish a long critical
article on Whitman.

IV

In printing Burroughs's "Walt Whitman and His 'Drum Taps,' "
the *Galaxy* published what O'Connor felt was "the first article . . .
that reveals critical power and insight, and a proper reverence, upon
the subject of Walt Whitman's poetry."[37] That this New York-based
magazine should accept an article previously rejected by the *Atlantic*
was appropriate for, as the *Nation* observed on April 26, 1866, the
Galaxy's "*raison d' etre*" is "partly a 'divine discontent' which pre-
vails in these parts with regard to the 'Atlantic Monthly,' and partly
the feeling, also widely diffused, that New York ought to have
a monthly of its own . . . ."[38] Where the *Atlantic* was decidedly
sectional, the *Galaxy* attempted to be national. As Stedman recalled
in 1903, at a dinner honoring the founding editors, William Conant
Church and his brother, Francis Pharcellus Church:

It was the first magazine after the war really to welcome above all
American contributions. It was given out at the office, also, that quality
and not reputation was a thing that was wanted. Best of all, we were
allowed to affix our names to our articles; and that gave young fellows
a chance, and consequently brought most of the talent to the aid of the
editors; and the magazine was run in this spirit for years.[39]

[36] *Atlantic Monthly*, VXL (Dec., 1877), 751.
[37] Whitman, *Correspondence*, I, 296. See footnote 63.
[38] *The Nation*, II (April 26, 1866), 534.
[39] Speech reprinted in *The Army and Navy Journal*, Jan. 24, 1903, pp. 509–510.

O'Connor, recognizing the opportunity for Whitman, brought his name to the attention of the Churches.[40]

Until the magazine ceased publication in January, 1878, Whitman was considered a "regular contributor," as W. C. Church explained in responding to Stedman:

New York, April 27, 1880

Dear Sir

I cannot understand Walt Whitman's making himself a party to the false statement concerning the Galaxy which you quote from the *West Jersey Press* and which, you tell me, Whitman sent you, for he knows perfectly well that he was treated with entire courtesy from first to last by the Editors of the Galaxy.

In the second volume of the Galaxy we published an eulogistic article upon "Walt Whitman and his 'Drum Taps' " by John Burroughs (see the number for December 1st, 1866, page 607). This was followed at intervals by three poems and two prose articles written by Whitman and signed with his name. These articles in the order of publication were as follows:

1. "A Carol of the Harvest for 1867" (poem) Sept. 1867, p. 605.[41]
2. "Democracy" (prose article) published Dec. 1867, p. 919.
3. "Personalism" (prose article) May, 1868, p. 540.
4. "Brother of All with Generous Hand" (poem) January 1870, p. 75.[42]
5. "O Star of France" (poem) June 1871, p. 817.

If we ever declined any of Walt Whitman's contributions, which I do not now recollect, it was certainly done in terms of entire courtesy and such as we should use to a contributor to whose articles our pages were ordinarily open.

I find a letter from Whitman acknowledging the receipt of a check for $60 for his first contribution "A Carol of the Harvest." In it he alludes to a "piece," "Ethiopia Commenting" which we did not publish, apparently for the reason that we preferred the article "Democracy" which we did publish, & which he offered us in the same letter.

Whitman put his own price on his contributions, and, so far as I can recollect, it was paid. In reference to his article "Democracy" he says "it is partly provoked by, and in some respects a rejoinder to Carlyle's Shooting Niagra."

[40] Edward F. Grier, "Walt Whitman, *The Galaxy,* and *Democratic Vistas,*" *American Literature,* XXIII (Nov., 1951), 332–350.
[41] Retitled "The Return of the Heroes."
[42] Retitled "Outlines for a Tomb."

I recall the fact that we were beset by a variety of contributors who wished to burn incense to Walt Whitman as a sort of demi-God, and it is to our failure to appreciate some of these contributors that the statement which appeared in the New Jersey paper is to be ascribed, I presume. One of these contributions was, I remember, written by a cultivated English woman, and though we could not use it, it interested me very much as offering a sort of psychological study of the effect produced by Whitman upon a woman of earnest nature who had been hedged about all her life by English conventionality, & to whom his voice came as that of one who had awakened her from the dead *"Fabitha Cuiui."*[43]

There are many things I might tell you of Whitman, and which enter into an estimate of his *personal* character but I presume they are already known to you.

Very Truly Yours,
W. C. Church

To.

Mr. E. C. Stedman
71 W. 54 St.

Whatever the personal matters to which Church refers, the important point is that he was able to separate his impression of Whitman's personal character from his professional judgment of his work. In this he was unlike T. B. Aldrich, who wrote Stedman, "There is something unutterably despicable in a man writing newspaper puffs of himself. I don't believe a charlatan can be a great poet. I couldn't believe it if I were convinced of it!"[44]

Church's listing of the Whitman record should be corrected in the following way: the *Galaxy* did reject "Orbic Literature," the third and last section of *Democratic Vistas.*[45] It printed an additional poem, "A Warble for Lilac-Time" (May, 1870). Also, Burroughs praised Whitman's work in the course of several of the magazine's articles.[46] In 1871, "Lucy Fountain," noting that Whitman is "greatly admired by all but his own countrymen," quoted Swinburne's opin-

[43] Possibly Mrs. Anne Gilchrist, "An Englishwoman's Estimate of Walt Whitman," *Radical* (Boston), VII (May, 1870), 345–359.

[44] Ferris Greenslet, *The Life of Thomas Bailey Aldrich* (Boston, 1908), p. 140. Letter dated Nov. 27, 1880.

[45] See Grier, pp. 347–348.

[46] John Burroughs, "Before Genius," *Galaxy*, V (April, 1868), 421–426. "Emerson," *Galaxy*, XXI (Feb. and April, 1876), 254–259, 543–547. "What Makes the Poet?" *Galaxy*, XXII (July, 1876), 55–60.

ion that Whitman is "one of the great geniuses of our time."[47] In January, 1877, "To Walt Whitman," an eulogistic poem by Joaquin Miller, was published. Whitman was not modest in placing price tags on his work and yet the *Galaxy*, financially the weakest of the four magazines, paid what he asked.

Colonel Church's letter resolves doubts about the magazine's treatment of Whitman which have been raised in two previous articles on the subject. Portia Baker concludes that the *Galaxy's* favorable treatment extended only until 1871. She feels that the unfavorable reviews of the first two sections of *Democratic Vistas* led to the rejection of the third and that, as the magazine became more conventional, Whitman became "a figure of little consequence."[48] There is nothing in Church's letter to indicate that this had been the case. On the contrary, Whitman remained "a contributor to whose articles our pages were ordinarily open," but evidently, he did not submit anything after 1871. I have not found any contradictory evidence. The rejection of "Orbic Literature" may simply have been the result of its "extreme length."[49] Finally, if Whitman had become a figure of "little consequence" to the magazine, it would be hard to see why it would print "To Walt Whitman." The poem comments on Whitman's slighting remarks in the *West Jersey Press*. It advises the poet to forget the entire, demeaning business:

> O titan soul, ascend your starry steep
> On golden stair to gods and storied men!
> Ascend! nor care where thy traducers creep.
> For what may well be said of prophets when
> A world that's wicked comes to call them good?
> Ascend and sing![50]

Edward F. Grier, noting that Whitman's "position as a *Galaxy* author was important to his personal fortunes and his literary reputation," argues that the "most significant" aspect of the relationship is that the *Galaxy* published the first two sections of *Democratic*

[47] "Lucy Fountain," *Galaxy*, XII (Aug., 1871), 230–234.

[48] Portia Baker, "Walt Whitman's Relations with Some New York Magazines," *American Literature*, VII (Nov., 1935), 278.

[49] Grier, p. 348.

[50] Joaquin Miller, "To Walt Whitman," *Galaxy*, XXIII (Jan., 1877), 29.

Vistas, the "most important prose statement of his idealism." But in concluding his account of Whitman's relationship with the *Galaxy*, he finds two later references to the magazine which, "instead of rounding off the story neatly, leave it in confusion." There is the *West Jersey Press* charge that the *Galaxy* insulted Whitman and a letter of January 24, 1877,

to John Burroughs about the manuscript of *Birds and Poets*, Burroughs' fourth book. After suggesting a change in the order of the constituent essays and approving the title, he remarked in passing that he had not yet received a manuscript from Church. What this manuscript was and why Whitman was expecting a manuscript from either of the Churches a year after he had publicly accused them of insulting him, are, barring the appearance of more letters, more difficult to discover than what song the Sirens sang.[51]

The appearance of Church's letter to Stedman frees us from the complexities of the Sirens' song. Whitman was in the habit of assisting Burroughs with his work and it is likely, as Edwin Haviland Miller suggests,[52] that he is referring not to his own manuscript but to Burroughs's "Our Rural Divinity," which appeared in the *Galaxy* in January. Church does not mention that Whitman had submitted anything at this time. And Church's letter should also help resolve any doubts about the *Galaxy*'s treatment of Whitman raised by the *West Jersey Press* article. Clearly, as Grier suspects, the "insulting" letter came from Holland, not Church. There is no reason to doubt Church's statement that Whitman "was treated with entire courtesy from first to last by the Editors of the *Galaxy*."

v

Because of *Harper's* great popularity, its treatment of Whitman is a matter of considerable importance. Alden, who edited the magazine from 1869 to 1909, paid Whitman what he requested for "Song of the Redwood-Tree" ($100) and "Prayer of Columbus" ($60).[53] Whitman, in the *West Jersey Press* article, admitted his early success with the magazine, but claimed that "imperative orders from head quarters have stopped anything further." This would have been an

[51] Grier, pp. 333, 350.
[52] Whitman, *Correspondence*, III, 76. See footnote 9.
[53] Ibid., II, 255, 259.

obvious charge for Whitman to make. The close supervision of Fletcher Harper, who guided the magazine from the time of its founding in 1850 until his retirement in 1875, was well-known in the literary community. In writing to Stedman, Alden specifically denied Whitman's charge:

> Franklin Square,
> New York, April 27, 1880
>
> Dear Sir,
>
> I have yours of the 26th. Seven years ago I accepted two poems by Walt Whitman—"Song of the Redwood-Tree," & "The Prayer of Columbus"—which were published in *Harper's Magazine* (February & March 1874). He has sent me, since then, poems which I felt obliged to decline, because they seemed to me not adapted to the magazine. I have never received any instructions from the Messrs. Harper respecting Walt Whitman's contributions. It would certainly give us greater pleasure to accept than to decline them.
>
> I have always been an admirer of Whitman's poetry. In so far as *imagination* marks the poet, (if we define imagination as thinking through types [*eidullia*]), he has no equal in this generation.
>
> Very truly yours,
> H. M. Alden
> Ed. *Harper's Mag.*
>
> Edmund C. Stedman, Esq.

I have not been able to determine the titles or dates of the poems Alden rejected. Whitman himself, in conversation with Traubel, gives this version of the relationship:

> The Harpers once accepted a poem, which induced me to send them others, but five or six were rejected in succession, some of them accompanied on their return with palliating notes: then I saw I was not wanted: I shut the door and withdrew.[54]

Alden's letter to Stedman expresses both a friendly attitude toward Whitman and a high regard for his work. From his denial that the management had given orders concerning Whitman, we might conclude that the poet was too hasty in shutting the door.

Alden, in stating that he rejected certain of Whitman's poems because "they seemed to me not adapted to the magazine," is refer-

[54] Traubel, I, 185.

ring to Fletcher Harper's broad editorial principles. As Charles
Nordhoff learned, Harper insisted that his magazine carry material
which would prove "intelligible, interesting, and useful to the
average American."[55] Such a maxim is certainly not a commitment
to literary excellence for its own sake. But it did allow *Harper's*
more flexibility and openness than its chief rival, *Scribner's*, which
was limited by Dr. Holland's narrow Puritan moralism. *Harper's*
was not afraid of Whitman's reputation. In printing "Song of the
Redwood-Tree," which celebrates the great westward migration of
the American pioneers, "a swarming and busy race settling and
organizing everywhere," it published a poem in tune with the
optimistic, expansionary tendencies of the age. But "Prayer of
Columbus" is a different matter.[56] One might not expect "the great
successful middle-class magazine" to print such a poem.[57] But it
would appear that Fletcher Harper's editorial principles were broad
enough, and Alden's perception was acute enough, to embrace the
best of Whitman's later work.

Two additional letters from Alden to Stedman testify to the
fundamental seriousness with which he approached Whitman's
poetry. Three days after the first letter, he wrote to clarify his
position.

Franklin Square,
New York, April 30, 1880

My dear Mr. Stedman,

In speaking of Whitman's imagination, I would not have you suppose
that I use the term as I would if I were applying it to Coleridge. I limited
it to the use of types (discovered by its own analysis); and in this sense
it is really more applicable to a Master of Science than to a poet. In the
poet the type is lodged in his own heart, and when the occasion comes—
when the mystery within him is confronted by the corresponding mystery
around him—it is felt, rather than seen nakedly as an intellectual image—
& he is noticed by it, & he must sing.

I do not think that this may be said of Whitman. The type is not so
much in his heart as in his thought; & its embodiment or outward expression has not the rhythm of the song. He has been called the most unconventional of poets but he seems to me one of the most conventional.

[55] Eugene Flaxman, *The House of Harper* (New York, 1967), p. 77.
[56] Whitman, *Leaves of Grass*, pp. 209, 421.
[57] Mott, II, 391.

He is conventional, but violates at the same time the law of conventional art. While the inward operation is so purely intellectual, it is outwardly expressed in the concrete—the absolutely *real*. In this way the conventionalism is disguised; it is as if, in decoration, the artist were to introduce real objects—birds, flowers, etc.—without conventionalizing them. Perhaps this comparison is not quite fair: but the point of it is that while Whitman is moved by thought, (often grand and elevating,) he does not give the intellectual satisfaction warranted by the thought, but a moving panorama of pictures. He not only puts aside his "singing robes," but his "thinking cap" also, and resorts to the stereopticon. Considered as art. [istic] results, I do not think Whitman's poems do full justice to his ability. They suggest greatness but do not adequately express it.

Pray excuse this long letter which I intended to be only a brief note.

Sincerely yours
H. M. Alden

Alden is bothered by Whitman's cataloguing. How can a true poetry be simply a listing of objects? If this is an accurate indication of his method, must we not conclude that his powers of imagination are of a distinctly inferior nature? It is a pertinent objection, and Stedman quoted extensively from Alden's letters in his "Walt Whitman" to illustrate the complaint. But Stedman goes on to explain the method, describing

a peculiar quality in these long catalogues of types,—such as those in the "Song of the Broad-Axe" and "Salut au Monde," or, more poetically treated, in "Longings for Home." The poet appeals to our synthetic vision. Look through a window; you see not only the framed landscape, but each tree and stone and living thing. His page must be seized with the eye, as a journalist reads a column at a glance, until successive "types" and pages blend in the mind like the diverse colors of a swift-turning wheel. Whitman's most inartistic fault is that he overdoes this method, as if usually unable to compose in any other way.[58]

While hardly a complete explanation of Whitman's cataloguing technique, it is a perceptive start. What is important is that Stedman meets a theoretical objection with an appeal to experience.

Alden, in writing to Stedman on November 16, 1880, testifies to the need for just such practical criticism of Whitman's poetic techniques.

[58] Edmund C. Stedman, "Walt Whitman," *Scribner's Monthly*, XXI (Nov., 1880), 59–60.

Harper & Brothers.

> Franklin Square, New York.
> Nov. 16, 1880

My dear Mr. Stedman,

A miserable little notice that I find in the Chicago *Inter-Ocean* (copied from the N.Y. *Sun*) of your Whitman paper prompts me to do what I meant to do some days ago—viz. express to you my opinion regarding the paper.

The complaints which are made seem to me a justification of your work in one very important respect. A well-considered, discriminating judgment of Whitman must of necessity offend those who do not discriminate in either their praise or their blame.

My first thought after reading your paper was that I had under-rated Whitman. Seeing him on all sides as you presented him, my estimate was raised. It is the only essay on Whitman that has anything like completeness. It is not an easy thing to bring together within the compass of a maga.[zine] article all that is essential to a fair judgment concerning a subject about which there is so much variance of opinion.

In *temper* the paper is a model of criticism. The strength does not depend upon the strain of extravagant expression.

I am glad that you exposed the delusion that it can ever be natural to put Nature herself "out of countenance." As you point out, the Greek idea in this matter was the true one.

What pleased me most was the comparison between Whitman and Wordsworth: such comparisons throw more light upon such a subject than direct assertion.

In conclusion, let me thank you for the graceful way in which you quoted from my letters to you.

> Yours Sincerely
> H. M. Alden

Although slow in coming in the American press, such temperate critical work as Stedman's "Walt Whitman" was essential for the broadening of Whitman's reputation.

The new letters from the four editors to Stedman reveal a situation very different from that described by Whitman in the *West Jersey Press* article. Only in the matter of "insulting notes" from *Scribner's* is there a firm basis for his charges. He may have overstated his situation purposely as a means of calling attention to his plight. If this was the case, he was definitely successful. On the other hand, Holland's angry letter may have affected him so deeply that he struck out against all of the major magazines—indeed, against the entire literary establishment.

Beyond disproving the *West Jersey Press* claims, these letters lead to the conclusion that Whitman's position with the monthlies was remarkably good. It would be hard to quarrel with Stedman's own interpretation. After receiving the letters from the editors, he wrote Howells on May 8, 1880:

I knew, of course, that Whitman would never have any just cause to complain of *you*—in any matter that might pertain to your official management. But I supposed, from his statement, that he at some time had endeavored to open relations with the *Atlantic*, and wished to know exactly what had occurred. The fact is that he has been well-treated by *Harper* and *exceptionally* favored by the *Galaxy*—and in my opinion never had any just claims to the honors of martyrdom.[59]

Only Dr. Holland's *Scribner's* was closed to Whitman, but, ironically, this magazine, in printing Stedman's "Walt Whitman," did much to extend the poet's reputation. Especially when we consider the radical nature of Whitman's challenge to the literary and cultural standards of his time, the major American monthlies treated him well in the years before 1880.

[59] Stedman and Gould, II, 106.

Walt Whitman's Catalogue: Rhetorical Means for Two Journeys in 'Song of Myself'
John B. Mason

WALT WHITMAN'S DEVOTED CRITICS in the nineteenth century, such as Edward Dowden, defended the poet's use of catalogues on the grounds that the catalogues were outgrowths of the poet's democratic spirit. Dowden wrote, "No single person is the subject of Whitman's song, or can be; the individual suggests a group, and the group a multitude, each unit of which is as interesting as every other unit, and possesses equal claims to recognition. Hence the recurring tendency of his poems to become catalogues of persons and things."[1] Although Dowden's position was defensive rather than critical, his comments point to the important relationship between the catalogues and Whitman's "unity through diversity," a relationship pursued more precisely by critics in this century. Modern examinations of the catalogues have helped to explain why Whitman used the catalogues, but these examinations have eschewed the issue of how the catalogues work.[2]

As modern critics have suggested, Whitman's catalogues express his transcendentalism. The catalogues also control the reader's involvement in the poet's movement from the singular to the cosmic. An examination of the catalogues in "Song of Myself" will show that the catalogues are written in such ways as to manipulate reader involvement. "Song of Myself" is a history of the poet's movement from loafing individual to active spirit. But the poet's movement is paralleled by the reader's movement from "assuming" to "resum-

---

[1] Edward Dowden, "The Poetry of Democracy: Walt Whitman," in *A Century of Whitman Criticism*, ed. Edwin Haviland Miller (Bloomington, Ind., 1969), p. 43.

[2] A convincing argument for the catalogues as an organizational technique in "Crossing Brooklyn Ferry" can be found in Stanley Coffman's " 'Crossing Brooklyn Ferry': A Note on the Catalogue Technique in Whitman's Poetry," *Modern Philology*, LI (May, 1954), 225–232. Coffman's scheme works especially well with this "short" poem, which features two major catalogues. The scheme is not so illuminating for longer poems such as "Song of Myself."

ing," and the poet controls both movements in the poem with the catalogues.

Whitman's poetry, from one point of view, is the working out of Emerson's statements in prose on the function of the poet as a "liberating god" who can show the innate spiritual connections among all physical things. In "The Poet," Emerson wrote, "For as it is dislocation and detachment from the life of God that makes things ugly, the poet, who re-attaches things to nature and the Whole—re-attaching even artificial things and violation of nature, to nature, by a deeper insight—disposes very easily of the most disagreeable facts." In spite of the poet's act of "re-attaching," Emerson saw the poet in a passive role. "The weakness of the will begins when the individual would be something of himself," he wrote in "The Over-Soul." For Emerson, death of egotism was prerequisite to participating in the Over-Soul. The idea is found also in "Nature": "I become a transparent eyeball; I am nothing; I see all; the currents of the Universal Being circulate through me; I am part and parcel of God." Whitman himself, in the preface to the 1855 edition, speaks of the United States as the greatest poem and of himself as a seer. If one views Whitman as a passive seer, his catalogues are easily explained: they would be his way of calling the roll for the nation; the greatest poem, and the function of the poet would be to describe rather than to order. Lawrence Buell explains, "Emerson, Whitman, and Thoreau all regarded art pragmatically, that is, as properly the expression of something beyond itself—call it vision, truth, or what you will; they were, in short, not trying to write poems but nature; and they were therefore convinced that the secret of design in art rested rather in the ability to perceive the natural order than in imposing an aesthetic order upon their perceptions."[3] Certainly evidence for Buell's view can be found in "Song of Myself." At the beginning of the poem, the poet is relaxed and inactive. "I loafe and invite my soul,/ I lean and loafe at my ease observing a spear of summer grass."[4] The poem's first major catalogue appears in section two after the poet has expressed a desire to dissipate into the atmosphere. "I am mad for it to be in contact with me" (*LG*, p. 29). Within

[3] Lawrence Buell, "Transcendentalist Catalogue Rhetoric: Vision Versus Form," *American Literature*, XL (Nov., 1968), 335.

[4] Walt Whitman, *Leaves of Grass*, ed. Harold W. Blodgett and Sculley Bradley (New York, 1965), p. 28. Hereafter *LG*.

that catalogue, the poet attempts to unite aspects of his own physiognomy with aspects of nature: "The sound of the belch'd words
of my voice loos'd to the eddies of the wind," and "The feeling of
health, the full-moon trill, the song of me rising from bed and meeting the sun" (*LG*, p. 30). This union between the poet and nature
reappears in later catalogues, especially in the catalogue that forms
section thirty-one. "I find I incorporate gneiss, coal, long-threaded
moss, fruits, grains, esculent roots, / And am stucco'd with quadrupeds and birds all over" (*LG*, p. 59). The poet announces his passive role in section twenty when he writes, "To me the converging
objects of the universe perpetually flow, / All are written to me, and
I must get what the writing means" (*LG*, p. 47).

The view of Whitman as a passive absorber easily explains the
poet's use of the catalogues, but the poet of "Song of Myself" is not
entirely or even essentially passive. He adopts a relaxed, even passive
role at the beginning of the poem, but in the course of the poem
he consciously expands the self into inclusive consciousness. As R.
W. B. Lewis states, "Traditional mysticism is the surrender of the
ego to its creator, in an eventual escape from the limits of names;
Whitman's is the expansion of the ego in the act of creation itself,
naming every conceivable object as it comes from the womb."[5]
Whitman's movement in "Song of Myself" is more than absorption;
it is also expansion. Emerson had declared in "The Poet," "Bare
lists of words are found suggestive to an imaginative and excited
mind." But Whitman knew that words alone would not be enough
to record his movement from the "I" to the cosmos, and, just as important, he knew that mere words would not provoke the reader to
resume the journey. In the preface, Whitman admitted that people
expect more than lists from the poet: "they expect him to indicate
the path between reality and their souls" (*LG*, p. 714). Whitman
was keenly aware of the dangers of extreme organicism. To be Emerson's ideal poet, he would have to be the poet of silence. As Howard
Waskow explains, "For the extreme organicist, neither the poet nor
the listener should have to approach the other party; for either party
can be the poet, and absolute spontaneity of expression should be
indistinguishable from absolute receptivity."[6] That Whitman's cat-

[5] R. W. B. Lewis, *The American Adam* (Chicago, 1955), p. 52.
[6] Howard J. Waskow, *Whitman: Explorations in Form* (Chicago, 1966), p. 59.

alogues are seldom mere lists of words may illustrate his lack of faith in the poetry that Waskow describes, a poetry which would ostensibly satisfy Emerson.[7] Within Whitman's catalogues in "Song of Myself," items are usually modified, directly by description or indirectly by contrast. Section fifteen is a roll-call of citizens, each one described in a complete sentence. The sentences are not lacking adjectives, but the strength of the catalogue lies in its descriptive verbs:

The peddler sweats with his pack on his back, (the purchaser higgling about the odd cent;)
The bride unrumples her white dress, the minute-hand of the clock moves slowly,
The opium-eater reclines with rigid head and just-open'd lips,
The prostitute draggles her shawl, her bonnet bobs on her tipsy and pimpled neck. (*LG*, p. 43)

When Whitman does list items without description, the very nature of the combinations is usually so startling that description is not missed:

Of every hue and caste am I, of every rank and religion,
A farmer, mechanic, artist, gentleman, sailor, quaker,
Prisoner, fancy-man, rowdy, lawyer, physician, priest. (*LG*, p. 45)

Gay Wilson Allen disapproves of the very term "catalogue" because the term suggests mere accumulation, whereas, according to Allen, each image is sharply focused within a Whitman catalogue.[8] And to show that the catalogues in "Crossing Brooklyn Ferry" are more than mere lists, Stanley Coffman has discovered that the catalogues in that poem are internally organized on the basis of evolution and provide an organization for the entire poem as well. Some of the catalogues in "Song of Myself" likewise appear to be more than haphazard in arrangement. The long catalogue (a catalogue within a larger catalogue) at the beginning of section thirty-three, for example, begins with a series of prepositional phrases. The poet is "afoot" with his vision, and he observes animal and human activity.

[7] In fairness to Emerson, it should be noted that he himself did not seem satisfied with the poet as a mere lister. He wrote in "The Poet," "The poet, by an ulterior intellectual perception, gives them [things] a power which makes their old use forgotten, and puts eyes and a tongue into every dumb and inanimate object."

[8] Gay Wilson Allen, *A Reader's Guide to Walt Whitman* (New York, 1970), p. 177.

The beginning of each line (with a few exceptions) brings the reader back to images of place. The prepositions give way to five lines which begin with the same predicate adjective: "pleas'd." The poet has observed and is pleased. The catalogue climaxes in an on-rush of participles:

> Storming, enjoying, planning, loving, cautioning,
> Backing and filling, appearing and disappearing,
> I tread day and night such roads. (*LG*, pp. 64–65)

The poet has moved from observation to action, reflecting the movement of the poet through the entire poem. Buell warns against seeing too much order in the catalogues. "One feels that whatever intricate design a catalogue may later seem to have, it is essentially an outpouring, intended to stir up, not to settle."[9] Buell's advice is probably good, but if an order within a catalogue can be discovered rather than superimposed, Whitman is obviously more than an organicist or a mere lister.

Whitman was not a mere lister because lists alone could not record the movement from inactive observation to active participation in the spirit that lies beneath all physical forms. His technical problem was that of finding an appropriate form which would both record that movement and involve the reader in a similar journey. David Daiches helps to explain how Whitman solved the first part of the problem. He sees Whitman's movement as one of lyric vision toward epic vision. He holds that Whitman's personal, confessional strain naturally required the "lyric pose," but that the poet was also aiming for a prophetic vision. The prophetic vision would require a rhetorical means of expanding the self. The movement, according to Daiches, is primarily expansive. "His technical problem was to find the appropriate kind of expansive imagery, the rhetorical means of enlarging the 'I' into a grand symbolic figure, both ideal observer and epitome of all that is observed, a benevolent god surveying his creation with infinite understanding and at the same time the suffering servant who participates in all human woe."[10] Although Daiches identifies the device as the catalogue, he does not show how it works toward the end that Whitman desired.

[9] Buell, p. 339.
[10] David Daiches, "Walt Whitman: Impressionist Prophet," in *Leaves of Grass: One Hundred Years After*, ed. Milton Hindus (Stanford, 1955), p. 110.

The expansion of self, for Whitman in "Song of Myself," is not easy. He has his reservations, and he knows that he is embarking on a dangerous journey:

Creeds and schools in abeyance,
Retiring back a while sufficed at what they are, but never forgotten,
I harbor for good or bad, I permit to speak at every hazard,
Nature without check with original energy. (*LG*, p. 29)

He will journey without the comforting aid of intellectual knowledge. The first seven sections of the poem are a "warming up," with the poet torn between his desire to explore the atmosphere (his relationship with nature) and his desire to linger on the grass in sensuousness and comfort:

Shall I postpone my acceptation and realization and scream at my eyes,
That they turn from gazing after and down the road,
And forthwith cipher and show me to a cent,
Exactly the value of one and exactly the value of two, and which is
ahead? (*LG*, p. 31–32)

The catalogues do offer the poet a way of beginning the journey. In the first seven sections they are short compared to those that will follow. They are used both positively and negatively. The catalogue in section two illustrates the positive reward that will come with the poet's merging his physiognomy with nature. The catalogue that begins section four presents the numerous tragedies, the "trippers and askers," that haunt the poet:

The real or fancied indifference of some man or woman I love,
The sickness of one of my folks or of myself, or ill-doing or loss or lack
of money, or depression or exaltations, (*LG*, p. 32)

"But they are not the Me myself," the poet concludes. But they do influence him once again to adopt the lounging pose. "Apart from the pulling and hauling stands what I am, / Stands amused, complacent, compassionating, idle, unitary" (*LG*, p. 32). The casual line, "Both in and out of the game and watching and wondering at it," seems more than anything else an attempt to disguise the poet's anguish in indecision. In section five, the poet invites the soul to lounge with him (the self) on the grass, and Whitman writes the most sensual lines in the poem:

I mind how once we lay such a transparent summer morning,
How you settled your head athwart my hips and gently turn'd over upon
   me,
And parted the shirt from my bosom-bone, and plunged your tongue to
   my bare-stript heart,
And reach'd till you felt my beard, and reach'd till you held my feet.
(LG, p. 33)

But idle sensuality is no more the answer than idle sensuousness.
The poet must go to the soul. The short catalogue which follows the
lines above is merely the poet's attempt to convince himself that the
self and the soul have already merged and that there is no need for
a journey. The sensual merger of the self and the soul which the
poet attempted was really onanism. And it is the child, a presexual
figure, in the next section who presents the question, "What is the
grass?" That is the question which the poet must answer with more
than idle, deductive speculations, which he at first offers. He can
answer only by leaving the idle pose behind.

    Most of the brief catalogues in the first seven sections are used to
entice the poet to remain. These are probably not the catalogues
Daiches has in mind when he speaks of the "grand symbolic stature"
of the poet. The first grand catalogue is section eight. There Whitman catalogues the extremes of humanity, from the innocent babe
to the criminal. Whitman typically adopts the overview when he
has accepted the risks that are inherent in a journey toward the
soul, and such is the case here. He begins by looking down at the
babe, a young couple, and a suicide. He maintains this lofty view
even as he leaves the catalogue for the scene of the girl and the
twenty-eight men in section eleven. From this position the poet
moves down into the world. In section fifteen, the longest catalogue
so far in the poem, the poet moves through humanity in its diverse
forms. The catalogue is a visual feast. Following the didacticism of
sections seventeen through twenty-five, the feast is audible. In the
extremely long catalogue that comprises section thirty-three, the
poet is totally involved with life, and the senses of touch, sight, and
sound are fully awake and working simultaneously:

   Scorch'd ankle-deep by the hot sand, hauling my boat down the
     shallow river, (LG, p. 61)

> Over the dusky green of the rhy as it ripples and shades in
>   the breeze; (*LG*, p. 62)

> Where the mocking-bird sounds his delicious gurgles, cackles,
>   screams, weeps . . . . (*LG*, p. 63)

The catalogues in sections twelve through forty-three record the
poet's expansion of the self, an opening of his perceptions to the
life around him and a willingness to approach life at its own level.
Whereas deduction would not answer the question "What is the
grass?" inductive experience with the forms of life does.

The poet has his moments of doubt, of course. The didacticism
which interrupts the catalogues is perhaps the way the poet re-
strains himself from too rapid an involvement with life, or perhaps
he again resists the loss of the self. The two narratives which follow
the grand catalogue of section thirty-three may also be restraints for
the poet, ways of bringing himself back to the comfort of facts and
surfaces. The "essence" of things may be a difficult burden to carry.
The extreme doubt expressed at the beginning of section thirty-eight
is similar to the doubt expressed by Christ as He hung on the cross:

> Enough! enough! enough!
> Somehow I have been stunn'd. Stand back!
> Give me a little time beyond my cuff'd head, slumbers, dreams, gaping,
> I discover my self on the verge of a usual mistake.

> That I could forget the mockers and insults!
> That I could forget the trickling tears and the blow of the bludgeons
>   and hammers!
> That I could look with a separate look on my own crucifixion and
>   bloody crowning. (*LG*, p. 72)

The poet has, in a sense, sacrificed himself: he has extended himself
to all life. But the expressed doubt merely allows the poet to expand
himself further, encompassing the gods of the universe in the catalogue in section forty-one and even the worshipers of false gods
in the catalogue in section forty-three. By the time the poet has
reached section forty-four, there is no need for the grand catalogue.
The journey has been traveled.

> All below duly travel'd, and still I mount and mount.

Rise after rise bow the phantoms behind me,
Afar down I see the huge first Nothing, I knew I was even there,
I waited unseen and always, and slept through the lethargic mist.

(LG, p. 81)

Without extending the Christian analogy too far, the poet looked on man, traveled with man, became a man and then arose following the great self-sacrifice.

The catalogues do solve the rhetorical problem for Whitman's journey. But there is also the problem of the reader's journey. In "A Backward Glance O'er Travel'd Roads," Whitman, in describing the "suggestiveness" of his verse, explains that the poem is a joint venture between the poet and the reader. "The reader will always have his or her part to do, just as much as I have had mine. I seek less to state or display any theme or thought, and more to bring you, reader, into the atmosphere of the theme or thought—there to pursue your own flight" (*LG*, p. 570). The last several sections of "Song of Myself" are directly addressed to the reader, explaining that the reader too has a journey to make:

> I bequeath myself to the dirt to grow from the grass I love,
> If you want me again look for me under your boot-soles.
>
> You will hardly know who I am or what I mean,
> But I shall be good health to you nevertheless,
> And filter and fibre your blood.
>
> Failing to fetch me at first keep encouraged,
> Missing me one place search another,
> I stop somewhere waiting for you. (*LG*, p. 89)

The journey for the reader is to be the same one the poet has made, from idle observation by the self to active participation in the spirit that lies beneath all physical forms. The journey for the reader, however, will be simpler, for he has had the path cleared by the poet. "Long enough have you dream'd contemptible dreams, / Now I wash the gum from your eyes" (*LG*, p. 84). "I act as the tongue of you" (*LG*, p. 85). The poet tells the reader that the reader must make his own way ("Not I, not any one else can travel that road for you, / You must travel it for yourself," *LG*, p. 83), but the path has been cleared. Whitman begins the poem with the comfortable statement, "I celebrate myself, and sing myself, / And what I assume you shall assume" (*LG*, 28). But the statement is not quite prophetic. It comes too easily for both the poet and the reader. The statements made by the idling self in the first seven sections regarding unification of the self and the soul are unconvincing. There has been no test, no purging, no journey. By the time the poet has traveled through life in its diverse forms, via the catalogues, however, the poet can readdress the reader with authority. This time he does more than tell the reader that he will accept the poet's assumptions:

My face rubs to the hunter's face when he lies down alone in his blanket,
The driver thinking of me does not mind the jolt of his wagon,
The young mother and old mother comprehend me,
The girl and the wife rest the needle a moment and forget where they are,
They and all would resume what I have told them. (*LG*, pp. 85–86)

The reader, then, will *resume*. He can resume the journey because the poet, through his sacrifice, has cleared the way.

Whitman was not above didacticism, but he knew that a mere statement of affinity with the reader would not be enough. He had to find a rhetorical means of engaging the reader so that he would resume the journey. In the preface, Whitman pointed to the need for such a device. "Without effort and without exposing in the least how it is done the greatest poet brings the spirit of any or all events and passions and scenes and persons some more and some less to bear on your individual character as you hear or read" (*LG*, p. 716). The device that would accomplish the goal he described is the catalogue.

The most obvious way in which the catalogues engage the reader is by forcing him into the act of condensation. The catalogues in "Song of Myself," especially the longer catalogues, cannot be "gulped down." They are accumulations of images. Yet, in a sense, they can be digested at once. Each catalogue results in a single image because the reader has been forced to condense. As Thomas Rountree explains, "In the use of catalogues Whitman seems to reverse the process of poetic condensation; the reader is to condense the catalogues for their essence. This gives a reciprocal seesawing of condensation between the poet (or poem) and the reader."[11] The task of condensation is not difficult in the short catalogues:

Whatever interests the rest interests me, politics, wars, markets, news-
papers, schools,
The mayor and councils, banks, tariffs, steamships, factories, stocks, stores,
real estate and personal estate. (*LG*, p. 77)

The reader does more than simply conclude that Whitman was correct in the line preceding the catalogue: "This is the city and I am
one of the citizens." He is forced to draw a single image of commerce that encompasses both process and product so that the two
are inseparable. Gay Wilson Allen probably gave too much or too
little credit to Whitman when he maintained that Whitman's catalogues are composed of clearly focused images. At times, especially
in the shorter catalogues, the images are blurred intentionally. In
this catalogue from section forty-one, the reader can hardly respond
to one image before another is thrown to him:

Taking myself the exact dimensions of Jehovah,
Lithographing Kronos, Zeus his son, and Hercules his grandson,
Buying drafts of Osiris, Isis, Belus, Brahma, Buddha,
In my portfolio placing Manito loose, Allah on a leaf, the crucifix
engraved,
With Odin and the hideous-faced Mexitli and every idol and image.
(*LG*, p. 75)

The alliteration helps to blur the names, and the personality of the
individual god is robbed by the poet's treatment of the gods as post-
age stamps in an album. The reader is to see one god who is unnamable.

The problem of condensation is more difficult in the longer catalogues, of course. Whitman may have sensed the problem when
he added the line "And of these one and all I weave the song of
myself" to the end of the long catalogue in section fifteen in a later
edition. Kenneth Burke confesses that "one inclines to skim through
them somewhat as when running the eye down the column of a
telephone directory."[12] But skimming almost seems to be intended

[11] Thomas J. Rountree, "Whitman's Indirect Expression and Its Application to 'Song
of Myself,'" *PMLA*, LXXIII (Dec., 1958), 552.
[12] Kenneth Burke, "Policy Made Personal: Whitman's Verse and Prose—Salient Traits,"
in *Leaves of Grass: One Hundred Years After*, ed. Milton Hindus (Stanford, 1955), p. 97.

by the syntactical parallelism found in so many of the catalogues. In the process of skimming, the reader searches for connectives— something to tie together the onrush of apparently disconnected images. At times, the task of condensation is made less difficult for the reader; the poet supplies the missing words, usually verbs, as in the catalogues that end sections thirty-six and forty-three. Whitman's way of expanding the self is to skim the universe, and he presents the universe to the reader in a similar fashion. Buell maintains that "if there is a limit to the length a catalogue can be sustained, it is not so much in the number as the quality of the items."[13] By "quality" Buell seems to mean freshness. Whitman's major source of freshness lies in sharp contrast, but the reader does not take long to become cynical. Repeated contrasts, after so long, become absurdly humorous. There does seem to be a limit to which the reader will try to synthesize, and Whitman probably reached the limit in section thirty-three.

The extreme length of some of Whitman's catalogues does help to serve the poet's aim of involving the reader. As James Miller notes, "Image follows image in such pell-mell rush that the reader, glutted with the concrete, pants for a generalization."[14] Such is the case in "Song of Myself," where in sections fifteen and sixteen, the reader is so gorged on visual images that he welcomes the didacticism in section seventeen which he might have otherwise rejected. Section seventeen presents a puzzle:

These are really the thoughts of all men in all ages and lands, they are
    not original with me,
If they are not yours as much as mine they are nothing, or next to nothing,
If they are not the riddle and the untying of the riddle they are nothing,
If they are not just as close as they are distant they are nothing.

(LG, p. 45)

What has preceded the passage were not thoughts at all but concrete images. If the reader has responded to the catalogues in the way Whitman hopes, the passage is superfluous, but if the reader has not undergone the experience himself, he is at least ready to hear an abstract account of the experience.

Muriel Rukeyser's comparison of the catalogues to a film script

[13] Buell, pp. 338–339.
[14] James E. Miller, *Walt Whitman* (New York, 1962), p. 69.

may seem little more than clever on first consideration, but her comparison does point to another feature of the catalogues which helps to involve the reader in his own journey to the cosmic. The feature is "cinematography."[15] No poem can be a motion picture, of course. Unlike the visual arts, poetry is bound by its essential temporal form. Whether or not a narrative form is chosen, images must follow one after another in poetry. Poems differ, however, in how closely they approach the purely spatial. Some poems, more than others, are able to produce numerous, even diffuse, images "simultaneously." Joseph Frank finds that the attempt to achieve the spatial form is the impetus in modern poetry:

Since the primary reference of any word-group is to something inside the poem itself, language in modern poetry is really reflexive: the meaning-relationship is completed only by the simultaneous perception in space of word-groups which, when read consecutively in time, have no comprehensible relation to each other. Instead of the instinctive and immediate reference of words and word-groups to objects or events they symbolize, and the construction of meaning from the sequence of these references, modern poetry asks its readers to suspend the process of individual reference temporarily until the entire pattern of internal references can be apprehended as a unity.[16]

Frank has in mind imagistic poetry, especially Pound's *Cantos*. His concept of the impetus in modern poetry, however, helps to explain how some of Whitman's catalogues encourage the reader to embark on his own journey. Whitman's goal is for the reader to form a single image of all of the catalogues in "Song of Myself." Inducing the reader to condense and to skim serves the goal. Presenting images simultaneously, or "cinematographically," serves the same end. When one views a motion picture, one views numerous images simultaneously. To challenge the viewer's perception even further, the picture frame is continually moving and probably changing. Whitman seeks to engage the reader in a similar fashion:

In me the caresser of life wherever moving, backward as well as forward sluing,
To niches aside and junior bending, not a person or object missing,
Absorbing all to myself and for this song. (*LG*, p. 40)

[15] See Muriel Rukeyser's *The Life of Poetry* (New York, 1949), pp. 80–85.
[16] Joseph Frank, "Spatial Form in Modern Literature," *Sewanee Review*, LIII (April, 1945), 229–230.

Within a Whitman catalogue, dozens, perhaps hundreds, of images are accumulated. With the addition of each image the picture is changed entirely; condensation by the reader is necessarily postponed until the end of the catalogue, and the reader is invited to skim, rushing to the end and the final image. One may feel induced to skim, but one never feels entirely satisfied in leaving a catalogue unfinished. To stop half-way is to perceive half of a moving picture.

The cinematography of the catalogues is easily seen in the catalogue that forms most of section eight:

The blab of the pave, tires of carts, sluff of boot-soles, talk of the
    promenaders,
The heavy omnibus, the driver with his interrogating thumb, the clank
    of the shod horses on the granite floor,
The snow-sleighs, clinking, shouted jokes, pelts of snow-balls,
The hurrahs for popular favorites, the fury of rous'd mobs,
The flap of the curtain'd litter, a sick man inside borne to the hospital,
The meeting of enemies, the sudden oath, the blows and fall,
The excited crowd, the policeman with his star quickly working his
    passage to the centre of the crowd,
The impassive stones that receive and return so many echoes,
What groans of over-fed or half-starv'd who fall sunstruck or in fits,
What exclamations of women taken suddenly who hurry home and give
    birth to babes,
What living and buried speech is always vibrating here, what howls
    restrain'd by decorum,
Arrests of criminals, slights, adulterous offers made, acceptances, rejections
    with convex lips,
I mind them or the show or resonance of them—I come and I depart.
                                                        (*LG*, p. 36)

Most of the images are of sound. The sounds are individual at first and at ground level. These sounds, however, merge to create the "blab of the pave." Individual sounds become soon lost in the sounds of the crowd. One sound does not replace another. The impassive stones that "receive and return so many echoes" bounce the sounds back and forth. The final image is one of joyous clatter. To Whitman, of course, the clatter is resonance. The poet also considers the scene a "show." And it is a show of images, but the reader does not see the show until the catalogue has come to its close.

Presenting the simultaneous activity of a city street is a small feat for Whitman. He attempts to present the simultaneous activity of the world in the massive catalogue of section thirty-three. Grammatical parallelism and repetition help the poet keep the reader moving through the catalogue, and the catalogue's organization keeps the reader from prematurely drawing the boundaries for the catalogue's total image. Too much organization would be as detrimental to Whitman's plan for a total image as no organization at all. Whitman stressed in the preface that his technique must be without effort and without exposure. The movement in this catalogue from prepositions of place to participles of activity, discussed earlier in this essay, is apparent only upon a rereading. The movement's organization, however, does help the reader to perceive that one image. The image is beyond description; it involves the simultaneous presentation of all human activity.

At the end of section thirty-three the poet has completed his journey, which has been the expansion of the self. The rest of the poem is concerned with the poet's role as a savior. At the end of section thirty-three the reader should have likewise made the journey for himself. He should have formed that one image of the universe in which he loses the ego, the image which Whitman calls the "huge first Nothing" because the image is out of the domain of language. The "journey," however, has not been a step-by-step process. The poet uses the metaphors of travel, but his metaphorical language should not lead the reader to assume that the poet is actually mapping a course for the reader. The poet, aware of the limitations created by the temporal nature of language, strives to create the impression of spontaneous expansion. The poet's preference for the present tense indicates his desire to escape temporal boundaries. His catalogues, by creating single images, serve the same end. The concept of the journey is used to communicate that which is beyond communication. At the beginning of the grand catalogue of section thirty-three, Whitman writes:

Space and Time! now I see it is true, what I guess'd at,
What I guess'd when I loaf'd on the grass,
What I guess'd while I lay alone in my bed,
And again as I walk'd the beach under the paling stars of the morning.

(*LG*, p. 61)

What the poet had guessed is that time and space are inseparable. And no longer is the poet bound by either. The narratives following section thirty-three, which have puzzled Whitman's readers, illustrate the poet's escape from the boundaries of space and time. In section thirty-four, the poet describes the defeat at the Alamo, and the account is expressed entirely in the past tense. Earlier in the poem, the past tense was used only when the poet's journey was endangered by preoccupation with sensuality (section five). The poet in section thirty-four is completely free to "travel" to the past. In section thirty-five, the narrative of the sea battle is told in a blending of the past and present tenses. Time and distance have been surmounted; they have become, in a sense, nonexistent. The poet speaks of a "perpetual journey," but the journey, for both the poet and the reader, is above time and space. The journey can be expressed only through paradox: it is both perpetual and instantaneous.

We have seen that although the view of Whitman as an organicist easily explains his use of the catalogues, it fails because the poet, at least in "Song of Myself," is essentially active. The poet is active in his movement away from the self and toward the universe or cosmos. The catalogues describe that journey, and, moreover, they enable the reader to resume the journey. The two journeys, however, are merely metaphors for processes which occur outside of time and space. The reader, through a process of skimming and condensation, forms a single image of each catalogue and finally a single image of that unnamable reward which awaits the poet and the reader.

Leaves of Myself: Whitman's Egypt in 'Song of Myself'
Stephen J. Tapscott

ALTHOUGH THE MYSTERIOUS RELIGION, culture, and language of the ancient Egyptians had for centuries been the subjects of speculation and of scholarly research, the critically incisive linguistic discoveries about hieroglyphics, and a popular cultural enthusiasm for Egyptology, were particularly nineteenth-century phenomena. In 1798, when a slab of basalt was unearthed by a French soldier digging near the town of Rashid, some thirty miles south of Alexandria, workmen discovered that the stone was apparently carved in three different languages, arranged sequentially.[1] Not until 1818, however, did Thomas Young decipher some particular names in hieroglyphic characters on the black slab, known as the Rosetta Stone; the three scripts were eventually identified as Greek, formal Egyptian hieroglyphics, and a cursive form of Egyptian known as demotic characters. By 1821 the celebrated French scholar Champollion had established that the Egyptian signs were alphabetic and hence capable of being deciphered; at the time of his death in 1831 Champollion had just completed his decisive *Grammar of Egyptian Hieroglyphics,* the proofs of which he corrected on his death-bed. (Walt Whitman, in his 1855 article on the treasures of the Egyptian Museum in New York, cites the legend of Champollion's handing those proofs to his publisher shortly before his death and saying: "Preserve these, they are my visiting-card to posterity." In "A Backward Glance O'er Travel'd Roads," in 1888, the older Whitman even identifies his own life-investment in *Leaves of Grass* with Champollion's attitude toward his life's work.)[2] Indeed, because such work on hieroglyphics

---

[1] Information about the Rosetta Stone and about subsequent interest in Egyptology during the nineteenth century is taken from E. A. W. Budge's *The Rosetta Stone* (London, 1929), especially Chapters 1, 2, 4.

[2] All quotations from Whitman's poetic works in this essay are taken from *Leaves of Grass: Comprehensive Reader's Edition,* ed. Harold Blodgett and Sculley Bradley (New York, 1965). Blodgett and Bradley use the standard edition (from the eighth edition, 1881) of "Song of Myself," but all quotations from the poem given here also appear, sometimes with minor changes, in the original 1855 edition of the poem. (See *Whitman's 'Song of*

had made many Egyptian writings comprehensible, the field of Egyptology grew hugely in scope and sophistication during the nineteenth century, opening new fields of study in related areas of Biblical scholarship, linguistics, cultural history, comparative religions, and literature, besides offering new sources of imaginative direction to many thinkers and writers. As Whitman wrote of the Egyptian Museum in New York, "It is a place to go when one would ponder and evolve great thoughts."[3]

Whitman showed a marked interest in Egyptian lore and myth throughout his life. Evidence in the notebooks shows that he knew, either through books and lectures or through conversation with professional Egyptologists, the work of several of the most prominent writers on Egypt, including Champollion. Whitman's *Life Illustrated* article of 1855 suggests that by then he was familiar both with the scholarly work of other major authorities, such as Rosellini, Wilkinson, and Lepsius, and also with popularized versions of Egyptology, such as George R. Gliddon's books and lectures, which Whitman also mentions in other contexts. As early as 1855, Whitman had shown an amateur enthusiasm for Egyptology and a familiarity with the largest historical and linguistic issues of the subject. By 1855 he had probably also read Christian Bunsen's theory of universal history, a theory that takes its initial hypothesis from the Hegelian concept of history as a manifestation of spirit, a notion to which Whitman, with his repeated assertion of the imaginative inclusiveness of the individual personality, would certainly have been receptive.[4] A friend and early literary biographer of Whitman offers evidence, further, that this youthful interest in things Egyptian continued throughout the poet's life: mentioning Whitman's habit of not completing books which he had begun to read, Dr. Richard Bucke notes that two notable exceptions were Whitman's thorough

Myself'—*Origin, Growth, Meaning*, ed. James E. Miller, Jr., New York, 1964.) Whitman's article on the Egyptian Museum is "One of the Lessons Bordering Broadway," reprinted in *New York Dissected*, ed. Ralph Adimari and Emory Holloway (New York, 1936), pp. 27–36. See also footnote 9.

[3] Whitman, "One of the Lessons," p. 40.

[4] Floyd Stovall, "Notes on Whitman's Reading," *American Literature*, XXVI (Nov., 1954), 339. Whitman also mentions Gliddon's popularity as a lecturer, in an essay for the *Eagle* of November 7, 1846. Bunsen's book of historical theory is entitled *Outline of the Philosophy of University History, Applied to Language and Religion* (London, 1854). Whitman also read Bunsen's *Egypt's Place in Universal History* some years later. (Stovall, p. 338); see also footnotes 14 and 15, below.

reading of books on Egypt, both published around 1879, by Renouf and Brugsch-Bey.[5] The notebook entries, particularly, are interesting because they often record the poet's initial impressions of concepts he encountered in his reading on the subject of Egypt; they reveal how Whitman met those religious concepts imaginatively and what his assimilative imagination did with the myths once he had received them.[6]

Apparently Whitman so thoroughly immersed himself in Egyptian lore during the early 1850's, in fact, that he identified himself imaginatively with Osiris, the god of vegetative regeneration and of the underworld, the most important god of the Egyptian pantheon.[7] One contemporary remembers the days when Whitman "paraded on Broadway, with a red shirt on, open in front to show the 'scented herbage of his breast' and compared himself with Christ and Osiris."[8] Most importantly, however, the influence of Whitman's reading and study becomes manifest in his work.

One of the most significant direct records of Whitman's general fascination with and particular interest in Egypt is an article about the Egyptian Museum (then at 659 Broadway in Manhattan), written for *Life Illustrated* magazine in 1855. The date of the article is important because Whitman's intense interest in Egypt coincides with the approximate time of composition of and with the first date of publication of "Song of Myself." In the article Whitman first acknowledges his own personal interest in the Museum and the educational conversations he has had with its proprietor, Doctor Henry Abbott: "We had the advantage, in many visits to the Egyptian Museum in Broadway, of an acquaintance with Dr. Abbott himself, and of passing many friendly evenings with him, and having his personal explanation of the objects in the museum."[9] In

---

[5] Dr. Richard M. Bucke, *Walt Whitman* (Philadelphia, 1883), p. 52.

[6] Stovall, p. 362.

[7] Gay Wilson Allen, *The Solitary Singer* (New York, 1955), pp. 121–122.

[8] See Esther Shepherd, "Possible Sources of Some of Whitman's Ideas and Symbols in 'Hermes Trismegistus' and Other Works," *Modern Language Quarterly,* XIV (March, 1953), 74.

[9] Whitman, "One of the Lessons," p. 38. Whitman did not sign the *Life Illustrated* piece, which was apparently written to support Dr. Abbott's campaign to persuade the city of New York to buy his collection. Internal evidence in the article and a comparison of it with Whitman's notes and with the facts of his biography, however, identify it almost certainly as his work; he also saved a copy of it among his papers, and notes to the piece appear in his *Notes and Fragments.* See the introduction and notes to the essay in Adimari

other prose works Whitman refers again to the educational aspects
of his friendship with Dr. Abbott: "The great 'Egyptian Collection'
was well up in Broadway," he writes later, "and I got quite acquainted with Dr. Abbott, the proprietor—paid many visits there,
and had long talks with him, in connection with my readings of
many books and reports on Egypt—its antiquities, history and how
things and the scenes really look, and what the relics stand for, as
near as we can now get."[10] In his article on this "Lesson Bordering
Broadway," Whitman praises ancient Egyptian science, religion,
law, and the sweeping scope of its national history, comparing the
most important events of that tradition with the most important
historical events of Western civilizations. Demonstrating a competent knowledge of the work of several well-known European Egyptologists, Whitman in a characteristically ebullient prose emphasizes
the educational possibilities of such an authentic collection in Manhattan, and he testifies to the fascination the collection held for him.
In fact, Whitman shows a particular interest in the Rosetta Stone
(the original of which was in the British Museum) and in the
process of deciphering hieroglyphics; we have already seen his
repeated use of the Champollion story. After mentioning the popular nineteenth-century interest in paleography, Whitman describes
the marvels of the Museum's hieroglyphic exhibits: "Around the
walls of the room are slabs of limestone, some of them very large,
each containing its spread of chiseled hieroglyphics. They are
wonderful...."[11]

Recalling Whitman's eventual identification of himself in the role
of life-poet with Champollion, decipherer of the secretive language
of the Egyptians, and noting also the contemporaneous date of
composition of "Song of Myself" with Whitman's interest in the
ideographic language of formal Egyptian hieroglyphics, we can
begin to look at "Song of Myself" in a new light. Even from its

---

and Holloway, p. 13. In 1954 Floyd Stovall reexamines the evidence and also attributes
the piece to Whitman (pp. 338–339); Blodgett and Bradley use the piece as source
material in their notes to *Leaves of Grass* (pp. 686–687n), and Gay Wilson Allen accepts
the piece as Whitman's (pp. 121–123). Of Whitman's reading the works cited in the
essay, Allen concludes, "the echoes, allusions, and references to Egyptology in *Leaves of
Grass* are so numerous that one must conclude that Whitman read the works closely and
took notes on them."

[10] P. 28; see also the notes to the article.

[11] P. 38, text.

earliest editions, "Song of Myself" contains a strain of images that deals with essentially the same process of "deciphering" a secret, vital, and ancient language: of "translating" the hints of the natural life of the Self in the open air (#47), of "long dumb voices" to be comprehended (#24), of words "unsaid" but perceived in nature by a personality that is itself "untranslatable" (#50, #52). This theme of "Song of Myself," the characterization of the role of the poet-Self as one who can "translate into a new tongue" (#21) the signs that the natural world offers him, clearly parallels the process of deciphering the hieroglyphics of a secretive language that so interested Whitman at this early stage of his career. The theme need not be traced exclusively to Egyptian sources, of course; by 1855 the metaphor of the "Book of Nature" was a literary commonplace, from the legacy of the Romantics, and the New England Transcendentalists had expanded the notion to an entire cosmology.[12]

The first time we meet the theme in Whitman's "Song of Myself," significantly, is in a section which connects the idea of translating the Book of Nature with the image of the grass itself. (This connection will become more significant when we come to discuss the personality of Osiris, the god of vegetative and spiritual regeneration, in Whitman's work.) In section 6 of "Song of Myself" the speaker, supine in the grass, sees in the grass an immediate symbol of universality:

> Or I guess it is a uniform hieroglyphic,
> And it means, Sprouting alike in broad zones and narrow zones,
> Growing among black folks as among white. . . .

To understand the grass is to "read" it, through a process of ideogrammic associations, as the speaker does from the moment the "child" brings a handful of grass to him. As section 6 continues, gradually the scope of the symbol enlarges until the hieroglyphic grass represents a semanteme which encompasses both mortality and the resurrection of the spiritualized body with a new speech:

> O I perceive after all so many uttering tongues,
> And I perceive they do not come from the roofs of mouths for nothing.

[12] The image appears, for instance, in sources Whitman certainly would have read. Emerson elaborates the idea in his essays at the time, especially in "The Poet" and "Nature"; Thoreau points to the same notion in the transcendental pastoralism of *Walden*, in 1854, and in England Carlyle, whom Whitman read in the 1840's, considers a similar idea of the individual's reading the world as a symbolic system.

I wish I could translate the hints about the dead young men and women,
And the hints about old men and mothers, and the offspring taken soon
    out of their laps.

What do you think has become of the young and old men?
And what do you think has become of the women and children?

They are alive and well somewhere,
The smallest sprout shows there is really no death. . . .

Eventually, in the process of bringing his listeners behind the poem
to the "origin of all poems," Whitman defines his object as the
invention of a new language—or, more specifically, as the authentic
transcription of the language he intuits conceptually (or "hiero-
glyphically," in untranslated potential) in all the world, even among
animals:

Oxen that rattle the yoke and chain or halt in the leafy shade, what is
    that you express in your eyes?
It seems to me more than all the print I have read in my life.

(#13)

The new language arises even from generic "things":

All truths wait in all things,
They neither hasten their own delivery nor resist it. . . .

(#30)

In a larger sense, the poet encompasses the "all" by listening to it:

Now I will do nothing but listen,
To accrue what I hear into this song, to let sounds contribute toward it.

(#26)

Or again:

I know I am solid and sound,
To me the converging objects of the universe perpetually flow,
All are written to me, and I must get what the writing means.

(#20)

This "endless unfolding of words of ages" sometimes involves listening to "voices indecent" from deep within the self, and the imaginative seizure of an almost Satanic energy:

I am the poet of the Body and I am the poet of the Soul,
The pleasures of heaven are with me and the pains of hell are with me,

The first I graft and increase upon myself, the latter I translate
   into a new tongue. . . .

(#21)

Nevertheless, this task of "translating" is always consistently identified with a movement of the soul toward a vitalistic divinity implicit
in the objects and life of nature. The essence of the natural world in
the hieroglyphics of its physical manifestations is to be read by the
eye of the poet: "I find letters from God dropt in the street. . ."
(#48).

In the final section of the poem, once he has thoroughly identified
himself internally and externally as a thing of nature among other
natural things, the poet begins to take on the same undecipherable
character of the hieroglyphs of nature:

There is that in me—I do not know what it is—but I know it is in me....

I do not know it—it is without name—it is a word unsaid,
It is not in any dictionary, utterance, symbol.

(#50)

In the final section of his "Song," the poet claims to merge with the
landscape, as an ideographic representation of his own eneriges in,
as he has said, "words simple as grass." At the end of the poem
Whitman becomes another of nature's organic utterances ("I too am
untranslatable, / I sound my barbaric yawp over the roofs of the
world,") and he passes on the paleographic task of comprehending
that natural language to the reader, who becomes the new Champollion:

I bequeath myself to the dirt to grow from the grass I love,
If you want me again look for me under your boot-soles. . . .

You will hardly know who I am or what I mean. . . .

(#52)

As the Egyptians three thousand years ago had implied, and as
Emerson had more recently insisted, the language of the individual
can fix him in time and yet can free him to suggest transhistorical
conclusions on the basis of his organic connection with the world.
Natural objects can be used as spiritual facts.

Christian Bunsen, whose book Whitman probably read in 1854,
shortly after its publication in the United States and shortly before

the publication of "Song of Myself,"[13] offers a similar metaphor for
the process of intuiting the presence of a Hegelian divine force
through human history, and his language and thought are strikingly
similar to the recurrent theme of Whitman's poem:

Indeed, if there exists a divine rule of human destiny and development in
the history of mankind, a philosophy of that history must be possible. . . .
the historian, who undertakes to interpret the great hieroglyph of the
times, and restore the Sibilline leaves of history, ought to believe, with
Pindar, in the divinely given beginning and end of man.[14]

The "Sibilline leaves" of history are a common enough concept, but
in more specifically linguistic forms Whitman may derive from
Bunsen his initial concept of the first grass as a "üniversal hieroglyph." In his chapter on the Egyptians in his *Universal History*
Bunsen praises the ability of the Egyptian language to build "ideographic signs" as units of language into a successive piling of concrete
images to express an abstract idea, a stylistic concept which Whitman must have found theoretically interesting, at least, during this
period of composition of "Song of Myself." Bunsen writes:

The ancient Egyptians had incontestably the germs of the composition of
words, to express, by the union of the two, a third or more abstract or
ideal notion, for which the language had no simple expression.[15]

As Ezra Pound will later discover, Egyptian hieroglyphics are ideogrammic; for Whitman in 1855, the discovery contributes to the
structure of the catalogue, his "translation" of the world's unified
diversity.

Simultaneously, another Egyptologist whose work Whitman knew
and with whom he claims (in the Egyptian Museum article) to have
had conversation was in 1855 in the process of completing work on a
theory strikingly parallel to this recurrent theme of Whitman's
poem.[16] Richard Lepsius, whose theories Whitman could very well
have heard either in conversation with him or with Dr. Abbott,
although the theories did not appear in print until 1855, organized a
system by which all spoken or written languages could be recorded

---

[13] Stovall, p. 339.
[14] Christian Bunsen, *The Outline of the Philosophy of Universal History*, I, 4.
[15] II, 61.
[16] Whitman, "One of the Lessons," p. 37.

in a uniform script, thus making the standardized alphabet a translatable and comprehensible vehicle of communication. In his section on ancient Egyptian hieroglyphics, Lepsius first describes their ideographic character and phonetic structure and then derives a general system by which hieroglyphic figures can be spelled out in a linear type.[17] It is inconceivable that Whitman could have had contact with Lepsius or with his work during this period without encountering Lepsius's latest, most arduous project; and, considered in the light of the common thematic concern of this work and "Song of Myself," it seems that Whitman could very well have had Lepsius's concept in mind when he wrote his own poem, that attempt to make comprehensible the incomprehensible, in a democratic language which the common man could understand. "Song of Myself" is an elaborated hieroglyph of the self.

Gay Wilson Allen, in an interesting article on Whitman's prosody, argues that much of Whitman's "democratic structure" of the catalogue may be drawn from his study of the parallelisms of Hebrew verse. I believe that the same claim might be offered for the influence of Egyptian literature on Whitman's style, based on the evidence of Whitman's continuing interest in the subject. Not only does what Allen calls an "enumerative style, the cataloguing of a representative and symbolical succession of images, conveying the sensation of pantheistic unity and endless becoming"[18] fit the ideographic theory of hieroglyphics offered by Bunsen and Lepsius, but also the theoretical underpinnings of the catalogue technique more closely conform to an Egyptian philosophy, as Whitman understands it, than to a Hebrew cosmology. Allen characterizes the philosophical implications of the use of the list technique: "Nowhere in the universe does he recognize caste or subordination. Everything is equally divine."[19] This equality of essence in the natural world, as Allen admits, is not characteristic of the monotheistic Hebrew religion, but it was a basic tenet of Egyptian belief. Whitman writes in the Museum article about the nature of Egyptian belief in universal

[17] K. Richard Lepsius, *Standard Alphabet for Reducing Unwritten Languages and Foreign Graphic Systems to a Uniform Orthography in European Letters*, 2nd ed. (London, 1863), pp. 193–200.

[18] Gay Wilson Allen, "Walt Whitman: The Search for a 'Democratic Structure,' " *Walt Whitman*, ed. Francis Murphy (Baltimore, 1970), p. 406.

[19] P. 406.

equality, "Before Isis and Osiris all human beings were equal."[20]
We may read "Song of Myself" as Whitman's cumulative hieroglyph, as much as his psalm, arranged to give shape to the secret
language which he claims to be translating: a transcendentalist's
language of which the script is the diversity of nature but the meaning of which is the unity of life beneath that appearance. The poem
is an instance of style recapitulating content in its democratic vital-
ism, and in the course of its broad inclusive sweep Whitman seems
to have borrowed concepts, images, and a linguistic structure from
his knowledge of Egyptian traditions.

The belief in the equality of life before the throne of the gods is a
concept of the Egyptian religion to which Whitman apparently
responded with fervor. Christians too, of course, believe that all men
are equal in the sight of God; but the hieratic Egyptians carried the
belief past the status of metaphor to a consistent and physical
thanatology, endowing animals, too, with a divine nimbus beyond
the power of death. Frequently in his notebooks Whitman writes
with respect about Egyptian religious belief:

Egyptian religion. . . . The central idea seems to have been the wonderfulness and divinity of life, the beetle, the bull the snipe here divine in that
they exemplified the inexplicable mystery of life. It was a profound and
exquisite religion.[21]

Compare this sentiment to many sections of "Song of Myself," in
which Whitman praises the life-force that moves through all things
and creatures:

The bull and the bug never worship'd half enough,
Dung and dirt more admirable than was dream'd,
The supernatural of no account, myself waiting my time to be one of
    the supremes. . . .

(#41)

The bull was an animal type of Osiris. The beetle, particularly, could
have been an appropriate image for Whitman of the self-sufficiency
of life, because its mythological significance in Egypt came from the
belief that the scarab-beetle was self-generating. Further, the Egyp-

---

[20] Whitman, "One of the Lessons," p. 32.
[21] Walt Whitman, *The Complete Writings of Walt Whitman*, ed. R. M. Bucke et. al.
(New York, 1902), VI, 55.

tians believed not only in the "wonderfulness . . . of all life" but also in the participatory unity of all distinct life in the life of the gods, particularly Osiris. Sir J. G. Wilkinson, whose book Whitman had almost certainly read between the time of its publication in 1854 and Whitman's Egyptian Museum article in 1855,[22] explains this doctrine more fully. Wilkinson also alludes to the themes of organic language and pregnant silence already noted in "Song of Myself":

> The fundamental doctrine [of Egyptian religion] was the unity of the Deity; but this deity was not represented, and He was known by a sentence, or an idea, being. . . . 'worshipped in silence.'[23]

If we read with a critical ear attuned to this extra dimension of Whitman, his religious interest in Egyptian mythology, we may hear echoes of this vitalistic concept in many passages of "Song of Myself." The speaker of the poem, who calls himself the "caresser of life wherever moving" (#13), observes:

> The sharp-hoof'd moose of the north, the cat on the house-sill, the
>   chickadee, the prairie-dog,
> The litter of the grunting sow as they tug at her teats,
> The brood of the turkey-hen and she with her half-spread wings,
> I see in them and myself the same old law.
>
> (#14)

And again,

> These are really the thoughts of all men in all ages and lands, they are
>   not original with me. . . .
> This is the grass that grows wherever the land is and the water is,
> This is the common air that bathes the globe.
>
> (#17)

Similar observations about Whitman's respect and wonder before a universal life-force have been made by other critics. For example, in his book *The Roots of Whitman's Grass*, R. Rajasekharaiah discusses Whitman's debt to Indian thought and to Vedic literature; he emphasized Whitman's fascination with the Hegelian or Indian "spirit" which pervades the physical universe and is its essential

---

[22] Stovall, p. 339; see also notes to "One of the Lessons," p. 206.

[23] Sir J. G. Wilkinson, *A Popular Account of the Ancient Egyptians* (New York, 1854), Chapter 5, p. 327.

reality.[24] The resultant readings of Whitman's poems, and the implicit links with Emerson's "Vedic" direction, are interesting and incisive. But by contrast the metaphysic of the Egyptian tradition does not emphasize the unreality of the natural world, its *maya* or deception of the senses, but rather asserts that the world-spirit is knowable only in its physical manifestations: a transcendental concept which seems at least as close to Whitman's attitude in "Song of Myself" as the Indian concepts do. Wilkinson writes that Egyptians "not only attributed to the sun and moon, and to other supposed agents, a participation in the divine essence, but even plants and stones were supposed to have some portion in it. . . ."[25] Whitman reflects this Egyptian respect for the world *an sich,* rather than as an analogy or cover for the real world of essences, and he observes this physical world closely in order to hear its "language." In the *Life Illustrated* article he writes, "The theology of Egypt was vast and profound. It respected the principal of life in all things—even in animals. It respected truth and justice above all other attributes of men. It recognized immortality."[26] Just how closely Whitman allies himself with this Egyptian theory of metaphysically naive realism may be further seen, for instance, in his Preface to the 1876 edition of *Leaves of Grass,* in which he insists that his "enclosing purpose" is "to express, above all artificial regulation and aid, the eternal Bodily Character of One's Self."[27] Throughout "Song of Myself," we find Whitman's repeated insistence on the physical reality and wonder of the physical body and on the participation of the body with the soul in the life of the individual. We also find Whitman's refusal to compromise the sensational reception of the world by any final form of transcendence: "I am the poet of the Body and I am the poet of the Soul," he insists. Although Whitman does admit that the mystical utterances of the universe cannot be immediately perceived but are to be intuited, he claims that "the unseen is proved by the seen, / Till that becomes unseen and receives proof in its turn." The physical body and its senses are the receptors and interpreters of those mysterious signals, for without the senses the soul would not

[24] T. R. Rajasekharaiah, *The Roots of Whitman's Grass* (Rutherford, N. J., 1970).
[25] Wilkinson, p. 329.
[26] Whitman, "One of the Lessons," p. 38.
[27] Whitman, *Leaves,* 1876 "Preface," p. 748.

receive the information it needs to distill the latent truth of its experience:

> Here or henceforward it is all the same to me, I accept Time absolutely.
>
> It alone is without flaw, it alone rounds and completes all,
> That mystic baffling wonder alone completes all.
>
> I accept Reality and dare not question it,
> Materialism first and last imbuing.
>
> (#23)

And, further,

> Divine am I inside and out, and I make holy whatever I touch or am touch'd from. . . .
>
> If I worship one thing more than another it shall be the spread of my own body, or any part of it. . . .
>
> (#24)

Like the Egyptian priests who considered the preservation of health an indispensable adjunct to the practice of piety (a tradition which Whitman marks in his notebooks),[28] Whitman in "Song of Myself" seems to consider the body not only an instrument of the soul but a full partner in the business of living and of achieving immortality:

> I have said that the soul is not more than the body,
> And I have said that the body is not more than the soul,
> And nothing, not God, is greater to one than one's self is. . . .
>
> (#48)

Whitman's admixture of immortality and materialism within the same set of conceptual images makes for a theory of immortality that locates the course and the realization of immortal life on earth, within a physical body, even while he recognizes the fact of individual death. The practice of mummification among the Egyptians was based on precisely this concept, that the body will again be unified with the soul. (Christianity, with its insistence on the mortification of the flesh as a necessary condition of salvation, treats the body with less literal respect; God, it asserts, will renew our bodies miraculously at the Last Judgment.) According to ancient

---

28 Whitman, *Complete Writings*, VI, 212.

Egyptian texts, however, the body lives in some mysteriously literal way even while it is interred in the pramids—hence the inclusion of food and tools in the Egyptian burial processions and tombs. Whitman knew and apparently respected this concept, as he indicates in his notebooks:

Materialism—that this earth is under a constant process of amelioration. . . that our immortality is *located* here upon the earth,—that we *are immortal*. . . . That the Egyptian idea of the return of the soul after a certain period of time involved a beautiful . . . nature . . . mystery [*sic*].[29]

In the Egyptian mythos the specific "period of time" after which the soul completely returns to the body is 5,000 years, and it is not coincidental that this same concept is exactly recapitulated in "Song of Myself":

My faith is the greatest of faiths and the least of faiths,
Enclosing worship ancient and modern and all between ancient and modern,
Believing I shall come again upon the earth after five thousand years. . . .
(#43)

Further, in the interim between the individual's death and the complete resurrection of the body in a united form, the physical body stays on earth, but, according to Egyptian tradition, if it is properly respected the body becomes a kind of spiritualized body, an analogue to the soul, which exists even during the individual's life. Thus an individual possessed, in effect, plural souls, each having different functions during the individual's life and, especially, after his death. This concept may go some distance toward explaining Whitman's notions of the self-soul split and of the multiplicity of spiritual personalities ("both in and out of the game and watching and wondering at it"); this Egyptian belief is also congruent with Whitman's respect for the body in its ultimately "spiritualized" reality, as a receptor of nature and as an instrument of immortality. In Egyptian religion this spiritualized body, called the sāhū, was both a physical body and a spiritualized eidólon of the self. (It is distinguished, for instance, from the kā soul, which is totally spiritual and goes to the gods immediately after burial, to be joined, if worthy, with the essence of Osiris.) This belief in the sāhū is the concept

[29] P. 151.

to which Whitman refers in the Egyptian Museum article, when he writes about the burial practices of the Egyptians: "The object in mummifying is supposed to have proceeded from the belief in Egypt that the body, if kept intact a certain time after death . . . would be reentered by the spirit and the double identity be resumed again."[30]

This dual knit of identity and the duality of the body and the soul, resolved in a regenerate spiritualized body, are recurrent themes throughout "Song of Myself." They appear, for example, in repeated addresses to the soul:

> This day before dawn I ascended a hill and look'd at the crowded
> heaven,
> I said to my spirit, *When we become the enfolder of those orbs, and the*
> *pleasure and knowledge of every thing in them, shall we be fill'd and*
> *satisfied then?*
>
> (#46)
>
> We found our way O my soul in the calm and cool of the daybreak.
>
> (#25)

How close this theme of Whitman's poem comes to a genuine echo of Egyptian tradition may be illustrated by a comparison with an example from Egyptian literature. One genre from that tradition is the lamentation, which usually takes the form of a conversation between the speaker and his soul, often at daybreak. (Whitman knew of this tradition, at least at second-hand, for he refers to it obliquely in his *Life Illustrated* article.) A conventional image of the separation of body and soul (or heart) and a travel-motif with the soul as guide appear, for instance, in the "Dispute with his Soul of One who is Tired with Life," in which the body and soul set out on the open road:

This is what my soul said to me: Cast aside lamentation, my comrade, my brother . . . I will abide here, if thou rejectest the West [the other world, land of the dead]. But when thou reachest the West, and thy body is united with the earth, then I will alight after that thou restest. Let us have an abode together. . . .[31]

---

[30] Whitman, "One of the Lessons," p. 38.

[31] Adolph Erman, ed., *The Literature of the Ancient Egyptians* (London, 1927), p. 92. Although this particular document was not fully edited, translated, and published in English until 1874—not in time for Whitman to have known it before the early editions

This interpenetration of body and soul, further, is the basis for the Egyptian faith in an immortality enjoyed with the full possession of sensual and spiritual faculties. A more modern (1895) commentator generalizes about the *Egyptian Book of the Dead*: "The Egyptians believed in a corporeal existence, or at least the capacity for corporeal enjoyment, in the future state. This belief may have rested on the view that the life in the next world was but a continuation of the life upon earth."[32] Significantly, this immortality was not viewed as an impersonal joining with an Emersonian world-soul, accompanied by a loss of distinct personality, but was considered a personal and particular life continued beyond death: the kā soul joined the spirit of Osiris even while the sāhū remained distinct and immortal. Wilkinson defines the concept as

the idea common to the Egyptians . . . that to die was only to assume a new form—that nothing was annihilated . . . and this dissolution was merely the forerunner of reproduction.[33]

This tone and this belief are carried through "Song of Myself":

> I know I am deathless. . . .
> I laugh at what you call dissolution,
> And I know the amplitude of time.
> (#20)

This audacious stance toward death can be possible only if it is supported by a strong belief in immortality (and, here, in the revivification of the body through a "physical" soul):

Distant and dead resuscitate,
They show as the dial or move as the hands of me, I am the clock myself.
(#33)

Probably the most striking example of this theme in "Song of Myself" is its first appearance in the poem, in sections 5 and 6, where the images of regeneration coincide with the images of the "grass":

---

of "Song of Myself"—nevertheless it is representative of the imagery, tone, and tradition of the address to the soul that characterize the Egyptian "lamentation" form. See, for instance, a "Complaint" on pp. 108–110 of Erman's collection, another example in which the speaker's "heart" is addressed on a walk through an extended landscape.

[32] E. A. Wallis Budge, ed., *The Egyptian Book of the Dead* (New York, 1895, rpt. 1967), p. xi.

[33] Wilkinson, p. 382.

The smallest sprout shows there is really no death,
And if ever there was it led forward life, and does not wait at the end to
   arrest it,
And ceas'd the moment life appear'd.

All goes onward and outward, nothing collapses,
And to die is different from what anyone supposed, and luckier.

We have already seen how the image of the grass functions within
the poem as a symbol both of regeneration and of the "untranslated"
language which the universe offers to Whitman's eyes and ears.
When its further development as an image of spiritual immortality
underlying vegetative regeneration becomes evident, a pattern begins to emerge. Clearly, in "Song of Myself" Whitman associates the
grass with the self that is reborn or regenerated after the death of
the individual body (although the body, too, is glorified because it
shares in the immortality of the composite personality). As we have
seen, this dual immortality is an important concept in Egyptian
religious thought also. It should not surprise us, therefore, to find
that the very image Whitman chooses to represent the sight of this
regeneration in the physical world, the grass, is the image consistently used in Egyptian writings to signify the growth at the
moment when the body becomes the sāhū, or spiritualized body. According to the *Egyptian Book of the Dead,* after death

the body does not lie in the tomb inoperative, for by ceremonies on the
day of burial, it is endowed with the power of changing into a sāhū, or
spiritualized body. Thus we have such phrases [in the *Book*] as 'I germinate like the plants,' 'thy flesh germinateth,' 'I exist, I exist, I live, I live,
I germinate,' 'thy soul liveth, thy body germinateth by the command of
Rā. . . .'[34]

[34] Shephard, p. 74. Shephard's article suggests that Whitman could have found many
of his initial ideas about spiritual regeneration implicit in the works of Hermes Trismegistus,
whose Gnostic doctrines contain much that the Coptic tradition inherited from the religion
of the ancient Egyptians. Provocative as the argument is, I think some qualification is
necessary: (1) there is no conclusive proof that Whitman had read Hermes Trismegistus
or showed interest in his work, except in reaction to a fictionalized character named
"Hermes" in a novel Whitman read; (2) Trismegistus' attitude of contempt for the physical
world, and in particular for the human body, would seem to work against the argument
that Whitman accepted the Gnostic doctrine of immortality of the spirit, without a
parallel respect for and immortality in the body. See the "Pymander," in *The Theological
and Philosophical Works of Hermes Trismegistus,* trans. J. D. Chambers (Edinburgh, 1882),
especially vii, #3; iv, #6; vi, #2; xiv, #7. Whitman was, however, eclectic enough to
have accepted part of Hermes's cosmology and to have rejected what did not appeal to him.

Grass and leaves, germination and regeneration, immortality and
the body: we have seen how all these themes seem to function in one
complex concept, both in Whitman's poem "Song of Myself" and
in the Egyptian mythological system for which he displayed such
an enthusiasm. Further, given Whitman's emphasis on personality
and on the importance of the self in a cosmology, it should not surprise us to learn that the Egyptians revered one divine personality
whose various attributes encompassed all of the concepts shared by
both Whitman's poem and the Egyptian religion. He is a vegetable
deity whose death and subsequent regeneration were annually
represented by the flooding of the Nile and the growth of the grass.
He is the god whose body was destroyed, reassembled, and re-
vitalized: Osiris. Most importantly, he is the one Egyptian god with
whom Whitman identified himself.

Originally, Osiris was considered the offspring of the intercourse
of heaven and earth (an archtypal situation which Whitman also
employs in "Song of Myself," as in sections 24 and 29). Osiris is
credited with creating humans and with teaching them agriculture.
When still a young man, Osiris was betrayed and mutilated, his
body cut into many pieces and spread over the land of Egypt. Everywhere a piece fell the ground became holy, and they fell in many
places: the cult of Osiris was wide-spread. But Osiris's sister-and-wife
Isis collected the pieces of her husband's body and rejoined them,
and he was revivified. He rules, according to the Egyptian myth, in
the underworld, where he is the king of the dead and where the
life-spirits of all who die are joined with his spirit: they assume his
name.[35] In accord with his role as judge and king, the hieroglyph for
"Osiris" (as Whitman would have known, having read Wilkinson),
is a large eye above a throne, like the emblem of an eye-and-pyramid
which still appears on the Great Seal of the United States and on the
one-dollar bill. This image of cosmic vision has many resonances in
"Song of Myself," with the poem's repeated theme of visual observation and of the eye-I of the speaker as his instrument of knowing
and of belonging to the landscape. The associations resonate closer to
home, as well, both in the Easter rituals of Christianity, by which
the risen Christ becomes both vegetative deity and lord of hell, and in
Emerson's famous image of the "transparent eyeball." Like the

[35] Budge, *Book of the Dead*, p. lix.

Osirian hieroglyph, like Emerson's observer, Whitman is "afoot with his vision." Supported by his wide and sympathetic reading, Whitman's syncretic style allows for all of these associations simultaneously. He associates himself with Osiris and with Christ, for instance, as part of the rhetoric of inclusiveness in "Song of Myself." The tradition from one source (such as the Egyptian) paradoxically buttresses the internalized traditions from other sources, "enclosing worship ancient and modern and all between ancient and modern."

Another critic has already mentioned Osiris in this connection with Whitman, noting how Whitman uses the image of the annual regeneration of the grass through Osiris to symbolize the concept of immortality. Esther Shepherd, in a provocative article that links Whitman with Christ, Osiris, Hermes Trismegistus, Jakob Boehme, and Heinrich Heine, among others, suggests that Whitman saw a particular hieroglyph of Osiris supine with blades of grass springing from his body, in a representation of his type as the god of spiritual and vegetable regeneration.[36] The iconography is common, having occasional variations upon the basic scheme, and Shepherd documents at least one instance of Whitman's having seen such a picture. She concludes that such a figure is the source of some of Whitman's imagery in his poem "Scented Herbage of My Breast."

Many other critics have noticed the "divine" tone in "Song of Myself," characterizing Whitman's particular notion of divinity as a belief in a vitalistic or animistic force. Gay Wilson Allen writes that

despite his announced intention to celebrate himself as a representative man, the 'I' of the poem is sometimes Walt Whitman blurting out personal confessions; sometimes the symbol of man, either modern or universal; and more often a personification of an animistic life force, such as primitive minds before the dawn of history worshipped in the stallion, the bull, or some other god of fertility. The latter motif was entirely conscious. . . . and in writing his poem he drew heavily on his accumulated knowledge of Egyptology and comparative religions. . . . The 'I' finally created in this poem resembles in many aspects the god of primitive myth, such as Egypt or Mesopotamia, where the divine was comprehended as immanent and the gods were *in* nature.[37]

[36] These facts are all generally known and are available in several sources, including Rosellini and Lepsius, which Whitman is known to have seen; see, for instance, Wilkinson, pp. 51ff.

[37] Allen, *Solitary Singer*, p. 163.

Recognizing the reasonable limits of any single critical light, we may nevertheless read "Song of Myself," in this Egyptian light, as a celebration of this "representative" aspect of the immanent and divine personality of the Self as a type of Osiris. The "translating" speaker-poet identifies himself with the god of the sprouting grass that makes possible both the wonder of the body and the immortality of the soul, and the evidence of that divinity is the physical body itself ("divine am I inside and out"). The metaphor extends equally well to the Self as a type of Christ, but Whitman's egalitarian attitude toward all life and all persons is the most notable doctrine of Egyptian religion, as well; and the Egyptian thanatology does fit, even closer than Christianity, the main tenets of Whitman's concepts of death and immortality. For the Egyptians all the dead become Osiris, participating in his essence in a future of perfect democracy. As Whitman summarizes the concept, "before Isis and Osiris all human beings are equal." With the scattering of the pieces of his mutilated body, Osiris comes to personify the divinity that exists immanently in nature, to be worshipped when the sign of his regeneration, his "hieroglyph," is recognized in the leaves of the grass that mark his immortality (and also the immortality of the dead who live in his essence). Whitman dramatizes his concept of human life in the face of this immortality, picturing himself "waiting my time to be one of the supremes" (#41), like one of the many "Osiris" figures of the Egyptian necropolis pictured waiting in line before the god's throne, waiting to be made gods.

Indeed, Whitman even began a poem entitled "Osirus" [sic], which he only partially completed, and this concept of a democratic divinity realized through the vegetation-god is exactly what seized Whitman's imagination:

Osirus—to give forms.
I am he who finds nothing more divine than simple and natural things are divine.[38]

It is clear how nearly this "form-giving" function corresponds to the personality of the speaker of "Song of Myself":

In all people I see myself, none more and not one a barley-corn less,
And all the good or bad I say of myself I say of them

(#20)

[38] Whitman, *Leaves*, p. 699.

and:

> I do not call one greater and one smaller,
> That which fills its period and place is equal to any.
>
> (#44)

Likewise, Whitman's statement of intention in his 1855 "Preface" also asserts this form-giving natural divinity:

in the vast clear scheme where every motion and every spear of grass and the frames and spirits of men and women and all that concerns them are unspeakably perfect miracles all referring to all and each distinct and in its place. It is also not consistent with the reality of the world to admit that there is anything in the known universe more divine than men and women.[39]

In his type as young man/sacrificial victim/vegetative deity, Osiris was the original "phoenix," and the cults of the Babylonian Thammuz and of the Greek Bacchus seem to have owed much to influence from Egyptian cults of Osiris. Wilkinson is articulate about the ancient identification of the cults, taking his cue from Plutarch. Coincidentally, several visitors to Whitman's home noted that the poet had a picture on his wall of Bacchus as a vivacious young man.[40] Whitman's identification of himself with the young vegetative gods (including Jesus, ultimately), whose rituals sprang from Egyptian religious practices, was apparently rather strongly impressed on his syncretic imagination. Throughout the "Song of Myself" Whitman wavers from a personal tone to a "Christian" sense of self, to a politically or socially remonstrative self, to this "divine" demiurgic self; the claims of each imply the other types of the same self. I should call the "divine" mode of the self Osirian, at least in parts, with the understanding that Whitman's "divine" role is not, finally, so limited to any single deific personality. At times, however, this Osiris-role in "Song of Myself" does appear in episodes of the poem, with conceptual images that correspond to events in the life of the mythic Osiris himself. Sections 28–29 of "Song of Myself," for instance, recall the ritual death and resurrection of Osiris. Betrayed by his brother, Osiris dies, but each year the Nile floods (reenacting Osiris's posthumous orgasm that generates his son Horus) and then the grass sprouts in the Nile delta (representing a

[39] P. 719.
[40] Allen, *Solitary Singer*, pp. 203, 372.

resurrection through the god). Whitman recasts the ritual as a personal experience of his sensually divine Self:

> I am given up by traitors,
> I talk wildly, I have lost my wits, I and nobody else am the
>   greatest traitor. . . .
>
> You villain touch! what are you doing? my breath is tight in
>   its throat,
> Unclench your floodgates, you are too much for me.
>
> Blind loving wrestling touch, sheath'd hooded sharp-tooth'd touch!
> Did it make you ache so, leaving me?
>
> Parting track'd by arriving, perpetual payment of perpetual loan,
> Rich showering rain, and recompense richer afterward.
>
> Sprouts take and accumulate, stand by the curb prolific and vital,
> Landscapes projected masculine, full-sized and golden.

A correspondence with the Osirian myth is at least implicit: Whitman seems to be using the myth to convey his own sense of orgasmic death (the "floodgates") and regeneration (the sprouting of plants). Besides its spiritual expansiveness, the Self of the poem can physically expand to include the landscape.

Finally, the Egyptian god Osiris achieves his gift of immortality for all by his sacrificial death and by the spreading of his body about the land to sanctify it; in short, he becomes the landscape. We recognize this same impulse in Whitman's poem, the desire to accommodate within one composite democratic individual all the people and land of a nation. In his "Preface" to the 1855 edition of *Leaves of Grass,* Whitman describes the necessary character of the new American poets, who are

to enclose old and new for America is the race of races. Of them a bard is to be commensurate with a people. . . . His spirit responds to his country's spirit . . . he incarnates its geography and natural life and rivers and lakes.[41]

Accordingly, he assumes this incarnation of the land in "Song of Myself":

> I find I incorporate gneiss, coal, long-threaded moss, fruits, grains,
>   esculent roots,
> And am stucco'd with quadrupeds and birds all over. . . .
>
>   (#31)

---

[41] Whitman, *Leaves,* p. 711.

Like Keats's concept of the poet's assimilative lack of identity, Whitman implies an essentially Osirian activity for the poet of the American States, the task of absorbing into his "fluid and swallowing soul" all the scenes and events which make a composite nation. Gay Wilson Allen, among others, describes Whitman's use of catalogues and lists as a technique which is essentially "democratic," for it recognizes no subordination of persons or ideas in its organization. In the light of our discussion about the Osirian myth of the generalized personal body of a deity and about the immanent unity in natural diversity that that story represents, such a "democratic" philosophy and technique appear clearly as concepts for which Whitman could have found theological, political, and stylistic parallels, if not his original inspiration, from his study of Egypt. Whitman's naturally democratic bent found at least a sympathetic parallel in the traditions of the oldest continuous civilization in history. To call the relation an "influence" adds a nuance of formative strength that I do not mean to suggest; Whitman was not so much "influenced" as he was fascinated by Egyptian lore, raiding that tradition and adding it, with many others, to the materials with which his vastly syncretic imagination worked.

And yet the theoretical analogies are strong. Formally, ancient Egyptian literature is full of examples of enumerative listings of places, of the parts of the body, of the wonderous effects of Osiris's death: images bound together by the implicit belief that all share in the life of Osiris through his generalized self. Further, the idea of the aggregative body-self, which is fundamental to the Osiris myth, to Whitman's sense of individuality, and (metaphorically) to the concept of democratic federalism, has important political implications as well as metaphysical ones. For Whitman, identifying himself with the Osirian role of "incarnating the geography," in effect imaginatively makes himself the United States, much in the same way as he refers to his general poem as the "epic of democracy," "the great psalm of the republic," and refers to the United States as the "composite nation," the "nation of many nations." The myth of Osiris seems to have been for Whitman a political as much as a spiritual (or spiritualized-physical) theme. The essential problem of American federated democracy, involving exactly this tension between unity and diversity, was to cause the American Civil War within a few years of the first publication of "Song of Myself."

Whitman's vision, then, of his enlarged self as the one Body which can incorporate all the diversity of his separate states into a unified imaginative whole found strong confirmation in the Egyptian Osiris, whose body was spread over both the North and South Kingdoms and who thus unified the lands of Egypt.

It is no coincidence, furthermore, that Whitman admiringly describes Sesostris, the legendary Pharaoh of Egypt and descendent of Osiris, in images that strongly recall Whitman's beloved Abraham Lincoln: "He was six feet ten inches high and nobly proportioned and supple," Whitman writes. "He was considerate of the common people. He conquered Asia and Europe, honoring most those that resisted him most. He was a rugged, wholesome, masculine person and in the list of Egyptian greatness comes first after Osiris."[42] Again, Sesostris is called in verse "the freer of slaves—divider among them of homesteads—maker of farmers."[43] If Egypt offers a model for the composite American Individual, it also offers an historical model for political leaders in times of internecine strife. When Whitman claims to transcend history in "Song of Myself," he does so not by denying its potency but by enlarging himself to include its models.

Finally, therefore, Whitman seems to be using the story of Osiris— and his own imaginative identification as assimilative American poet with that type—as a metaphor throughout "Song of Myself" for the American federated democracy. Implicit in this comparison is a continuity throughout history, running from the first dynastic civilization in the West to its (nineteenth-century) counterpart and superseding tally, the America that in Whitman's view encloses and completes the history of humankind. In his notebooks Whitman aligns the democracy of his contemporary America with the Osirian democracy of the living and the dead in ancient Egypt:

Egypt . . . represented that phase of development, advanced childhood, full of belief, rich and divine enough, standing amazed and awed before the mystery of life—nothing more wonderful than life, even in a hawk—a bull or a cat—the masses of the people reverent of priestly and kingly authority. The definite history of the world cannot go back farther than Egypt, and in the most important particulars the average spirit of man has not gone forward of the spirit of ancient Egypt.[44]

42 Whitman, *Complete Writings*, VI, 100–101.
43 Whitman, *Leaves*, p. 687.
44 Whitman, *Complete Writings*, VI, 103.

"Song of Myself" is Whitman's "hieroglyph" of the democratic individual, and Whitman's appropriating the Osirian myth as a personal myth to inform the poem has both metaphysical and political implications. In Egypt Whitman found a fascinating, consistent, and potent set of metaphors. Egypt was not the only source, of course, for many of these notions, nor was it the only culture in which Whitman was interested; but in his study of the literature, religion, art, and ideogrammic language of the ancient Egyptians, Whitman found a rich tradition which contributed to the imagery, to the conceptual underpinnings, and to the "democratic" structure of his own hieroglyphic poem.

Whitman's Use of the Middle Ages
David W. Hiscoe

O NE OF THE WONDERS to which Whitman sought to wake up the readers of *Leaves of Grass* was their particular, peculiar place in history. Unfortunately, in the twenty years since the publication of R. W. B. Lewis's *The American Adam,* critics by and large have assigned Whitman and his readers simply to "the party of Hope," representing the New Innocent "emancipated from history, happily bereft of ancestry," and "unspoiled by memory."[1] Yet the columns of historical data Whitman compiled between 1855 and 1856 in no less significant a place than the flyleaves of unsold copies of the 1855 edition[2] suggest—given Whitman's love of the symbolic act—that we, as he often said, "take warning." He is "surely far different from what you suppose" ("Are You the New Person Drawn toward Me," 2).[3] The spirit of the evolving book was to be embodied in things, in the historical fact, and, as Floyd Stovall's *The Foreground of Leaves of Grass* has shown us,[4] clearly Whitman was setting about to master his historical ancestry and to school his memory. The difference Whitman would have us suppose, I suggest, presents us a less naive poet, one who shared historical ground with Hawthorne and Melville, sympathetic to both the parties of Hope and Memory yet confined to neither.[5]

Aside from the American past, Whitman most often turned to the Middle Ages in Europe as a prop for his dramatization of the Self

---

[1] *The American Adam: Innocence, Tragedy and Tradition in the Nineteenth Century* (Chicago, 1955), pp. 5, 45.

[2] "Notes on English History," *Notes and Fragments Left By Walt Whitman,* ed. R. M. Bucke, in *The Complete Prose Works of Walt Whitman,* ed. R. M. Bucke, Thomas Harned, and Horace Traubel (1902; rpt. Grosse Point, Mich., 1967), X, 39.

[3] All quotations from Whitman's poetry are from *Leaves of Grass: Comprehensive Reader's Edition,* ed. Harold Blodgett and Sculley Bradley (New York, 1965). All quotations from Whitman's prose, unless otherwise noted, are from the New York University edition of *Collected Writings,* parenthetically documented as *PW*.

[4] (Charlottesville, Va., 1970).

[5] *The American Adam,* p. 7.

that might arise in the American democracy. His manipulation of
the period in *Leaves* nicely demonstrates the peculiar neutral terri-
tory Whitman strategically created out of the past. On the one hand,
a reader professing to admire medieval literature or culture is constantly invited to leap from his seat and contend for his life when
picking up Walt Whitman. In "The Song of the Broad-Axe," for
instance, the tool lying in the grass

> has served all,
>
> . . . . . .
>
> Served all great works on land and all great works on the sea,
> For the mediaeval ages and before the mediaeval ages,
> Served not the living only then as now, but served the dead.
> (151–165)

The following stanza reveals, with that characteristic Whitmanian
humor which it is dangerous to miss, just how the axe served the
dead in the medieval past:

> I see the European headsman,
> He stands mask'd, clothed in red, with huge legs and strong
>   naked arms,
> And leans on a ponderous axe,
> (Whom have you slaughter'd lately European headsman?
> Whose is that blood upon you so wet and sticky?) (166–170)

In the new world, the axe is to be no longer a murderous weapon on
the scaffolds of "foreign kings" and "priests" (177) but a tool with
which to carve out the new shapes of America:

> I see the blood wash'd entirely away from the axe,
> Both blade and helve are clean.
>
> . . . .
>
> I see the headsman withdraw and become useless,
> I see the scaffold untrodden and mouldy, I see no longer any
>   axe upon it,
> I see the mighty and friendly emblem of the power of my own
>   race, the newest, largest race. (178–183)

Safely in the camp of Hope, told what to think of the Middle Ages,
given a comfortable theory of history by Walt Whitman, we are apt
not to notice that the last detail in the stanzas of catalogs of new
forms that follow is "The shape of the step-ladder for the convicted
and sentenced murderer, the murderer with haggard face and pin-

ion'd arms,/ The sheriff at hand with his deputies, the silent and white-lipp'd crowd, the dangling of the rope" (231–232). The axe may be building new cities, but executioners still tread scaffolds; only the form of death has changed. One must remember that the new man of *Leaves* stands on the same firm legs and shares the same strong naked arms as his medieval counterpart and that the strong bird may become pinioned among the equal brood as well as any-where else. Whitman has just stuck our heads between our legs to unfix our vision, a technique Emerson recommends for its ability to make us look at the world with fresh eyes.[6] Time and again in *Leaves of Grass* Whitman used the same strategy: the reader is given a "proper" view of the role of the past, of the Middle Ages, in his life only to have Whitman's kosmos soon contradict itself. Constantly placed at the third point of the sort of triad Alfred Marks has shown to be characteristic of Whitman's thinking,[7] the audience is made to resolve the dialectic of Hope and Memory. Investigation of Whit-man's knowledge of the Middle Ages and his use of that knowledge promises to clarify the nature of the resolution he expects from his reader.

A frustrated scholar could, however, easily make a case for decid-ing that Whitman's use of the period is more a problem than a strat-egy. In *Democratic Vistas,* for instance, Whitman, in a quite schol-arly footnote, sends readers interested in discovering more about the "enchanting" literature of the time to, among other things, Walter Scott's *Border Minstrelsy,* Percy's *Ballads,* George Ellis's *Specimens of Early English Metrical Romances,* the poems of Walter of Aqui-tania, and the German *Nibelungen* (*PW* II, 366). Characteristically, no edition of Walter of Aquitania's poems was available in transla-tion in the nineteenth century;[8] indeed, Walter is a character in sev-eral sagas, not an author at all. A little digging, however, reveals a two-page cursory treatment of the hero in "Provençal & Scandinavian Poetry," an article from *The Edinburgh Review* on which Whitman made extensive notes in 1848.[9]

---

[6] *The Complete Works of Ralph Waldo Emerson,* ed. Edward Waldo Emerson (Boston, 1903–1904), I, 51.

[7] "Whitman's Triadic Imagery," *American Literature,* XXIII (March, 1951), 99–126. See also Millie D. Jensen, "Whitman and Hegel: The Curious Triplicate Process," *Walt Whitman Review,* X (June, 1964), 27–34.

[8] Stovall, p. 180.

[9] LXXXVIII (July, 1848), 23–24.

Ellis's *Metrical Romances* offers a more tantalizing disappointment. Horace Traubel recalls Whitman's giving him a copy of the book and solemnly declaring, "It is a textbook for me—a sort of work-tool: I have made use of it time and again."[10] The scholar goes lusting off, plows through the six hundred pages of Ellis's book, and finds nothing to connect it to Whitman's works, unless it were the lists of heroes in "Song of the Expositon" or, more likely, the recurring references of a less enchanted Whitman to the "interminable ballad romances of the middle ages" (*PW* II, 557, 590). More pertinently, Ellis discusses Percy's *Ballads*,[11] and we have, perhaps, a source of Whitman's knowledge of his sources of knowledge.

Ellis's *Specimens*—Whitman surely admired at least the title—indicates the way in which Whitman, like most Victorians, was exposed to medieval poetry. The prose translations in which the tales were cast completely miss the word play, the gaming with style and tone, and the manipulation of detail that created the interest and meaning of the stories for an audience probably quite familiar with each story's plot. Ellis, by his own admission, was baffled by the tales he presented. The legends of Roland and Charlemagne, for instance, he thought "absurdities . . . accepted in lieu of authentic history in a credulous age."[12] Artistically, they seemed notable mainly for "monotony."[13]

Whitman's other medieval readings were in German epics, in Dante, and in Chaucer. William A. Little concluded that if Whitman read the *Nibelungenlied* at all he did not read it carefully and that more than likely his knowledge of it came from secondary sources.[14] He owned a copy of John Carlyle's translation of the *Inferno* and sententiously recorded in his notes that the Middle Ages believed Dante took an actual journey in Hell with Virgil.[15] He reviewed Charles Deshler's 1847 edition of *Selections from the Poems of Geoffrey Chaucer* in the *Daily Eagle,* heavily annotated his own copy, and

---

[10] *With Walt Whitman in Camden* (1908; rpt. New York, 1961), II, 464.

[11] (London, 1848), pp. 16–18.

[12] *Ibid.*, p. 344.

[13] *Ibid.*, p. 13.

[14] "Walt Whitman and the *Nibelungenlied*," *PMLA*, LXX (Dec., 1965), 562–563.

[15] "Preparatory Reading and Thought," in *Notes and Fragments*, IX, 93. A short description of Whitman's personal copy of Carlyle's *Inferno* may be found in Peter Van Edmond, "Bryn Mawr College Library Holdings of Whitman Books," *Walt Whitman Review*, XX (June, 1974), 42–43.

kept at least part of it for the rest of his life.[16] Deshler's book, however, contains curiously little of Chaucer's poetry, a good bit of the volume being taken up with a long introduction, and the fragments of Chaucer he does present are arranged under such sections as "Rural Descriptions" and "Paintings: Female Characters." The only evidence that the book made an impression on Whitman is an editorial from the *Eagle* titled with a quotation from Chaucer's translation of *The Romance of the Rose*.[17]

Whitman's declarations on the Middle Ages, then, were more the stuff of myth than knowledge. The form of the myth he created about Chaucer, which culminates in no less than a detailed phrenological description of the poet, is suggestive of much he did with the Middle Ages in his poetry. In the reading he is known to have done concerning Chaucer can be seen two distinct methods of dealing with the history of the period. Dugald Stewart's introductory overview of human history for the first volume of the eighth (1860) edition of *Encyclopedia Britannica* set forth the view that gave the Middle Ages its name:

The long interval commonly known by the name of the *middle ages,* which immediately preceded the revival of letters in the western part of Europe, forms the most melancholy blank which occurs, from the first dawn of recorded civilization in the intellectual and moral history of the human race.[18]

Stewart's medieval world lay in the grip of "the vices and corruptions of the Romish church" (p. 14), and nineteenth-century commentators, in the grip of their poet-as-Bard-theory, readily found a place for Chaucer in this scheme. Deshler, for instance, insistently returned to the poet's Catholicism and made much of the "chivalrous bias of his nature."[19] The author of "Chaucer," a lengthy 1848 review of Chaucerian criticism in *The North British Review,* presented the poet—in phrasing that again must have appealed to Whitman—as a "speciman of the man of his time."[20] Whitman cut the article from the journal,

[16] (New York). The Feinberg Collection in the Library of Congress contains Whitman's copy.

[17] 8 Dec. 1847. See Stovall's discussion, pp. 233–234.

[18] Whitman knew at least some of the entries in this edition in one form or another. See Floyd Stovall, "Notes on Whitman's Reading," *American Literature,* XXVI (Nov., 1954), 348–349.

[19] *Selections,* p. 40.

[20] X (Feb., 1849), 314.

made extensive underlinings and marginal notes in preparation for a lecture entitled "The Poet" that was apparently never delivered, and kept the article all his life.[21]

The *Review* article baldly presents history as a progress toward the flowering present. Chaucer did not rise against the tyrannous religious, political, and philosophical systems of his time either because he "was not bold enough to be a reformer" or, at best, because "he felt, as England and Europe felt at that time, that the hour for the downfall of the priesthood had not yet arrived, that they still had a part to play and functions to discharge in the history of the world."[22] Isaac D'Israeli, whose *Amenities of Literature* Whitman admiringly reviewed,[23] could argue, taking the opposing side, that Chaucer was "a revolutionary" driven from court because "he openly joined with a party for 'the people' ";[24] but the assumption remained that to revolt or not to revolt was the issue of the day, that the individual defines himself through his relation to the progress of the historical world.

Oddly enough, however, the *Review* article Whitman found so interesting argued, in eagerness to attack the subjectivity of Shelley, Byron, and Keats, a quite different view of man's relationship to history. Chaucer, in spite of the historical circumstances in which he lived, was "above all . . . a cheerful and hopeful man"[25] who found the source of his poetic powers in his day-to-day "discharging of the duties of the ordinary English citizen."[26] In the daily life of contact with the usual existence, the Self finds a force—Whitman would later call it sanity—that transcends historical considerations. The reviewer

[21] "Shorter Notes, Isolated Words, Etc.," in *Notes and Fragments*, IX, 227. The comments on the manuscript are Bucke's. Whitman's note in the margin of his copy, now in the Trent Collection at Duke University, suggests that the "lecture" Whitman finally delivered was broader than Bucke realized. When the reviewer argues that "It is an extremely common error, both with vulgar narrators and careless readers, to lay hold of the points of dissimilarity between distant ages and those in which they live, to the almost total exclusion of the often much more important features of resemblance" (p. 159), Whitman underlined the passage and, beside one of those fine pointing hands he drew to indicate striking concepts in his readings, remarked that this is "an important thought to open [his proposed but never written] 'History of Brooklyn' " or, more intriguingly, given the history of the Self soon to simmer into *Leaves*, "any History." The importance of the concept is emphasized by the four different pens and colored pencils with which the article is marked.

[22] P. 319.

[23] *Brooklyn Daily Eagle*, 9 Mar. 1847.

[24] (New York, 1847), I, 178. Deshler also creates a Chaucer who struck the "first blow which the people administered to priestly arrogance and imposture" (p. 18).

[25] P. 319.

[26] *Ibid.*, p. 308.

presented, in passages Whitman scored twice in his copy, a Chaucer who, being bathed in "the Elysium . . . [of] human sympathies,"[27] obtained "that peculiarly healthy and normal character which . . . is to be attributed to his having taken so large a share in the actual business of the world."[28] Accordingly, "the masculine air of his delineations is what strikes us most. His characters are large and strong." Whitman returned to this passage three times for scoring. And, since Chaucer "does not think of himself as too good for the world, nor the world too bad for him,"[29] he may present even "grossness and immorality . . . freely and unshrinkingly,"[30] sure that here rather than in "lingering long in the regions of metaphysical and logical abstractions"[31] is a source of truth. Thus, in spite of the culture in which he lived, Chaucer had found ground to stand and tell the nobility "straw for your gentillesse."[32]

Given these two conflicting views of Chaucer, the first suggesting that history is progress, that one might remember and build on the past but inevitably must reject it, and the other implying that human life transcends culture, Whitman created his own Chaucer. The poet, Whitman wrote in the margins of the *Review* article, was given to writing poems for "poetical-disposed genteel persons."[33] The logical sequel to such judgment was to join those "who have left all feudal processes and poems behind them, and assumed the poems and processes of Democracy" ("By Blue Ontario's Shore," 185). Whitman, however, also joined Chaucer. The poet, he decided in his notes, was

a strong wholesome man with large perceptive organs, friendly, amative, of independent spirit—possessed of true English tastes, rude, fond of women, fond of eating and drinking, not to be quelled by priestcraft or kingcraft.[34]

What we are given here, of course, sounds suspiciously like the sort

[27] *Ibid.*, p. 326.
[28] *Ibid.*, p. 307.
[29] *Ibid.*, p. 326.
[30] *Ibid.*, p. 325. Whitman, as one might guess, scored this vigorously.
[31] *Ibid.*, p. 315.
[32] *Ibid.*, p. 299. The words, of course, are actually Harry Bailey's to the Franklin (*The Works of Geoffrey Chaucer*, ed. F. N. Robinson, 2nd. ed. [1933; rpt. Boston, 1957], V, 695). Deshler (pp. 2, 6, 16, 61) covers much the same ground, again in both language and stance similar to those which appear in *Leaves*.
[33] "Preparatory Reading," p. 86.
[34] *Ibid.*, pp. 86-87.

of phrenology Walt Whitman, a Kosmos, conjured for himself.[35] Chaucer, living in the dark Middle Ages and writing for a feudal audience, achieved the Self of the democratic man four hundred years before *Leaves of Grass*. What then for the process of history and America with her equal brood? This antithesis Whitman played upon throughout his published prose and poetry.

Much of the vigor of Whitman's writing derives from his working out of the first stance. Americans are heir to the "medieval navigators" who "awaken'd" to that vast "Something swelling in humanity now like the sap of the earth in spring/ The sunset splendor of chivalry declining" ("Passage to India," 143–146), and they are challenged by Walt Whitman, the new Columbus,[36] to live hopefully in a universe in which "the celestial laws are yet to be work'd over and rectified" ("Song of Myself," 469). One must begin "Outbidding at the start the old cautious hucksters" (1027). The "bat-eyed and materialistic priests" ("Song of the Open Road," 130) are to be replaced by the new religion of Democracy so that "the lifeless cross . . . , Europe's dead cross, may bud and blossom" ("Prayer of Columbus," 39) in the New World.

This position, with its rejection of the medieval past, stands at the center of both his theory of literature and his practical criticism. From it, Shakespeare is regarded with suspicion as the very "tally of feudalism" (*PW* II, 522).[37] One finds in Dante only "the usual distinctions of good and evil";[38] Carlyle seems "Feudal at the Core" (*PW* I, 261); Tennyson "exhale[s] that principle of caste which we Americans have come on earth to destroy" (*PW* II, 476); Scott's novels are damned for their anti-democratic bearing.[39] In another of those flagrantly symbolic dramas with which Whitman made both poetry and kitsch, a passage in *Specimen Days* shows us Whitman putting down Scott's "Lay of the Last Minstrel" and "Marmion" and begin-

---

[35] For Whitman's actual description see Edward Hungerford, "Walt Whitman and His Chart of Bumps," *American Literature*, II (Jan., 1931), 350–384. And cf. Michael Dressman, "Whitman, Chaucer, and French Words," *Walt Whitman Review*, XXIII (June, 1977), 77–82.

[36] For a discussion of Whitman's own identification with Columbus see Gay Wilson Allen, *The New Walt Whitman Handbook* (New York, 1975), p. 43.

[37] Commentary on Whitman's view of Shakespeare is surprisingly extensive. See Floyd Stovall, "Whitman, Shakespeare, and Democracy," *Journal of English and Germanic Philology*, LI (Oct., 1952), 457–472.

[38] "Preparatory Reading," p. 92.

[39] *Brooklyn Daily Eagle*, 26 Apr. 1847.

ning to ponder the makings of a new "Mississippi Valley Literature" (*PW* I, 222–223). "Those immensely overpaid accounts," the Troy story, the stuff of medieval romance, the "German, French, and Spanish castles," "Merlin and Lancelot and Galahad," are declared unalterably "Pass'd! pass'd! for us, forever pass'd" ("Song of the Exposition," sections 2 and 3). And good riddance. Who has time for "the aimless sleepwalking of the middle ages" ("Preface 1855," 710)?

The business of the poet of the present is to establish the new accounts. As Whitman concluded in the margins of an article documenting the continuing European interest in the poetry of the troubadours, "the English poet has reminiscences and constantly extols them. The American poet has a future, and must extol it."[40] Writers of "other lands in quite all past ages and mainly at present show justifying greatness in their special, exceptional heroes and eminences, and kings and martyrs, sages, warriors, bards, intellectualists, or what not."[41] The new poet is to replace these with the type of the Divine Average, with that Self that has its sleeves rolled up and the top of its undershirt showing:

To offset chivalry, indeed, those vanished countless knights, old altars, abbeys, priests, ages and strings of ages [Whitman's cataloguing technique can be a fine tool of sarcasm as well as evoker of the Ideal], a knightlier and more sacred cause today demands, and shall supply, in a New World, to larger, grander work, more than the counterpart and tally of them. (*PW* II, 423)

This new work—Whitman, his hat jauntily cocked, was fond of calling his contribution to it "the New Bible"[42]—will produce types, characters, kosmoses, a new literature, with "at least as firm and as warm a hold in men's hearts, emotions and belief, as in their days, feudalism or ecclesiasticism" (*DV, PW* II, 368).

Another form Whitman's attitude toward history takes is what Robert Falk calls his "Hegelian-evolutionary reading of the universe in which the past contains the seeds of the future."[43] Though the past is not to be fanatically rejected, the growth metaphor still controls. The new Self knows that "Immense have been the preparations for

[40] "Preparatory Reading," p. 90.
[41] *Ibid.*, p. 16.
[42] "Meaning and Intention of 'Leaves of Grass,'" in *Notes and Fragments*, IX, 6.
[43] "Shakespeare's Place in Walt Whitman's America," *Shakespeare Association Bulletin*, XVII (Apr., 1942), 88.

me" ("Song of Myself," 1157), that it has antecedents in "the trouba-
dour, the crusader, and the monk" ("With Antecedents," 8). "The
present," *Democratic Vistas* proclaims, "is but the legitimate birth of
the past, including feudalism" (*PW* II, 362), and we, Walt Whitman,
you and I,

> . . . touch all laws and tally all antecedents,
> We are the skald, the oracle, the monk and the knight, we
>   easily include them and more. ("With Antecedents," 17–18)

We may take the metaphor out of the realm of flowers, but progress
remains the principle of history:

> For what is the present after all but a growth out of the past?
> (As a projectile form'd, impell'd, passing a certain line,
> still keeps on,
> So the present, utterly form'd, impell'd by the past).
> ("Passage to India," 13–15)

The past, then, is "middling well as far as it goes—but is that all?"
("Song of Myself," 1025). The 1855 *Preface* suggests a program for
obtaining something more interesting, more complete:

America does not repel the past . . . accepts the lesson with calmness . . .
is not so impatient as has been supposed . . . perceives that the corpse is
slowly borne from the eating and sleeping rooms of the house . . . perceives that it waits a little while in the door . . . that it was fittest for its
days . . . that its action has descended to the stalwart and wellshaped heir
who approaches . . . and that he shall be fittest for his days. (709)

The past is manure, but, as the Walt Whitman soon to be under our
boot-soles knew, such stuff is useful and contains a certain beauty.

Nevertheless, the central image of Whitman's book, as well as
much he says throughout his poetry and prose, precludes regarding
history as progress alone: the grass may grow by every road, but it
also sprouts in every time. When crossing Brooklyn Ferry, one sees
that "It avails not, time nor place" (20); and the Self's thoughts,
Whitman explains, "are really the thoughts of all men in all ages and
lands, they are not original with me" ("Song of Myself," 355). Or,
as an early commentator put it: "One must not say originalities, for
Whitman himself disclaims originality—at least in the superficial

sense. His notion explicitly is that there is nothing actually new."[44] The writer, of course, was Whitman.

Given this "vast similitude" which "interlocks all/ . . . All nations, colors, barbarisms, civilizations, languages,/ All identities that have existed or may exist on this globe, or any globe,/ All lives and deaths, all of the past, present, future" ("On the Beach at Night Alone"),[45] Whitman may also view history from the end of the tug-rope of reality opposite to Progress:

The most immense part of ancient history is altogether unknown. Previous to ten thousand years ago there were surely empires, cities, states, and pastoral tribes and uncivilized hordes upon the earth.

Do you suppose that history is complete when the best writers get all they can of the few communities that are known and arrange them clearly in books? Sublime characters lived and died and we do not know when or where—full as sublime as any that we now celebrate over the world . . . .

Upon America stood many of these vast nations . . . . In the trance of the healthy brain of man. Time, the passage of many thousands of years, the total vacuity of our letters about them, their places blank upon the map, not a mark or a figure that is demonstrably so. With all this they lived as surely as we do now.[46]

Thus, Whitman can conclude in one of his proposed but undelivered lectures that "With respect to . . . morals, virtue or to heroism and the religious incumbency the old principles remain"[47] and can praise Poe for setting his tales against "the background of the eternal moralities" (*PW* I, 232). The celestial laws to be rectified have become, it seems, "the elementary laws" which "never apologize" ("Song of Myself," 411).

From this corner of Whitman's triad, the poet, standing apart from history, is to chant "the same monotonous old song" ("By Blue Ontario's Shore," 272) for that "ever new, yet old, old human race" (*PW* II, 478). In fact, all the arts address themselves to human characteristics which operate regardless of historical culture:

good theology, good art, or good literature has . . . features shared in common. The combination fraternizes, ties the races—is . . . under laws

44 "Meaning and Intention," p. 12.

45 To call this notion Hegelian, or even Emersonian, as do Blodgett and Bradley (p. 261), seems a little shortsighted.

46 "Preparatory Reading," pp. 49–50.

47 *Ibid.*, pp. 168–169.

applicable indifferently to all, irrespective of climate or date, and from whatever source, appeals to emotions, pride, love, spirituality, common to humankind. (*DV, PW* II, 411)

Whitman's "New Bible"—the literature of Democracy—is to be, then, only a form of the same one read by medieval man, by the Chaucer who shares Walt Whitman's phrenology, for "if the time ever comes when iconoclasm does its extremest in one direction against the Books of the Bible in its present form, the collection must still survive in another" (*PW* II, 548).

On the one hand were the bat-eyed priests of the Middle Ages; on the other was Whitman's reaction, recorded by Traubel, to a letter, received anonymously and addressed to "the American poet," urging him to read the history of Lourdes and offer votive masses:

When I was in Washington it was surprising how many Catholic priests I came to know—how many took the trouble to get acquainted with me . . . I think we were unified on the strength of the . . . spirit that was patent behind our differences or technology, theology—our differences of lingo, name. . . . Of course I haven't a particle of faith in Lourdes—in faith cures—bones of saints, . . . but this postal has for me a meaning quite apart from the literal yes or no of Lourdes—a meaning at least of sympathy.[48]

Again, cultural forces, history, even the Party of Hope, are transcended by the base of all metaphysics.

Why, then, the dialectic and how would Whitman have us synthesize it? The essay "Nature and Democracy—Morality" with which Whitman ended *Specimen Days* suggests the strategy:

Perhaps indeed the efforts of the true poets, founders, religions, literatures, all ages, have been, and ever will be, our time and times to come, essentially the same—to bring people back from their persistent strayings and sickly abstractions, to the costless average, divine, original concrete. (*PW* I, 295

It is, of course, Whitman against whom the charges of iconoclasm and persistent straying are usually put, charges he invites, begs for. The weapon of attack is usually tradition, which Walt has chucked out the window, beginning his studies, as he does, childishly loitering about, admiring his feet. The charges are admirably consistent. For

---

[48] *With Walt Whitman*, I, 371–372.

T. S. Eliot, Whitman was "satisfied—too satisfied,"[49] a man who in his chase after strange gods forgot man's fallen nature. George Santayana, anticipating Lewis's analysis of Whitman's Adamic stance, returned the same diagnosis:

Walt Whitman has gone back to the innocent style of Adam, when the animals filed before him one by one and he called each of them by its name.

In fact, the influences to which Walt Whitman was subject were as favourable as possible to the imaginary experiment of beginning the world over again. Liberalism and transcendentalism both harbored some illusions on that score; and they were in the air which our poet breathed. Moreover he breathed this air in America, where the newness of the material environment made it easier to ignore the fatal antiquity of human nature.[50]

"Goodbye original sin, goodbye the fall of man," sighs George Bowering.[51] Whitman, of course, did want to talk of Adam, but Lewis and the rest are ignoring the other edge of the broad-axe. Whitman also consistently argued a view of man which tallies rather nicely with that of his medieval antecedents.

Human nature he saw strangely divided between the good and the bad, and, as he noted in the margins of an article on the habits of ancient man, one need not go to foreign continents to view "men's brutish nature"; there are, after all, plenty of "Rocky Mountain and California aborigines" about.[52] In Mosby's raids one could easily find "the human heart everywhere black" (*PW* I, 81). And the condition is one of those that transcend culture:

the three Presidentiads preceding 1861 show'd how the weakness and wickedness of rulers are just as eligible here in America under republican, as in Europe under dynastic influences. (*PW* I, 24)

For the individual, the human nature is "the same old role, the role that is what we make it, as great as we like, / Or as small as we like, or [with a characteristic Whitmanian triad] both great and small" ("Crossing Brooklyn Ferry," 84–85). One chooses his own nature.

49 "Whitman and Tennyson," *Nation and Anthenaem*, XL (Dec., 1926), 426.

50 *The Poetry of Barbarism*, in *Interpretations of Poetry and Religion* (New York, 1900), p. 178.

51 "The Solitary Everything," *Walt Whitman Review*, XV (March, 1969), 19.

52 "Preparatory Reading," p. 54.

The "thorn'd thumb"—Paul's thorn in the flesh (II Cor. 12:7)—is still "inexplicable" ("Song of Myself," 1066);[53] it is still possible to knit "the old knot of contrariety" ("Crossing Brooklyn Ferry," 71); and "those men and women" still "pass unwittingly the true realities of life, and go toward false realities" ("Thought [Of persons]," 6). Those who choose this nature are "unwaked somnambules walking in the dusk" ("Thought," 8). "Is it you," Whitman asks, that is "Outside fair costume, within ashes and filth" ("A Hand-Mirror," 2)? Beware, he warns, of that "Another self, a duplicate of every one, skulking and hiding it goes"; to accept it is to choose "death under the breast-bones, hell under the skull-bones" ("Song of the Open Road," Sec. 13). Those who deprive themselves of their proper nature are the "diseas'd person," the "rum drinker," and those of "venereal taint" ("Song of the Open Road," 137), and they must face the inevitable compensatory law of nature shared by Whitman, Emerson, and Boethius: "The law of drunkards, informers, mean persons," of which "not one iota thereof can be eluded" ("To Think of Time," 86).

The ability to choose the proper nature lay, for the Middle Ages, in the province of Reason, a term, of course, as equivocal as "human nature," but again one which medieval thinkers defined in a manner suitable to Whitman. For both it exists, to be sure, in the mystical moist night air rather than the charts and diagrams of the classroom. Even Aquinas, the source of Eliot's trust in the concept, defined the term as "an inclining toward the good, . . . a natural inclination to know the truth about God" (*Summa Theologica,* II: II: 94) and, after ranging the proofs and figures in columns in the *Summa,* is said to have ended his life levitating about rooms, traveling through walls, and mocking the users of words. Reason, then, is the intuition that allows one to know instinctively one's own nature, a nature that *Genesis* (1:26), Augustine (*De doctrina Christiana,* I: XXII: 20), and Whitman ("From Noon to Starry Night," 56) insist contains within itself the image of God. In the margins of the "Chaucer" article, Whitman copied, in a slightly changed form and without quotation marks (one can see his lecture forming itself), the reviewer's decision that in Boethius's works "the middle ages first became ac-

---

[53] Blodgett and Bradley's gloss of this passage as "WW's version of the familiar metaphor" for "an image of vexation" is rather shameful.

quainted with the flattering doctrine that man, by the exercise of his reason, becomes superior to the dominion of fortune,"[54] a concept Whitman almost certainly meant to ridicule. Yet, the source of Boethius's concept of reason was in the Stoic philosophers, and Whitman ended *Specimen Days* with Marcus Aurelius's claim that morality, the fruit of Reason, is "only a living and enthusiastic sympathy with Nature" (*PW* I, 295).[55] In the margins of an article on the "objective nature of truth" in Kant's writings, Whitman showed that he planted Reason in the same granite to which Boethius is mortised and tenoned:

It remains, I say, to be inquired . . . whether there is not probably also something in the soul, even as it exists under present circumstances, which being itself adjusted to the inherent and immutable laws of things . . . does not afford a clue to unchangeable standards and tests.[56]

Whitman saves the term from the "genteel little creatures" (*DV, PW* II, 388) with whom it is such a favorite by "unfixing" and redefining it. This "latent eternal intuitional sense in humanity . . . this perennial regulation" (*DV, PW* II, 421), becomes the "Perfect sanity" ("Song of the Answerer," 53) of Whitman's "tally." "A man is tallied," a man is acting reasonably, when "he realizes here what he has in him" ("Song of the Open Road," 86), and the unchanging standards of tally are the laws of the universe, the most basic of which is man's creation in the image of God. Though Whitman readily conceded that it is easy to pervert that image in one's self, he insisted that "there is perfection in you also" ("Crossing Brooklyn Ferry," 130).

The antithesis Whitman creates in his poetry and prose between two attitudes toward the past, toward the traditions he represents by the Middle Ages, functions to force the reader to grapple with these elementary laws. He is presented with a quandary, one of Walt Whitman's contradictions. He is given a world which must be founded on new principles, which must reject the past, and then is told that the only worthy principles are the eternal ones, the same as those available to that rejected past. That synthesis which fixes us again on solid ground, with undizzied eyes, must take place, as it

[54] "Shorter Notes," in *Notes and Fragments*, IX, 227.
[55] Gay Wilson Allen is currently preparing an essay on Whitman and stoicism.
[56] "Preparatory Reading," p. 185.

should in a democratic world, in the individual reader. He must complete Whitman's vision, creating a future distinct indeed from the past because this time, perhaps, each individual, awakened to the possibility, may fulfill his nature. The nation of readers, each a simple, separate person, is, En-Masse,

> After all not to create only, or found only,
> But to bring perhaps from afar what is already founded,
> To give it our own identity, average, limitless, free
> To fill the gross the torpid bulk with vital religious fire,
>
> . . . .
>
> These also are the lessons of our New World;
> While how little the New after all, how much the Old, Old World!
>
> Long and long has the grass been growing,
> Long and long has the rain been falling,
> Long has the globe been rolling round.
> ("Song of the Exposition," 4–14)

Whitman and Motherhood:
A Historical View
Myrth Jimmie Killingsworth

T HE theme of motherhood presented Walt Whitman with philosophical problems which had a direct bearing on the quality of
his poetry. That theme contributes directly to the success of "Out of
the Cradle Endlessly Rocking," but the majority of his poems on
motherhood are notoriously bad. Critics have often agreed with
D.H. Lawrence: "Whitman's 'athletic mothers of these states' are
depressing. Muscle and wombs: functional creatures. . . . The
woman is reduced, really, to a submissive function. She is no longer
an individual being with a living soul. She must fold her arms and
bend her head and submit to a functioning capacity. Function of sex,
function of birth."[1] Lawrence's first concern is social; he asserts
that Whitman was oblivious of women's claims to social functions
other than those of sex and birth. Charles W. Eldridge, recalling
Whitman's conversations among the O'Connor circle in the 1860s,
had also held that the poet was "one of the most conservative of
men. He believed in the old ways; had no faith in any reforms. . . .
He delighted in the company of old fashioned women, mothers of
large families preferred, who did not talk about literature or reforms. . . ."[2] But Lawrence's criticism is also literary: Whitman's
mothers are dull and stereotypic; they lack individual character.

This assessment of Whitman's social views, in light of the most
recent histories of Victorian culture, is unfair, because it judges
his thought by twentieth-century standards and does not recognize
the historical context in which the female characters appear. A
number of recent critics have affirmed Whitman's good intentions
in the area of women's rights and have even seen him as an early
champion of feminism.[3] In fact, he shared the views of many of the

---

[1] "Whitman," *Nation and Athenaeum,* 29 (July 23, 1921), 616–18.
[2] Quoted in Gay Wilson Allen, *The Solitary Singer* (New York: Macmillan, 1955), p. 370.
[3] See, for example, Lottie L. Guttrey, "Walt Whitman and the Woman Reader,"
Walt Whitman Review, 22 (1976), 102–10; Kay F. Reinartz, "Walt Whitman and

social radicals of his day, in particular the notion that the female is superior to the male because of her maternal capacity. Today feminists reject this notion as quaint, patronizing, and even repressive, but in the nineteenth century the feminist movement was young, and its critique of society had not been refined. Whitman thus became tangled in a confusion that was as much cultural as it was personal, and the badness of his poetry dealing with motherhood may be traced to this confusion. Before examining the poetry itself, I think it necessary to touch on his notion of female superiority as presented in his prose writings and place it into the context of nineteenth-century American social thought.

In *Democratic Vistas,* Whitman gives particular attention to women and the fictional models available to them. The transcendental "pedestalism" with which sentimentalists coaxed women into submission has no place in the American literature he calls for; he rejects the middle-class ideal of the doll-like, fragile, yet morally superior female.

I say a new founded literature . . . underlying life, religious, consistent with science, handling the elements and forces with competent power, teaching and training men—and, as perhaps the most precious of its results, achieving the entire redemption of woman out of these incredible holds and webs of silliness, millinery, and every kind of dyspeptic depletion—and thus insuring to the States a strong and sweet Female Race, a race of perfect Mothers—is what is needed.[4]

"Dyspeptic depletion" and "webs of silliness" suggest that he recognized the signs of neurasthenia, the condition of "nerves" which came to be a mark of class, education, or occupation for the nineteenth-century woman.[5] In *Specimen Days,* when Whitman complains that the women he saw on his trip to the West were " 'intellectual' and fashionable, but dyspeptic-looking and generally doll-like," his criticism is again directed toward the fashionably neurasthenic woman. He was, however, careful to put "intellectual" in quotation marks. His admiration of George Sand, Frances Wright, and Mar-

Feminism," *Walt Whitman Review,* 19 (1973), 127–37; Harold Aspiz, *Walt Whitman and the Body Beautiful* (Urbana: Univ. of Illinois Press, 1980), chap. 7.

[4] *Prose Writings of Walt Whitman,* ed. Floyd Stovall (New York: New York Univ. Press, 1964), II, 372.

[5] See John S. Haller and Robin M. Haller, *The Physician and Sexuality in Victorian America* (New York: Norton, 1974), pp. 3–43.

garet Fuller demonstrates his acceptance of genuine intellectuality in women. And the full context of his remarks in *Specimen Days* proves that his criticism is not sexist but class-oriented: "The ladies . . . are all fashionably drest, and have the look of 'gentility' in face, manner and action but they do *not* have, either in physique or the mentality appropriate to them, any high native originality of spirit or body, (as the men certainly have, appropriate to them)."[6]

In these prose works Whitman is hardly conservative; he openly criticizes the middle-class establishment. And against this background we should read his encouraging words to women in *Democratic Vistas:* "sane athletic maternity, [is] their crowning attribute, and one ever making the woman, in loftiest spheres, superior to the man." The phrase "in loftiest spheres" refers to the ideal state, but the circumlocution is perhaps too subtle. Clearly enough it expresses Whitman's longing for the ideal and his dissatisfaction with the actual state of womanhood and maternity. Along with this social criticism—which is all the more discreet for being contained in a footnote—Whitman offers some suggestions for improving the condition of motherhood:

I have sometimes thought, indeed, that the sole avenue and means of a reconstructed sociology depended, primarily, on a new birth, elevation, expansion, invigoration of woman, affording, for races to come, (as the conditions which antedate birth are indispensable,) a perfect motherhood.[7]

To the transcendental "elevation" of woman, his program thus added "expansion" and "invigoration"—important romantic and even radical values. Woman's range should be expanded beyond conventional limits; female emancipation was necessary for the realization of "sane athletic maternity"; good motherhood should be the foundation of a new society.

The ideas of Whitman's political prose, when compared to those of his contemporaries, appear quite radical. Much of the rhetoric of the period, though it might seem deferential to mothers, was in fact a sugar coating for an unpleasant reality. Susan Conrad has said, "As female opportunities for wide social action shrank, the rhetoric of domesticity expanded, as if in compensation, to enhance the important of the 'woman's sphere.' " "Home Economics" was

[6] *Prose Writings,* I, 225–26.
[7] *Prose Writings,* II, 372n.

created in order to increase the appeal of domestic labor.[8] The woman was said to be superior in morals or religiosity—the virtues perfectly suited for child-raising—but inferior physically and intellectually. The world outside the home was not "safe" for the fragile creature "inferior to man yet somehow akin to angels."[9] Anyone who unreservedly advocated the doctrine of female superiority met with an unenthusiastic or even hostile reaction; such was the case, for instance, with Eliza Woodson Farnham's *Woman and Her Era,* which even feminists were reluctant to accept.[10]

And yet in the sentimental literature of the day, especially the periodical literature written by women or for a female audience, one very often finds, coordinate with the eloquent defenses of submissive virtues, praise of motherhood broad enough to suggest female superiority. Whitman had more in common with sentimental authors than many critics have admitted. One shared trait was the near-satiric tone (unusual for Whitman the poet) employed discreetly but with purpose in his prose critiques of social life. In a magazine as conservative as *Godey's Lady's Book,* there appeared social criticism similar in tone and content to Whitman's. Usually it took the form of subtle but biting reminders that the contributors and editors were not without discontent.[11] In magazines like *The Ladies' Companion* and *The Ladies' Pearl,* there were the same questionings and rumblings as found in *Godey's,* signifying an awareness of new directions in social thought and an interest in women's education, legal defenses against cruel husbands, and men's responsibility in marriage.[12] Even the conventional "Jennie June" (Jane Cunningham Croly) betrays an occasional bitterness. Speaking of old maids who must care for the children of others in lieu of having their own, she sardonically remarks, "Such a mission . . . the old maid may prefer to selling herself body and soul for a home and the title of 'Mrs.' "[13]

[8] *Perish the Thought: Intellectual Women in Romantic America* (New York: Oxford Univ. Press, 1976), p. 100.

[9] The phrase is Haller and Haller's; see *The Physician and Sexuality,* pp. 47–48.

[10] Sidney Ditzion, *Marriage, Morals, and Sex in America* (New York: Octagon, 1969), p. 240.

[11] See Ann Douglas, *The Feminization of American Culture* (New York: Knopf, 1977), p. 73.

[12] Ditzion, p. 123.

[13] *Jennie Juneiana: Talks on Women's Topics* (Boston: Lee and Shepherd, 1864), pp. 123–24.

But the rhetoric of these discontented sentimentalists was doomed to failure. In *The Feminization of American Culture,* Ann Douglas identifies the cause of this failure as the tendency of authors like Sarah Hale to pursue "feminist goals by largely anti-feminist means." Since the reformers' arguments "were contained within traditional, if strategically rephrased, notions of the feminine role," much of the force was allowed to dissipate, and the precise implications of the reformers were not always understood.[14] If Charles Eldridge mistook Whitman's "radical" view of motherhood for a more conservative position, Whitman's own rhetoric must be partly blamed. The occasional lapse into conventional diction, especially evident in *Democratic Vistas,* often clouds the meaning of passages; and, one imagines, Whitman's conversation was similarly imprecise. The sudden insertion of the words "lofty spheres," for example, into a bland statement of social principles would have called up associations of domestic rhetoric—the "woman's sphere," her "lofty moral nature"— a rhetoric which would have threatened the success of his design to present a progressive point of view.

Whitman was not the only unconventional thinker who failed to recognize the ineffectiveness of the conventional rhetoric. Almost every sex radical in the gilded age worshipped motherhood, even though few of them were otherwise noticeably sentimental. The early pre-Galtonian eugenicists, "free lovers" like Stephen Pearl Andrews and John Humphrey Noyes, maintained with Whitman that women are superior to men because of their maternal function. The work of Havelock Ellis, moreover, is evidence that the motherhood mystique was still well established at the turn of the century, although certain American feminists and sex reformers such as Lillie D. White had begun to reject it in favor of a more rational approach.[15] But early eugenic thought, to which most late nineteenth-century sex reformers and social purity advocates subscribed, "had always contained the assumption that reproduction was not just a function but the purpose, in some teleological sense, of a woman's

---

[14] Douglas, *Feminization*, p. 45.

[15] On Ellis, see Paul Robinson, *The Modernization of Sex* (New York: Harper and Row, 1976), pp. 36–37; on White, see Hal D. Sears, *The Sex Radicals: Free Love in High Victorian Culture* (Lawrence: Regents Press of Kansas, 1977), pp. 245–48.

life."[16] The eugenic impulse of the romantics ironically aligned them with their opposition, the middle-class patriarchy.

Whitman's interest in eugenics—often interpreted as an interest in evolution—most likely derives from the hereditarian doctrines of the phrenologist Orson Fowler. As John Humphrey Noyes, famous for his experiments in "stirpiculture" (controlled human breeding), suggested in 1870: "Phrenologists, popular physiologists and reformers of various kinds have long been carrying over the laws of Darwin into the public conscience. . . ."[17] Clearly Whitman shared in that public conscience; among the Whitman papers in the Harned Collection at the Library of Congress is an old binding for a copy of Orson Fowler's *Hereditary Descent: Its Laws and Facts Applied to Human Improvement,* which complains that "the most important [science] of all, Parentage, and the means of thereby improving the race, remains enshrouded in comparative darkness. How long shall this species of ignorance be tolerated, and even fostered?"[18] A similar attitude also takes the form of a question or challenge in *Democratic Vistas*: "Will the time hasten when fatherhood and motherhood shall become a science—and the noblest science?"[19] And in the original (1856) version of "A Woman Waits for Me" (first titled "Poem of Procreation"), the narrator/hero declares to his ideal woman: "O I will fetch bully breeds of children yet!"[20] Besides being aesthetically offensive (mainly because of the ridiculous pun on "bully"), the diction of this line might have been morally offensive to Whitman's audience because it suggested the "breeding" experiments which free lovers like Noyes carried out in hopes of improving the race. Whitman may have dropped the line either for artistic reasons or because he did not wish to become associated with the likes of Noyes. Even in its latest version the poem retains its eugenicist theme, now portrayed in imagery drawn from horticulture or agriculture rather than from stirpiculture.

> Through you I drain the pent-up rivers of myself,
> In you I wrap a thousand onward years,

[16] Linda Gordon, *Woman's Body, Woman's Right: Birth Control in America* (New York: Penguin, 1977), p. 134.

[17] "Scientific Propagation," *Modern Thinker*, 1 (1870), 99.

[18] *Hereditary Descent* (New York: Fowlers and Wells, 1853), p. 5.

[19] *Prose Writings*, II, 397.

[20] *Leaves of Grass*, Norton Critical Edition, p. 101n. Further references to Whitman's poems are to this edition (LG) by page number.

On you I graft the grafts of the best-beloved
of me and America,
The drops I distil upon you shall grow fierce
and athletic girls, new artists, musicians,
and singers . . .
I shall demand perfect men and women out of
my love-spendings,
I shall expect them to interpenetrate with others,
as I and you interpenetrate now . . .
I shall look for loving crops from the birth,
life, death, immortality, I plant so lovingly
now. (LG, p. 103)

Here and in many other passages Whitman's debt to Fowler is clear. In *Hereditary Descent* Fowler had written: "We investigate and apply . . . [parentage's] principles to the improvement of stock, yet its far higher application to the improvement of humanity is almost totally neglected."[21] Like many early eugenicists, he believed that parentage involved a grave responsibility, because he thought that moral as well as physical traits were inherited. The choice of a companion—"the most important business of life"—should be based on two factors: the prospective spouse's ancestry and his or her moral and physical condition. For example, he wrote: "in order that descendents may inherit the longevity of their ancestors, two things are indispensable—that none of these ancestors have either married weakly companions, or broken their health by repeated abuses before the birth of any such descendents, and that the descendents themselves have also so far obeyed the physical laws as to have preserved their own health unimpaired. . . ."[22] As Edward H. Dixon, a physician known to both Fowler and Whitman, put it, the soul or moral nature of the parent is "daguerreotyped upon the brain and nervous system of his offspring."[23]

Fowler was devoted to the motherhood mystique and, like Whitman, used highly idealized terms when he wrote of mothers. His book *Creative and Sexual Science* calls the mother "the queen among

---

[21] P. 5.

[22] Ibid, pp. 66 and 92.

[23] *The Organic Law of the Sexes: Positive and Negative Electricity and the Abnormal Conditions that Impair Vitality* (New York: Redfield, 1861), p. 4.

women, the pattern female as such."[24] He also claimed that children
develop their ability to love sexually through their experiences of
parental love: "parentage begets all those other tender ties ["connubial love," "parental endearment," and so on], and thereby contributes incalculably to human virtue and enjoyment in every department of life. . . ."[25] The same argument reappears in an even more
direct form in an unsigned article published in the *American
Phrenological Journal*. The author, probably Fowler, suggests that
"the sex drive . . . commences . . . even in childhood though in a
limited degree till puberty. Its first work is to attach boys to their
mothers, and fathers to their daughters."[26] This passage, most interesting because the initiatory capacity for sexual excitement is allotted
only to the males (fathers and boys), contains in a crude form the
ideas Freud would refine and systemize. Whitman's 1856 poem "On
the Beach at Night Alone" also suggests that the mother's love is
prerequisite to love in all its forms, including sexual love. The
speaker is not really "alone," for there with him is the sea, the
mother of all life: "the old mother sways her to and fro singing her
husky song" (LG, p. 260). In lines omitted from the 1867 edition of
Leaves of Grass and afterward, the meditation runs:

> I am not uneasy but I am to be beloved by young
>   and old men, and to love them the same,
> I suppose the pink nipples of the breasts of
>   women with whom I shall sleep will touch the
>   side of my face the same,
> But this is a nipple of a breast of my mother,
>   always near and always divine to me, her
>   true child and son, whatever comes.   (LG, p. 632)[27]

The mother is glorified in not only the spiritual realm but the
physical realm as well. She holds the key to sex, life, love, and death;
through her comes the knowledge that "a vast similitude interlocks
all" (LG, p. 261).

The intense devotion to motherhood in Whitman and Fowler

---

[24] (1870; rpt. Chicago: Follett, 1971), p. 61.

[25] Fowler, *Hereditary Descent,* p. 17.

[26] "Amativeness I," 10 (1848), 242.

[27] See Edwin Haviland Miller, *Walt Whitman's Poetry: A Psychological Journey* (New
York: New York Univ. Press, 1968), pp. 59–60.

may even have been their primary motive for advocating a recognition of female sexuality—not a popular stance in Victorian times—and sexual reform in general. A common belief in nineteenth-century medical folklore was that in order to conceive healthy offspring or even to conceive at all, a woman must enjoy sexual relations and achieve orgasm.[28] Whitman and Fowler might have based their encouragement of female sexuality on this belief. In "A Woman Waits for Me," Whitman's hero proclaims: "Without shame the man I like knows and avows the deliciousness of his sex/Without shame the woman I like knows and avows hers." He will be the "robust husband" of "those women that are warm-blooded and sufficient for me" and therefore "worthy of me" (LG, p. 102).

But when Whitman tried to sexualize the mother figure, he ran into severe difficulties. In "On the Beach at Night Alone" sexuality and motherhood exist comfortably together because the mother's role is that of teacher rather than temptress or lover; all sexual longing is located in the child at the breast. But in other poems, when Whitman tries to unite the volatile sexual female and the great mother, the two figures collide rather than meld.

Close readers of "A Woman Waits for Me" will notice that a double standard affects the portrayal of an ideal sexual couple. Though the poet claims that his waiting women are "not one jot less" than the forceful first-person hero, and though they know and avow the "deliciousness" of their sex, the hero's own aggressiveness and his assurance that "I do not hurt you any more than is necessary for you" imply a degree of reluctance on the part of the women. This is at odds with his stated intention to "dismiss myself from impassive women" and to "go stay . . . with those women that are warm-blooded and sufficient for me" (LG, p. 102).[29] Illuminating here are the comments made by Elizabeth Cady Stanton in an 1883 diary entry on "A Woman Waits for Me": "He speaks as if the female must be forced to the creative act, apparently ignorant of

[28] See Carl M. Degler, "What Ought to Be and What Was: Woman's Sexuality in the Nineteenth Century," *American Historical Review*, 79 (1974), 1475.

[29] Edwin H. Miller reads "A Woman Waits for Me" as a "masturbatory rape dream" involving a "fixation upon power." See *Walt Whitman's Poetry*, p. 137. Harold Aspiz sees the poem an "arrogant male chauvinism." See "The 'Body Electric': Science, Sex, and Metaphor," *Walt Whitman Review*, 24 (1978), 140. See also *Walt Whitman and the Body Beautiful*, pp. 196–98 and 220–21, in which Aspiz attempts, with little success, to reconcile this arrogant tone with the themes of female liberation and human perfection.

the fact that a healthy woman has as much passion as a man, that she needs nothing stronger than the law of attraction to draw her to the male."[30] Even the poem's syntax bespeaks this uncertainty. In line 9 the man "knows and avows *the deliciousness of his sex*," while in line ten the woman "knows and avows *hers*" (my italics). Though it is clear that by "hers" Whitman means "the deliciousness of her sex," his hesitancy to sexualize the future mother is quietly evident in this syntactical castration.

But the inconsistencies of "A Woman Waits for Me" are minor compared to those of "I Sing the Body Electric," which, though it contains some of the poet's best lines, is sadly uneven as a whole. Section 5 encourages women to enjoy their sexuality: "Be not ashamed women, your privilege encloses the rest, and is the exit of the rest,/ You are the gates of the body, and you are the gates of the soul." These lines are part of Whitman's portrayal of the sexualized ideal, which begins:

> This is the female form,
> A divine nimbus exhales from it from head to foot,
> It attracts with fierce undeniable attraction,
> I am drawn by its breath as if I were no more than
>   a helpless vapor, all falls aside but myself
>   and it,
> Books, art, religion, time, the visible and solid
>   earth, and what was expected of heaven or fear'd
>   of hell, are now consumed,
> Mad filaments, ungovernable shoots play out of it,
>   the response likewise ungovernable. . . . (LG, p. 96)

The female body with its transcendent power is not specified as the mother's—at least not right away. The lines which follow, describing sexual union metaphorically as the blending of night and day at dawn, suggest a concern more materialistic than that of the lines celebrating the "divine nimbus" of the female, though the theme of uncontrollable mystic ecstasy continues:

> Hair, bosom, hips, bend of legs, negligent falling
>   hands all diffused, mine too diffused,
> Ebb stung by the flow and flow stung by the ebb,

---

[30] Quoted in Gordon, *Woman's Body, Woman's Right*, pp. 98–99.

> love-flesh swelling and deliciously aching,
> Limitless limpid jets of love hot and enormous,
>   quivering jelly of love, white-blow and
>   delirious juice,
> Bridegroom night of love working surely and softly
>   into the prostrate dawn,
> Undulating into the willing and yielding day,
> Lost in the cleave of the clasping and sweet-flesh'd
>   day. (LG, p. 96)

In the lines that follow, the two somewhat contradictory views of the sexual female—the mystic and the erotic one—are reconciled: "This the nucleus—after the child is born of woman, man is born of woman,/This the bath of birth, this the merge of small and large, and the outlet again" (LG, p. 97). Physical sexuality is thus associated with the production of personalities, first as mere individuals (the child is born of woman) and then as mature personalities who through sexual experience rise to a new awareness (man is born of woman). The major theme of the poem is therefore reflected—the body and soul are one, and the action of one is dependent on and largely indistinguishable from the other.

Whitman's reconciliation of the mystical female and the erotic female is not, however, altogether satisfactory, as the following lines demonstrate:

> The female contains all qualities and tempers them,
> She is in her place and moves with perfect balance,
> She is all things duly veil'd, she is both passive
>   and active,
> She is to conceive daughters as well as sons, and
>   sons as well as daughters. (LG, p. 97)

The yoking of opposites, particularly "passive and active," results in meaninglessness. Some of the terms—"tempers," "in her place," and "duly veil'd"—recall the rhetoric of sentimentalism. The lines closing Section 5 are so vague that D.H. Lawrence could take them as evidence that Whitman valued submissiveness as a feminine virtue:

> As I see my soul reflected in Nature,
> As I see through a mist, One with inexpressible
>   completeness, sanity, beauty,

> See the bent head and arms folded over the breast,
>   the Female I see.   (LG, p. 97)

Other poems indicate that Whitman did not think that woman
exists merely for man's enjoyment and for the propagation of man's
race. On the contrary, he advocated the full development of the
female personality for its own sake. But he was trapped by his own
rhetoric. His intention was to use the motherhood mystique as a
means of winning favor for his feminist notions. His treatment of
prostitution in Section 8 of "I Sing the Body Electric," for example,
follows the logic that it is wrong to put the female's body on auction
not only because this involves the selling of a soul (the body is the
soul), but also because even the prostitute is a potential mother—
"the teeming mother of mothers" (LG, p. 99). Largely because of
this rhetorical stance, his portrait of woman as a social ideal is contradictory and confusing.

Whitman's difficulty is decidedly Victorian. The mother as a
physical being is unreal to him, and the only way he can successfully and consistently portray her is as the hopelessly untouchable,
mysterious ideal. In a short *Drum-Taps* poem, the speaker stands
dumbfounded before the mystery of madonna and child:

> I see the sleeping babe nestling the breast of its mother,
> The sleeping mother and babe—hush'd, I study them
>   long and long.   (LG, p. 275)

A Freudian, of course, would turn to Whitman's biography for
an explanation of this psychology and would find a wealth of
material indicating a close, perhaps abnormally close, relationship
with his own mother. But the culture from which he sprang en-
couraged a mystified and glorified mother-son bond. Mesmerism,
animal magnetism, spiritual marriage, Christian mysticism—all were
preoccupations of Victorian culture, and the motherhood mystique
fused with other "spiritual" interests and inspired bizarre literary
outbursts. "I wanted to be a Christian," said Henry Ward Beecher
of his youthful religious experiences; "I went about longing for God
as a lamb bleating longs for its mother's udder." The mother-son
relationship took on an intensity bordering on the sexual in the
novels of the day and in the bereavement literature. In an 1852
memorial narrative, a young boy about to die piteously tells his

mother that he wishes "we could die with our arms around each other's neck."[31]

In this tradition Whitman memoralized his own mother in a poem first published in 1881, about eight years after her death and at a time when he feared he was approaching death:

> As at thy portals also death,
> Entering thy sovereign, dim, illimitable grounds,
> To memories of my mother, to the divine blending,
>   maternity,
> To her, buried and gone, yet buried not, gone not
>   from me,
> (I see again the calm benignant face fresh and
>   beautiful still,
> I sit by the form in the coffin,
> I kiss and kiss convulsively again the sweet old lips,
>   the cheeks, the closed eyes in the coffin;)
> To her, the ideal woman, practical, spiritual, of all
>   of earth, life, love, to me the best,
> I grave a monumental line, before I go, amid these
>   songs,
>   And set a tombstone here.   (LG, p. 497)

Though it appears that Whitman's emotions so overcame him that he could not achieve aesthetic distance, current information about nineteenth-century sentimentalism suggests that his treatment of motherhood was quite the norm. In "As at Thy Portals Also Death," he has chosen to speak in two distinct "voices," each of which complements yet serves as a point of comparison for the other, and each of which is more or less conventional. The first voice, that of the first four and last three lines, speaks the public idealized language of tombstones and funeral orations. The second, that of the three lines within parentheses, whispers in the language of sentimentalism, with its mystic relation between mother and son. The mother in Victorian culture was the high priestess of the religion of sentimentalism. In the words of Jennie June, "A woman is not a woman until she has been baptized in her love and devotion to home and

---

[31] Quoted in Douglas, *Feminization*, pp. 133 and 205.

children." By becoming a mother the woman experiences "a glimpse of divinity."[32]

Whitman's most important use of the motherhood mystique is found in "Out of the Cradle Endlessly Rocking." Here the poet suggests that the complete human being, especially the artist, must transcend himself during his development and must experience "otherness." Largeness of self is only possible through self-abnegation; fullness of life depends on knowledge of death. By vicariously experiencing the pain of a mockingbird singing for its lost mate, the narrator, the boy-poet, steps outside himself and outside the safety of his previous experience. The bird, the narrator's "dear brother," sings of love and death, each of which involves self-denial and is necessary for the young poet to understand if he is to become the "chanter of pains and joys, uniter of here and hereafter" (LG, p. 247). The poet of selfhood has paradoxically drawn self-denial into his song. Considering the context of nineteenth-century sentimentalism, it is not surprising that Whitman associates the theme of self-denial with the mother figure, for she represents the ideal of selflessness. The child is part of the mother's self until birth, when he achieves partial selfhood. The child attains full selfhood, it would seem, when he is able to care for his own needs. But "Out of the Cradle" suggests that independent selfhood is actually impossible. In the poem the mother is represented as the great ocean beside which the child-poet hears the bird sing. The ocean is described as "some old crone rocking the cradle, swathed in sweet garments" (LG, p. 253). Even while the bird introduces the child to the pains of love and death, the old mother hisses and churns behind him. He is free to retreat to her at any moment, and in fact he does turn to the sea for the answers to the questions forced on him by his experience with the bird. It is the sea, the mother, who

> Whisper'd me through the night, and very plainly
>   before daybreak,
> Lisp'd to me the low and delicious word death,
> And again death, death, death, death
> Hissing melodious, neither like the bird nor like
>   my arous'd child's heart,

[32] Croly, *Jennie Juneiana*, pp. 31–32.

But edging near as privately for me rustling at my feet,
Creeping thence steadily up to my ears and laving
    me softly all over,
Death, death, death, death, death.   (LG, pp. 252–53)

Richard Chase has remarked that Whitman was "titillated by death"
and that, in "Out of the Cradle" and other poems, "he forms a
sentimental attachment to it."[33] Whitman's devotion to motherhood
and his association of the mother with the selflessness of love and
death seem to lend support to Chase's charge. As in the most
blatantly sentimental literature of his day, love and death are
strangely confounded in Whitman's poetry, and the relation of
mother and son is more powerfully and emotionally portrayed than
are those of mother and father or son and (female) lover. And yet
quite obviously "Out of the Cradle" is one of the great poems of
our literature, whereas most nineteenth-century sentimental literature is, at best, interesting. Ann Douglas characterizes sentimentalism
as mere "self-absorption, a commercialization of the inner self" and
distinguishes it from romanticism, "a desperate effort to find in
private resources an antidote and an alternative to the forces of
modernizing society."[34] Since intense heterosexual love was a forbidden subject for most Victorians, domestic emotions were mon-
strously exaggerated, and death was the focal point for these
intensified feelings. In such treatments of death, the authors' intentions are difficult to discover; perhaps they were trying to deal with
death in a serious philosophical way, but more likely they were
merely titillating an audience (or themselves) or playing an emotional game to release frustrations. Though "Out of the Cradle"
exhibits many of the conventions, it is not a sentimental poem, but
a serious attempt to give in the form of spiritual autobiography an
account of the poet's first experience of cosmic wholeness—hardly
a subject treated very often in *The Ladies' Pearl*.

The theme of motherhood as it is treated in Whitman's poems,
whether good or bad, is decidedly Victorian. Many literary historians
think of Whitman as the father of modern poetry, and certainly he
deserves the honor if nothing but his poetic technique is considered.

[33] " 'Out of the Cradle' as a Romance," in *The Presence of Walt Whitman*, ed.
R. W. B. Lewis (New York: Columbia Univ. Press, 1962), p. 68.
[34] Douglas, *Feminization*, p. 255.

But few modern poets could be comfortable with Whitman's loose and often entangled weave of love and sex and death and motherhood, with his furious knotting and unknotting of the themes, or with his inability to break entirely free from the characterizations of the ideal mother as his culture depicted her.

The Last Eleven Poems in the 1855
Leaves of Grass
Ivan Marki

"SONG OF MYSELF," as we all know, has a way of leaving its readers exhausted; it is small wonder, therefore, that the eleven
poems that follow it in the first edition of *Leaves of Grass* have received relatively little critical attention, and that little has usually
been spent on the individual poems in themselves.[1] Their function
in the volume as a whole, the order in which they are introduced, or
their relationship to one another as well as to the splendid pieces that
precede them are rarely discussed. Bliss Perry assumed that these
poems were mostly passages excised from "Song of Myself," and he
treated them accordingly; his assumption was taken up by Frederik
Schyberg, who called them simply "cuttings," and most critics have
gratefully followed their lead.[2] Yet, difficult as it is to speak in the
same breath of, say, "Song of the Answered" or "I Sing the Body
Electric" and what Edwin H. Miller has called "the first great poem
in American literature,"[3] it is even more difficult to imagine the
volume without them, nor is it just long familiarity that makes them
appear indispensable to the book. The study of the formal structure
constituted by these "other" poems indicates that without them the
first edition would be incomplete, because its story would be unfinished and its drama unresolved.[4]

---

[1] Throughout this essay, Whitman's poems are identified by the title they bear in *Leaves
of Grass: The Comprehensive Reader's Edition* [*CRE*], eds. S. Bradley and H. W. Blodgett
(New York: New York Univ. Press, 1965); the text, however, is that of the first edition,
and quotations are identified by line numbers in *Walt Whitman's Leaves of Grass: His
Original Edition*, ed. M. Cowley (1959; rpt. New York: Penguin, 1976). Whitman's idio-
syncratic punctuation of pauses and ellipses has been retained in the quotations; ellipses not
in the original are enclosed in square brackets.

[2] *Walt Whitman*, trans. E. A. Allen (New York: Columbia Univ. Press, 1951), p. 123.

[3] *Walt Whitman's Poetry: A Psychological Journey* (Boston: Houghton Mifflin, 1968),
p. 85.

[4] Stephen A. Black comes to a similar conclusion at the end of an argument based on
psychological observations. "Song of Myself," he argues, only begins the "definable psycho-

To be sure, by the time "A Song for Occupations" begins most moments of highest intensity have passed in both story and drama.[5] The rambling, eccentric, and fascinating "Preface" has introduced the person whose physical outlines have furnished the book its frontispiece. His "processes of consciousness," in which "elemental impulses of self-assertion" are "invariably followed by compulsive gestures of self-denial," reveal a tension which not only makes him capable of becoming the paragon he calls "the greatest poet" but quite simply forces him to attempt the transformation. This transformation is the subject of "Song of Myself." We discover in it that the speaker-protagonist's self-assertion and self-denial are rhetorical manifestations of a vicious circle of desire (associated with images of the soul, sexual gratification, the Mother, warmth) and guilt (associated with images of the grass, suffering and dying, the Father, cold), and this vicious circle turns his relationship to the Other into abject terror of Nothingness, of death. He can control this tension only by adopting a pose of all that he is not and then developing it into an identity. His "apparently spontaneous, improvised meditations . . . provide, in fact, an inventory of the moment in which he had to become the hero he had not been, to resist the threat of destruction he perceived in the grass because he had to seek to stay alive through joy with his soul. . . . The poem, [therefore,] is the ceremony of verbal gestures which perpetuates . . . the mythic instant when the 'I' utters forth himself as 'the greatest poet' with a primal, indeterminate and 'untranslatable' 'yawp' sounded over the 'fathomless' darkness of his fears and anxieties." Though at the end he has attained a tremendous, splendid victory, it is, for all that, only a qualified one. The forces that menaced him have been only contained, not defeated. As "A Song for Occupations" opens, the issue between the Other and the "I" is still unresolved. He knows it, and we know it. "This is unfinished business with me . . . how is it with you?" (l. 4) he begins, and we must, indeed, agree with him.

logical movement" that the other poems are needed to complete. Through this movement "Whitman sought to identify himself as a bard whose poems might be exchanged with external objects in return for gratification of basic needs." He thus erected a finally efficient "line of defense" against the "intolerable anxiety" that arose from his "inability to satisfy his needs through ordinary 'adult' relations with external objects." *Whitman's Journeys into Chaos: A Psychoanalytic Study of the Poetic Process* (Princeton: Princeton Univ. Press, 1975), pp. 137–38.

[5] The following outline recapitulates some of my major conclusions in *The Trial of the Poet: An Interpretation of the First Edition of* Leaves of Grass (New York: Columbia Univ. Press, 1976), especially pp. 149, 205, and 227.

Apart from our sense that the statement begun in the Preface—indeed, with the frontispiece—has not been concluded, the first and certainly most obvious clue to the continuity between "Song of Myself" and the other poems is typographical. The title "Leaves of Grass," which introduced "Song of Myself," heads now in the same typeface "A Song for Occupations" as well as the next four poems: "To Think of Time," "The Sleepers," "I Sing the Body Electric," and "Faces." Not only does this arrangement identify these pieces as distinct utterances, it also groups them together and distinguishes them from the last six poems, which bear no titles. "Song of the Answerer," "Europe: The 72nd and 73rd Years of These States," "A Boston Ballad," "There Was a Child Went Forth," "Who Learns My Lesson Complete," and "Great Are the Myths" are separated from one another only by a bold-face initial and by a horizontal double line running from margin to margin whenever the preceding poem does not conclude at the bottom of the page. (Only "Europe" and "There Was a Child" do.) Whitman, of course, looked at the printed page with the professional eyes of the editor and printer, and his preoccupation with the layout of his books is a very familiar story; we should also recall that never again was he to have the degree of control he had in 1855 over the visual design of his volume. The manipulation of the title, therefore, can hardly be casual; it invites us to consider the poems divided into the two groups it has established.

This division, moreover, is not likely to be based on the length of the poems. Although even the longest in the untitled group of six, "Great Are the Myths," with its 67 lines, is shorter than "Faces," which is, with its 85 lines, the shortest among the five titled poems, the disparities in length among the titled poems are much greater: the 204 lines of "The Sleepers" make it more than twice as long as "Faces" and nearly twice as long as "I Sing the Body Electric," which has 119 lines. Thus, beyond alerting us to the fact itself of this structural division, the "visual prosody," of course, cannot give us much help. To discover by what principles of organization the division was established and the order determined for the poems in each group, we must examine the form of the poems themselves. Two qualities seem distinctive about it: they all have closed structures, and they are all dominated by catalogues.

The first item seems both the most conspicuous and the least helpful: the structure of each of the eleven "other" poems appears as clear-cut, conventional, and closed as the structure of "Song of Myself" was obscure, unconventional, and open. Either in the rhetorical or in the narrative sense, they all have a beginning, a middle, and an end. No fewer than five of them follow a question-and-answer pattern, which sometimes frames—as in "To Think of Time" or "I Sing the Body Electric"—and always neatly concludes the poem, even when the answer is itself a rhetorical question, as in "Song of the Answerer," or not very clear, as in "A Song for Occupations" or "Who Learns My Lesson Complete?" "A Boston Ballad" and the wretched "Europe" are narratives, and so is "The Sleepers," whatever else it may be besides: it tells the story of a dream or a trance, from falling asleep to waking up. "Faces," "There Was a Child," and "Great Are the Myths" all play variations on a theme. They are the freest, most loosely structured among the "other" poems, yet, for all their freedom, in at least two of them the vestiges of a narrative are also present: the tone of "There Was a Child" is that of a fairy tale— ironically appropriate to the poem—and "Faces" hints at a story of homecoming as it finds its way through "sauntering the pavement" (l. 1) back to "the justified mother of men" (l. 85). Closed structures obviously reinforce the impression of independent pieces and tend to confirm the view that we are dealing with a miscellany of "cuttings" from the major statement, not with an organized sequence; therefore, they cannot answer our questions about the organization of the poems and their function in the volume.

The catalogues will help us to work our way out of the difficult pass. Examples of the paratactic series, which Whitman developed into possibly the most distinctive formal convention of his verse, first appear in the volume in the Preface and, of course, abound in "Song of Myself," but there is a wealth of catalogues in the eleven "other" poems as well. The "variations on a theme" are, of course, catalogues in themselves, but long catalogue-passages run through the entire sequence, not excepting the two apprentice pieces. Their presence is so obvious that it needs no elaboration.

Catalogues generate a mode of vision which can and does persist even after the words themselves have ceased.[6] This serial momentum,

---

[6] Cf. *The Trial of the Poet*, pp. 35, 43–44. Other readers have, of course, come to similar conclusions, e.g., Lawrence Buell, "Transcendental Catalogue Rhetoric: Vision Versus

if one may call it that, is often strong enough to suppress or weaken the effect of virtually all other devices of organization. If it does not force the reader, it nevertheless allows him to move past barriers such as titles or apparently closed structures, and thus, in the present case, it enables us to consider each of our two groups of poems as coherent not only typographically but poetically as well.

Naturally, to find transcendental catalogues in closed structures seems, if not absurd, at least paradoxical.[7] The paradox is resolved, however, as we recognize whereas the catalogues in the earlier portions of the volume are relentlessly paratactic, in the catalogues of the eleven "other" poems parataxis is, one might say, severely compromised, though not entirely destroyed. First, these catalogues all have a coda, a formal conclusion. For instance: "These become part of the child who went forth every day, and who now goes and will always go forth every day,/ And these become of him or her that peruses them now" ("There Was a Child," ll. 31–32), or, "When the psalm sings instead of the singer,/ When the script preaches instead of the preacher,/ . . . When a university course convinces like a slumbering woman and child convince,/ . . . I intend to reach them my hand and make as much of them as I do of men and women" ("Occupations," ll. 171–72, 175, 178). Unlike these, the most important catalogues in the first version of "Song of Myself" draw no conclusion; they just fall silent instead and allow the paratactic impulse to do its work.

As they have beginnings and ends, the later catalogues have middles, too: the rhetorical or emotional burden of their statement falls invariably in the center, sometimes with an almost mathematical precision. In "Faces," for example, the middle of the poem-catalogue consists of these lines:

> I saw the face of the most smeared and slobbering idiot they
>   had at the asylum,
> And I knew for my consolation what they knew not;
> I knew of the agents that emptied and broke my brother,
> The same wait to clear the rubbish from the fallen tenement;
> And I shall look again in a score or two of ages,

Form," *American Literature*, 40 (November 1968) 325–39, or John B. Mason, "Walt Whitman's Catalogues: Rhetorical Means for Two Journeys in 'Song of Myself,'" *American Literature*, 45 (March 1973) 34–49.

    [7] Cf. Buell, p. 339.

And I shall meet the real landlord perfect and unharmed,
    every inch as good as myself.   ("Faces," ll. 41–46)

This was the passage that, according to Whitman himself, generated the entire poem, which, we may recall, concludes by discovering the mother: the reference to "my brother," unfortunate "offspring taken soon out of [his mother's] lap" ("Song of Myself," l. 105), occurs in the forty-third of the poem's eighty-five lines.[8] Similarly, in "The Sleepers," in which the narrative consists of a loose catalogue of episodes, the climactic lines of parricidal rage are heard only a little more than halfway through the poem:

Now Lucifer was not dead. . . . or if he was I am his sorrowful
    terrible heir;
I have been wronged. . . . I am oppressed. . . . I hate him that
    oppresses me,
I will either destroy him, or he shall release me.
Damn him! how he does defile me,
How he informs against my brother and sister and takes pay
    for their blood,
How he laughs when I look down the bend after the steamboat
    that carries away my woman.
Now the vast dusk bulk that is the whale's bulk. . . . it
    seems mine,
Warily, sportsman! though I lie so sleepy and sluggish,
    my tap is death.   ("The Sleepers," ll. 126–34)

Though clearly a catalogue, "The Sleepers" is also one of the poems we have identified as having a plainly closed structure: Whitman's perfect touch in adapting the catalogue to the structural requirements he imposed on these poems is just another "incomparable thing" done "incomparably well" in the first *Leaves*. For it is easy to recognize now that the closed structures that seemed only to confirm that these poems are simply "cuttings" can help to prove the contrary, since they, too, establish the formal center of the poems as their center of gravity as well. Thus, far from being incompatible, closed structures and catalogues reinforce each other and together constitute the formal technique characteristic of these eleven poems: focusing on the middle, or "centering."

---

[8] Cf. Horace Traubel, *With Walt Whitman in Camden*, II (New York: D. Appleton, 1908), 56–57.

In the remaining three of the group of five titled poems, this device of "centering" brings into prominence "the greatest poet's" condescending reassurance, in "A Song for Occupations," to the "foolish child" (l. 100) who asked, "Can each see the signs of the best by a look in the lookingglass? Is there nothing greater or more?" (l. 98), then the marvelous *non sequitur* in "To Think of Time" with which he staunches the torrent of anguish that "the future would be nothing to you" (l. 4): "What will be will be well—for what is is well" (l. 65), and finally, in "I Sing the Body Electric," his apostrophe to women: "You are the gates of the body and you are the gates of the soul" (l. 61). Mother and father, brother, child, woman, body, soul, and desperate affirmation: the thematic relevance is obvious. In each poem, "centering" precipitates, so to speak, the significant forms in the "business" left "unfinished" by "Song of Myself."

If we now combine "centering" with the momentum of the catalogues, we reach the principle of organization that makes sense of the typographical grouping and can thus help us to recognize in the eleven "other" poems the resolution of the drama of the first *Leaves*. Though each poem is properly "centered" in itself, that is, catalogued, argued, and narrated, we can also trace through the five titled poems a catalogue of a larger scope and through it a single story and a single argument.[9] This larger catalogue begins to gather strength in the lists of occupations in the group's first poem and continues in "To Think of Time" with the grim description of the sick-room of the person who has just died:

> When the dull nights are over, and the dull days also,
> When the soreness of lying so much in bed is over,
> When the physician, after long putting off, gives the silent
> and terrible look for an answer,
> When the children come hurried and weeping, and the brothers
> and sisters have been sent for,
> When medicines stand unused on the shelf, and the camphor-
> smell has pervaded the rooms, [. . .]   (ll. 12–16)

This serial momentum becomes metaphorically visible, then, in an image of procession: "Slowmoving and black lines creep over the whole earth. . . . they never cease. . . . they are the burial lines"

---

[9] Cf. *The Trial of the Poet*, pp. 241–42.

(l. 30); from this point on, the sequence through "To Think of Time," "The Sleepers," and "I Sing the Body Electric" is dominated by this processional movement. The variations of the "burial lines" yield in "The Sleepers" to the protagonist's own progress, "swiftly and noiselessly stepping and stopping" (l. 2), among the sleepers. His movements then become "a dance" (l. 32), in which he is whirled around and moved ahead by a variety of dream images. This processional dance begins with the romp of the "gay gang of blackguards" (l. 41) and ends with the protagonist's shimmering vision of the sleepers as "they flow hand in hand over the whole earth from east to west as they lie unclothed" (l. 180). "The bodies of men and women" that "engirth" the speaker continue the series ("I Sing the Body Electric," l. 1), as "the natural perfect and varied attitudes" (l. 26) of the human form parade by. "All is a procession," the protagonist exclaims, "The universe is a procession with measured and beautiful motion" (ll. 78–79). Finally, just as it evolved from the sheer momentum of a catalogue, the metaphor of the procession recedes into a catalogue again as the sequence of the five titled poems concludes with the delightful, inventive list of images in "Faces."

The moment of the murderous rage of the "I" against the father is "centered" thus not just in "The Sleepers" but in the entire sequence, and it is logically correlated to his discovery of the mother, which forms the sequence's coda:

> The melodious character of the earth!
> The finish beyond which philosophy cannot go and does not
>   wish to go!
> The justified mother of men! ("Faces," ll. 83–85)

The successively longer dream episodes in "The Sleeper" that precede the crisis slow down the easy rush of images with which "A Song for Occupations" begins the catalogue and thus creates the effect of an increasingly labored and anxious progression toward a dreaded but inevitable confrontation.

This scheme not only accounts for the grouping together of these five poems, but it also locks them into place: "The Sleepers" must be in the center, and "Faces" must conclude the group. The shifts from list to procession to list again and the pattern of gathering speed and momentum, then slowing down as the crisis approaches, and finally picking up speed again once it is passed both require that the other poems remain in this order, too. The ordering is reinforced by what one might call the thematic tonality of the poems. In "A Song for Occupations," this is space ("Will you seek afar off? You surely come back at last" [l. 164], the speaker remarks); it is, of course, time in "To Think of Time" and body in "I Sing the Body Electric," and the faces listed in the last poem in the group indicate the soul: "They show their descent from the Master himself" (l. 57). In yet another act of "centering," "The Sleepers" is framed by poems that recall the four corners of the world of "Song of Myself": space, time, body, and soul.

The group of the six untitled poems parallels the group of the five titled ones. Although the entire sequence is fainter, much less emphatic than the one that precedes it, and its serial momentum is based on the incantatory repetition of single words and sounds rather than full-fledged catalogues, particularly toward the end, the main outlines are clear enough. The sequence "centers" the "I's" childhood memory of his parents in "There Was a Child Went Forth":

> The mother at home quietly placing the dishes on the supper-
>   table,
> The mother with mild words. . . . clean her cap and gown. . . . a
>   wholesome odor falling off her person and clothes as
>   she walks by:
> The father, strong, selfsufficient, manly, mean, angered,
>   unjust,
> The blow, the quick loud word, the tight bargain, the
>   crafty lure, . . .   (ll. 14-17)

The passage—the only one in which the couple that haunts the entire volume actually appears—corresponds to the climactic moment in "The Sleepers" and brings "the blow, the quick loud word" of the father into ironic juxtaposition with the threat of the entranced protagonist of "The Sleepers": "Warily, sportsman! though I lie so sleepy and sluggish, my tap is death" (l. 134). Another important juxtaposition is established by the coda of the second sequence; instead of the mother, the protagonist in the end discovers death: "Sure as the stars return again after they merge in the light, death is great as life" ("Great Are the Myths," l. 67). Analogies with the other patterns that organize the first group are only vestigial. "Song of the Answerer" is thematically similar to "A Song for Occupations," and the two historical poems together correspond to "To Think of Time." It is difficult to see further correspondences between the two groups, but those that do exist are sufficient both to fix the order of the shorter pieces and to indicate their relationship to the longer ones.

Through these two corresponding sequences, the "business" of the first *Leaves* is finished at last. "Song of Myself," the self-genesis of "the greatest poet," could not be a story; his confrontation with the forces that would destroy him must be a story, and the structure outlined in this essay helps us to trace it through the text. It is, of course, the very simple and very old one in which the hero must enter the darkness and overcome the horror that lives in it before he can obtain his reward. In the first *Leaves*, the hero is the self-created "I," and the darkness is the dreaded yet irresistibly attractive world of the "grass," the Other, in which the terrifying figure of the Father, looming in manifold shapes of guilt, bars the way to the "soul," to "the peace and joy and knowledge that pass all the art and argument of the earth" ("Song of Myself," l. 82) awaiting the "I" in the Mother's lap. In "The Sleepers," the father-dragon is slain, and in "Faces" the guerdon is granted. "There Was a Child Went Forth" and "Great Are the Myths" retell in the sober, detached tones of wakeful memory and wakeful perception the story that "The Sleepers" and "Faces" enact with the intensity of possession. In "There Was a Child," the "I" is an adult remembering his childhood; in "The Sleepers," he is, as George B. Hutchinson recently explained, a shaman in a trance, enduring and then triumphing over, as Roethke would have it, his "dark time."[10]

These eleven poems are hardly "cuttings," then. They are indispensable to the volume, since in them is the story told and the drama resolved that "Song of Myself" has generated. In the huge shapes that populate them, we recognize the dimensions that, according to some views at least, establish Whitman's centrality in American poetry. In mother, father, and death we can glimpse what Harold Bloom has described as "the giant forms" of Eros, Dionysus, and Ananke, the "divinities" whose "troublesome relations account for

---

[10] "Parallels to Shamanism in 'The Sleepers,'" *Walt Whitman Review*, 26 (June 1980), 43–52.

much of the peculiar individuality of post-Emersonian American poetry."[11]

Whether or not this is, indeed, the quality that gives Whitman his rank in "the native strain," the three figures and their configuration in these poems also project some moods that only later will become explicit in *Leaves of Grass*. The moment when mother and death, Eros and Ananke will merge is implied in the powerful motion of the poems that conclude the first edition. Like two "hurrying tumbling waves" with "quickbroken crests and slapping" ("There Was a Child," l. 28), the two groups impel the "beautiful gigantic" "I" swimming naked through the eddies of the sea" ("The Sleepers," l. 81) toward his destiny, and in the music they make we can already hear, ever so faintly, "the strong and delicious word" that "like an old crone rocking the cradle" the "fierce old mother" will whisper to him ("Out of the Cradle Endlessly Rocking," ll. 133, 181–82).[12]

[11] "The Native Strain: American Orphism," in *Literary Theory and Structure*, eds. F. Brady, J. Palmer, M. Paier (New Haven: Yale Univ. Press, 1973), p. 288.
[12] *CRE*, p. 253.

Walt Whitman: The Spermatic Imagination
Harold Aspiz

I

A NUMBER of bravura passages in the first three editions of *Leaves of Grass* focus on those moments in which the Whitman persona becomes emotionally and sexually aroused, seeking and finding release in spermatic utterances. Consistently, these passages reflect fantasized experiences, as distinct from "reported" or "realistic" ones, and relate the persona's sexual excitement to his urge to speak and to write poems. Because the persona's virile physicality is generally pictured as an element of his vatic or bardic powers, Whitman's invention of a spermatic trope seems to have been an inevitable next step. Combining the images of the hero-poet as a sexually charged begetter, fantasizer, and speaker with some bizarre notions about the nature of sperm as the quintessential distillation of the body and the mind, Whitman fashioned a trope in which the persona's sexual arousal and visionary fervor lead him to an inspired vocalism which accompanies, or acts as a surrogate for, orgasm. Always associated with the Whitman persona's role as a poet or utterer, the trope mimics the inspired moments of literary creation with their interplay of sexual and creative drives.

Located in a borderland of the mind, between reality, on the one side, and the unconscious, on the other, these emotionally charged passages are a manifestation of American literary romanticism. On the one side, a radical reformist approach to sexuality, a sense of place and time, and the historic Whitman; on the other side, a boundless world of the imagination, the persona's cosmic arrogance, and the mythic selfhood which is the source and sanction of his art. *Leaves of Grass* is related to "the subterranean phallicism

in nineteenth-century American literature,"[1] as Whitman acknowledged when he observed that "Swedenborg was right when he said
there was a close connection—a very close connection—between
the state we call religious ecstasy and the desire to copulate. I find
Swedenborg confirmed in all my experience."[2] But although the
sexually charged works of Hawthorne, Poe, Melville, and Dickinson occur in a borderland of the mind similar to Whitman's,
those authors tend to show the sexual drive as sublimated or chan-
neled into expressions of art, spirituality, or various intellectual
passions. One sees the process at work in Owen Warland, Hawthorne's "artist of the beautiful"; in Pierre, Melville's callow would-
be author; in the exquisite Dickinson persona. Significantly, Whitman's spermatic trope inverts this romantic mode, stands the process
on its head, by channeling artistic, intellectual, and spiritual yearnings into bold and unusual expressions of sexuality.

The process of "locating the genitalia with the geography of the
soul"[3] had considerable currency in Whitman's day. The American
phrenologist Orson S. Fowler asserted that the "power to think,
love, hate, remember, reckon, sing, talk, worship . . . originate in
the male, and inhere in that life-chit he furnishes." He maintained
that "a powerful sexuality . . . so sexes [a man's] ideas and feelings
that they impregnate the mentalities of his fellow-men. Every
intellectual genius on record evinces every sign of powerful manhood, while the ideas of the poorly sexed are tame, insipid, emas-
culated, and utterly fail to awaken enthusiasm." Likewise,
Whitman's preface to *Leaves of Grass* (1855) and his anonymous
reviews cited his splendid physique and his prowess as a breeder
as indicators of his poetic genius.[4] A number of other writers also
associated sperm and an inspired literature. Emerson admiringly
observed that Plotinus had spoken of "spermatic words"; Emerson
himself demanded books that are "vital and spermatic, not leaving

[1] Edwin H. Miller, *Walt Whitman's Poetry: A Psychological Journey* (1968; rpt.
New York: New York Univ. Press, 1969), p. 124. For the image of the borderland,
see *The Haunted Dusk: American Supernatural Fiction*, ed. Howard Kerr, John W.
Crowley, and Charles L. Crow (Athens: Univ. of Georgia Press, 1983), pp. 2–3.

[2] Horace L. Traubel, *With Walt Whitman in Camden*, ed. Gertrude Traubel, V
(Carbondale: Southern Illinois Univ. Press, 1964), 376.

[3] John B. Humma, "The Interpenetrating Metaphor: Nature and Myth in *Lady
Chatterley's Lover*," *PMLA*, 98 (1983), 80.

[4] *Creative and Sexual Science* (Philadelphia: National Publ. Co., 1870), pp. 126,
220–21. For Whitman's self-reviews, see *Walt Whitman: The Critical Heritage*, ed.
Milton Hindus (New York: Barnes & Noble, 1971), pp. 34–48.

the reader where he was," as well as "initiative, spermatic, prophesying, man-making words." He attributed to great writers the ability
to use spermatic language that can fertilize the thoughts of the
"great bands of female souls who can only receive the spermatic
aura, and brood on the same but add nothing." For Emerson, as
for Whitman, spermatic words have been said to "impregnate the
person at the receiving end, but they make him pregnant with a
male thought which when uttered is capable of impregnating
others."[5]
The emphasis on the well-sexed male was associated with an
amalgam of ideas about the sanctity of sperm: a lingering scientific
and popular belief in pangenesis ("each part of the body contributed
a fraction of itself to the sperm by way of the blood"), in "the
hereditability of acquired characteristics," and in the vital linkage
between the brain and the sexual organs.[6] In Whitman's day, many
doctors still credited the ancient notion that the "seminal fluid"
was a discharge of the brain. With the attainment of adolescence,
the cerebellum was thought to become involved in the production
of "Semen, or Life Fluid," with which to beget children and (with
the fluid retained in the body) to strengthen man's physical organism and "every fibre of his being." Dr. Frederick Hollick
alleged the interrelatedness of the nervous and sexual systems and
of "the nervous substance and the seminal fluid," theorizing in
terms of the electro-biology of the period that the mind and the
sexual organs were like "two poles of a Galvanic Pile," connected
by the spinal marrow, the right side of the brain paired electrically
with the left testicle or ovary, and vice versa. Fowler put it bluntly:
"Semen comes from the mind." Such notions account in part for
the era's anxiety over masturbation and sexual excess, which could
purportedly drain the life essence of abusers and afflict them with
spinal consumption and brain fever. It was deemed folly to waste
what Pythagoras had called "the flower of the blood" and the

[5] Erik Ingvar Thurin, *Emerson as Priest of Pan: A Study in the Metaphysics of
Sex* (Lawrence: Regents Press of Kansas, 1981), p. 174; the citations from Emerson's
notebooks and journals are quoted ibid, pp. 173–74. Alcott says that "Mettle [sperm]
is the Godhead proceeding into the matrix [womb] of Nature to organize man . . . the
creative jet!" See *The Journals of Bronson Alcott*, ed. Odell Shepard (Boston: Little,
Brown, 1938), p. 121.

[6] Ben Barker-Benfield, "The Spermatic Economy: A Nineteenth-Century View of
Sexuality," in *The American Family in Social-Historical Perspective*, ed. Michael
Gordon (New York: St. Martin's Press, 1973), p. 341.

American gynecologist Dr. Augustus Kinsley Gardner termed the "fecundating fluid" that inspires energy, longevity, and creativity and represents "the concentrated powers of man's perfected being . . . the purest extract of the blood."[7]

Dr. Alice B. Stockman, gynecologist, Whitmanite, and sexual reformer, related the fertile fluid to the fertile imagination, arguing that semen which is reabsorbed "into the system . . . adds enormously to man's magnetic, mental, and spiritual force" and that this retained semen

may be coined into new thoughts, perhaps new inventions, grand conceptions of the true, the beautiful, the useful; or into fresh emotions of joy, and impulses of kindness and blessing all around. This is, in fact, but another department of procreation. It is the procreation of thoughts, ideas, feelings of good will, intuitions of truth—that is, it is the procreation on the mental and spiritual planes, instead of the physical. It is just as really a part of the generative function as is the begetting of offspring. It is by far the greater part, for physical procreation can ordinarily be participated in but seldom, while mental and spiritual procreation may and should go on through all our earthly lives—yea, through our immortal existence.[8]

The likelihood that nineteenth-century spermatic notions could appeal to a major poet is confirmed in an essay by Ezra Pound, in which he suggests that the brain originated as "only a sort of great clot of genital fluid held in suspense or reserve," and that this "fluid" is involved in the formation of mental images. Drawing on the antic theories that had identified the brain fluid with semen, he remarks: "Given, that is, two great seas of this fluid, mutually magnetized, the wonder is, or at least the first wonder is, that human thought is so inactive." And in imagery reminiscent of the moment when the Whitman persona thrusts his phallus into the center of the American continent, Pound identifies the sexual drive

---

[7] John S. Haller, Jr., and Robin M. Haller, *The Physician and Sexuality in Victorian America* (Urbana: Univ. of Illinois Press, 1974), pp. 195–97; Fowler, *Creative and Sexual Science*, p. 948; Barker-Benfield, "The Spermatic Economy," p. 341; Henry C. Wright, *Marriage and Parentage: or, The Reproductive Element in Man* (1855; rpt. New York: Arno Press, 1974), pp. 28–31.

[8] *Karezza: Ethics of Marriage* (1896: rpt. New York: Arno Press, 1974), pp. 43–44, 99–100. For somewhat similar statements, see D. H. Jacques, *Hints Toward Reforms* (New York: Fowler and Wells, 1859), pp. 56–57; Dio Lewis, *Chastity; or, Our Secret Sins* (1874; rpt. New York: Arno Press, 1974), p. 317n.; Eliza B. Duffey, *The Relation of the Sexes* (1876; rpt. New York: Arno Press, 1974), pp. 179–80; Frank C. Fowler, *Life: How to Enjoy and How to Prolong It* (Modus, Conn.: n. p., 1896), p. 110.

with the creative urge: "Integration of the male in the male organ. Even oneself has felt it, driving any new idea into the great passive vulva of London, a sensation analogous to the male feeling in copulation." According to Pound's sexist formulation, man creates ideas, whereas woman represents "utility" and conservation. (Compare Emerson's "great bands of female souls.") Thought, Pound insists, is "a chemical process, the most interesting of all transfusions in liquid solution. The mind is an up-spurt of sperm." As if to equate the shaping spirit of a poet's imagination with semen, Pound calls the substance "conscious of form," possessing "a capacity for formed expression," a new species of creatures or of new ideas resulting from "a single out-push of a demand made by a spermatic sea of sufficient energy to cast such a form." Finally, Pound voices the familiar idea that withholding the sperm may enable one to "super-think."[9]

II

The phallicism of the Whitman persona has physiological, spiritual, and esthetic implications. In section 22 of "Song of Myself," he declares:

> I moisten the roots of all that has grown.
> Did you fear some scrofula out of the unflagging pregnancy?[10]

The euphemistic moistening exemplifies the scattering of the spermatic persona's fertilizing seed; the earth's immunity to scrofula (akin to the consumption that was often attributed to too-frequent pregnancies and to sexual excess) complements his "unflagging" sexual prowess.[11] Like the literature of genetic reform, which generally assumed that the laws of plant and animal breeding were

[9] Postscript to Rémy de Gourmont, *The Natural Philosophy of Love* (New York: Boni and Liveright, 1921), pp. 206–19. Personae whose sexual arousal results in a spiritual clarification and a spermatic utterance are portrayed by Lawrence, Genet, Styron, Leonard Cohen, Erica Jong, and others.

[10] *Leaves of Grass: Facsimile Edition of the 1860 Text*, ed. Roy Harvey Pearce (Ithaca: Cornell Univ. Press, 1961), p. 52. All poems are cited from this edition; omissions in the poems are indicated by ellipses. For some more prosaic echoes of the spermatic trope, see also *Democratic Vistas*, in *Prose Works 1892*, ed. Floyd Stovall (New York: New York Univ. Press, 1964), pp. 395–97, 404–05, 419–20, 424–26.

[11] On consumption resulting from sexual excess, see Edward H. Dixon, *A Treatise on Diseases of the Sexual System* (New York: Robert M. DeWitt, 1867), p. 237; Lewis, *Chastity*, p. 246; J. H. Kellogg, *Plain Facts for the Young and Old* (1888; rpt. New York: Arno Press, 1974), pp. 250, 345, 469.

applicable to humans, *Leaves of Grass* tends to associate sexual and agricultural concepts. In section 40 of the same poem, boasting that "this day I am jetting the stuff of far more arrogant republics," the persona proposes to inseminate all "women fit for conception" and to "start" a brood of "bigger and nimbler babes" for America (p. 85). In "Myself and Mine" he resolves to perfect himself so that he will be able to "chisel . . . the heads and limbs of plenteous Supreme Gods" and to disseminate "Every hour the semen of centuries" (pp. 224, 226).

His very poems are perceived as seed or semen. In "Proto-Leaf" he declares that "the following poems are indeed to drop in the earth the germs of a greater Religion" (p. 13). In "So Long!" vocal and genital images combine as the throat of the dying persona issues its last electric screams, which, like his semen, fructify the earth:

> Curious enveloped messages delivering,
> Sparkles hot, seed ethereal, down in the dirt dropping,
> Myself unknowing, my commission obeying, to question it
>   never daring,
> To ages, and ages yet, the growth of the seed leaving, . . .

As a result of this seeding, readers in the future may catch "a melodious echo, passionately bent for—death making me undying"; for with this poetic insemination the persona has planted his own voice, his own book, and his immortal self. Thus his declaration that "Who touches this, touches a man," seems to refer to a new Whitman, reborn by godlike fiat from the persona's spermatic plantings (pp. 454–56). And in another shocking image that relates the seed-semen figure to the persona's immortality, the short lyric "To Him that was Crucified" pairs the Whitman persona and Christ as twin seminal begetters of a new spiritual progeny, both of them moving among mankind, saturating the world with their seed, and "transmitting the same charge and succession. . . . Till we saturate time and eras, that men and women of races, ages to come, may prove brothers and lovers, as we are" (p. 397). (The "charge" ambiguously suggests both Christ's commandment to love one another and the supposed electrical nature of sexual begetting.)

The link between the persona's phallicism and his vocalism—whatever it may imply in psychological or sexual terms—is the basic element of the spermatic trope. The connection between voice and phallus is clearly asserted in "Chants Democratic 12" ("Vo-calism"), which declares that the "limber-lipped" orator (Whitman had toyed with the idea of becoming an orator) must undergo a vast range of experiences before he can attain "the divine power to use words" and before these words can "debouch" from his "loosened throat" as inspirational revelations of life and nature's laws. After maturing and experiencing "chastity, friendship, pro-creation, prudence, and nakedness,"[12] a "complete faith," and many clarifications, "it is just possible there comes to a man, a woman, the divine power to use words" (pp. 183–85). Similarly, the celebration of the "chaste and electric currents" of the persona's genitalia ("love-branches! love-root! love-apples!") in the closing lines of "A Song of Joys" gives way to the imagined joys of oratory—"quell[ing] America with a great tongue . . . speak[ing] with a full and sonorous voice" (p. 268). And in "Salut au Monde!" after enacting the passive (feminine) role of a spirit medium and being ravished by an influx of spirit so that what he sees and hears "widens" within him as though he were a pregnant woman (pp. 243–44), the persona becomes a phallic utterer, disseminating what he has absorbed during his mystic state, "penetrating" his ideas (to use Ezra Pound's phrase) into the "passive vulva" of America. "What cities the light or warmth penetrates," he exclaims at the poem's conclusion, "I penetrate those cities myself" (p. 257).

The most sustained examples of the spermatic trope are associated with the portrayals of the poet-persona in various "Children of Adam" poems, "Song of the Answerer," "By Blue Ontario's Shore," and the middle sections of "Song of Myself."

In sections 24 and 25 of "Song of Myself" the persona's sper-matic attributes form a link with the cosmos. "Disorderly, fleshy, sensual, eating, drinking, breeding," the electrical "afflatus surg-ing" through him, he utters "the pass-word primeval"; he becomes the voice of the voiceless, "of cycles of preparation and accretion, / And of the threads that connect the stars—and of wombs, and of

---

[12] Here "chastity" means a prudently regulated sex life. Compare "the chaste wife," "the chaste husband," "the great chastity of maternity," "the great chastity of paternity," *Leaves of Grass*, pp. 139, 307. The radical sex reformer Ezra H. Heywood cites similar usages by Benjamin Franklin, Robert Owen, and John Humphrey Noyes, in *Cupid's Yokes: or, The Binding Forces of Conjugal Life* (1876; rpt. New York: Arno Press, 1974), pp. 5n., 13.

the fatherstuff" (pp. 54–55). Caressed by nature's genitalia, he voices a series of tender invocations to his phallic self:

> Root of washed sweet-flag! Timorous pond-snipe! Nest of
>   guarded duplicate eggs! it should be you! ...
> Trickling sap of maple! Fibre of manly wheat! it shall
>   be you! ...
> Winds whose soft-tickling genitals rub against me, it
>   shall be you!
> Broad, muscular fields! Branches of live oak! Loving
>   lounger in my winding paths! it shall be you! (p. 56).

Doting on his "luscious" self, he beholds "A morning-glory at my window"—the objectification of the ecstatic moment about to erupt into a phallic and vocal utterance:

> Something I cannot see puts upward libidinous prongs,
> Seas of bright juice suffuse heaven. (p. 57)

The up-spurts into the interstellar spheres of his mystic semen, possibly reflecting his self-induced orgasm or the workings of his vivid imagination, are hyperbolical expressions of the persona's generative force, his powers of utterance, and his quenchless spirit. In keeping with the spermatic trope, the sexual climax is transformed into vocalism: the phallic utterance of the persona's semen becomes the seminal utterance of the poet's words.

> My voice goes after what my eyes cannot reach,
> With the twirl of my tongue I encompass worlds, and volumes
>   of worlds.
>
> Speech is the twin of my vision—it is unequal to measure
>   itself;
> It provokes me forever,
> It says sarcastically, *Walt, you understand enough—why don't
>   you let it out then?* (p. 58)

Like a primordial god, he has projected his semen into the womb of the universe, and the magnificence of his voice harmonizes with the music of the spheres.

In sections 27 through 30 of "Song of Myself," declaring that "Mine is no callous shell," perhaps to differentiate himself from mere self-abusers,[13] the persona places his own hand on the "head-

---

[13] Masturbation "renders its victims like sole-leather when compared to skin: a lifeless texture, frigid, stoical, benumbed, automatic . . . struck with a kind of mental fatuity, inert . . ." (Fowler, *Creative and Sexual Science*, p. 811).

land" (a thrice-repeated term denoting the unplowed land at the end of a plowed furrow) and thus arouses himself by "a touch . . . quivering me to a new identity." He is temporarily distraught as "prurient provokers" strain "the udder of my heart for its withheld drip." But after an apparent spasm in which (to use the words of section 22) he appears to "moisten the roots of all that has grown," he rejoices in the

> Parting, tracked by arriving—perpetual payment of perpetual loan,
> Rich showering rain, and recompense richer afterward.
>
> Sprouts take and accumulate—stand by the curb prolific
>   and vital,
> Landscapes, projected, masculine, full-sized, and golden.
>   (pp. 62–63)

The "perpetual payment" and the "recompense" the persona boasts of, after the hysteria and guilt induced by masturbation have subsided into a self-satisfied calm, are related to one of the most puzzling lines in the entire poem: "A minute and a drop of me settle my brain" (p. 63). Sexual experts, it will be recalled, generally held that the loss of semen would result in debility and mental derangement unless sufficient semen has been conserved to maintain physical and mental well-being. When one has learned to retain semen during sexual union, according to Dr. Stockham, "in the course of an hour the physical tension subsides, the spiritual exhilaration increases, and not uncommonly visions of a transcendent life are seen and consciousness of new powers experienced."[14] Apparently, the "prurient provokers" who threaten to rob the "udder" of the Whitman persona's heart of its "withheld drip" have failed; he has retained enough of his semen (in Pound's phrase) to "super-think." Perhaps the persona was only fantasizing the sensations of sexual ecstasy while conserving the flower of his blood in order to conjure up these "full-sized" and "golden" visions. In any case, following his intense sexual excitement and the subsequent restoration of his spermatic balance, he is inspired to voice the most sustained utterance in all of Leaves of Grass: section 31 ("I believe a leaf of grass is no less than the journey-work of the stars"), section 32 ("I think I could turn and live

---

[14] Stockham, Karezza, p. 26; see also pp. 43–44, and Gardner, Conjugal Sins, pp. 161–62.

with animals"), and section 33—the 130-line catalogue in which he is "afoot" with his vision and wondrously articulate.

"By Blue Ontario's Shore" illustrates the observation that when true artists "make love" to the world "it answers in joy, and gives birth to things that work."[15] In this poem, the persona, like a continental titan, embraces his nation in order to impregnate it with his own spermatic virtues:

> Attracting it body and Soul to himself, hanging on its
> neck with incomparable love,
> Plunging his semitic muscle into its merits and demerits,
> Making its geography, cities, beginnings, events, glories,
> defections, diversities, vocal in him,
> Making its rivers, lakes, bays, embouchure in him . . .
> spending themselves lovingly in him,
> If the Atlantic coast stretch, or the Pacific coast stretch,
> he stretching with them north or south,
> Spanning between them east and west, and touching whatever
> is between them . . .
> Through him flights, songs, screams, answering those of
> the wild-pigeon, coot, fish-hawk, qua-bird, mocking-
> bird, condor, night-heron, eagle; . . . (pp. 112–13)

The persona stretches himself flank to flank against the continent, "Plunging his semitic muscle" (corrected to "seminal" in the 1871 edition) into its bodies of water, which become "embouchure to him" and "spend" themselves in him. The "embouchure" imagery is ambiguously oral and vulval: "embouchure" denotes the mouth of a river, the opening out of a valley into a plain, or the manner of blowing a wind instrument; "spending" signifies orgasm, as do "spends" (p. 115), "love-spendings" (p. 304), and similar usages by Lord Rochester, Ik Marvell, Herman Melville, and Philip Roth. The reciprocal "spending" of the implicitly female North American continent during this embrace reflects the notion, once credited, that women also release a fecundating fluid, analogous to sperm, during orgasm.[16]

[15] Wayland Young, *Eros Denied: Sex in Western Society* (New York: Grove Press, 1966), p. 255.

[16] Young, *Eros Denied*, pp. 235, 295–96; Barker-Benfield, "The Spermatic Economy," p. 342; G. J. Barker-Benfield, *The Horrors of the Half-Known Life: Male Attitudes toward Women and Sexuality in Nineteenth-Century America* (New York: Harper and Row, 1976), p. 12; Philip Roth, *Zuckerman Unbound* (New York: Farrar, Straus and Giroux, 1981), p. 198.

"By Blue Ontario's Shore" establishes the political and esthetic motivations for the persona's titanic couplings. Only an intense interaction between America and her poet—tantamount to their sexual embrace—can instill the nation with the democratic virtues embodied in its poet:

> Bravas to States whose semitic impulses send wholesome
>   children to the next age! . . .
> By great bards only can series of peoples and States be
>   fused into the compact organism of one nation . . .
> Of all races and eras, These States, with veins full of
>   poetical stuff, most need poets, and are to have the
>   greatest, and use them the greatest,
> Their Presidents shall not be their common referee so
>   much as their poets shall. (p. 115)

The presence of "poetical stuff" in Mother America's veins reiterates the notion of a female fecundating fluid and lends a spermatic nuance to the persona's declaration that America "will advance to meet" her poetic counterpart ("the likes of itself") and that "his country absorbs him as affectionately as he has absorbed it" (p. 120). A dozen lines later the persona melodramatically demands that Mother America reward the sexual exertions of her beloved poet with the bestowal of language:

> Give me the pay I have served for!
> Give me to speak beautiful words! take all the rest; . . .
>   (p. 121)

The ending of this long and diffuse poem confirms that America has identified with her poet ("what is it finally except myself") and that she has gifted him with words, or, rather, with clues to the "beautiful, terrible, rude forms," the symbols which he alone can translate into poems by filtering them through his bardic self (p. 125).

About 1860, when Whitman was frequenting Pfaff's restaurant, the hangout of New York's bohemians, the drama critic William Winter (provoked by Whitman's backhanded praise for the poetic "tinkles" of Winter's gifted young friend Thomas Bailey Aldrich) baited Whitman "to oblige me with his definition of 'the Poet,'" and Whitman replied, "A Poet is a Maker." "But Walt," protested Winter, "what does he make?" According to Winter, Whitman assumed "a bovine air of omniscience," and said, "he makes

Poems."[17] Seen in perspective, Whitman's terse comments show
that he had defined himself as a maker in the venerable sense, a
vatic or bardic creator, different in essence from the tinkling ver-
sifiers of the day. This is his message in an 1860 poem, later
incorporated into "Song of the Answerer," which calls the verses
of mere singers partial and momentary but asserts that the true
poet is "the master," the luminous words of whose poems reconcile
mankind with the source of all wisdom and constitute a higher
order of cognition than any other science:

> He [the poet] is the glory and extract, thus far, of
>   things, and of the human race.
>
> The singers do not beget—only THE POET begets, . . .
> All this time, and at all times, wait the words of poems;
> The greatness of sons is the exuding of the greatness
>   of mothers and fathers,
> The words of poems are the tuft and final applause of science.
>   (pp. 215–16)

A closely related passage in the preface to *Leaves of Grass* (1855)
says that underlying "the structure of every perfect poem" is the
seed of scientists, of whose "fatherstuff must be begotten the sinewy
races of bards."[18] In calling the poet a begetter and calling his
words "the tuft and final applause of science," "Song of the Answerer" makes poetry the highest flowering of the imagination; in
this sense, "tuft" may connote a garland or a bouquet. But when
"tuft" is related to the "exuding" of the spermatic "fatherstuff"
and is recognized as another of Whitman's poetic code words for
the phallus (like "sweet-flag," "bunch," or "boss"), we may then
perceive the "words of poems"—and of this phallic poem—as a
"tuft," that is, as a spermatic utterance.

The "Children of Adam" group identifies the sexual drive with
the urge to utter poems. The spermatic trope is brilliantly encap-
sulated in "Enfans d'Adam 12":

> Ages and ages, returning at intervals,
> Undestroyed, wandering immortal,

---

[17] Winter, *Old Friends; Being Literary Recollections of Other Days* (New York:
Moffat, Yard, 1909), pp. 140–41.
[18] *Leaves of Grass: Comprehensive Reader's Edition*, ed. Harold W. Blodgett and
Sculley Bradley (New York: Norton, 1968), p. 718.

Lusty, phallic, with the potent original loins, perfectly
    sweet,
I, chanter of Adamic songs,
Through the new garden, the West, the great cities, calling,
Deliriate, thus prelude what is generated, offering these,
    offering myself,
Bathing myself, bathing my songs in sex,
Offspring of my loins. (p. 313)

Here the speaker with "the potent original loins, perfectly sweet,"
personifies the physiological Adam who can inaugurate a perfected
race for the new world by virtue of the preservation within his
loins of the best seed; he exemplifies Whitman's statement that a
new American literature "can only be generated from the seminal
freshness and proportion of new masculine persons."[19] Aroused
simultaneously by his sexual drive and by his urge to utter poems,
the new Adam celebrates that mysterious and "deliriate" moment
in which the poem is born—or at least begotten. "What is generated . . . these . . . Offspring of my loins" here specifically
designate the "Children of Adam" poems as well as this very poem,
which is both the creative act—duly recorded—and the artifact
of that act.

Even those "Children of Adam" poems which chiefly glorify
the procreative powers imply that the persona's sexual deeds encompass his acts of artistic creativity. "Enfans d'Adam 4" ("A
Woman Waits for Me") endows the persona with "the moisture
of the right man," who drains "the pent-up rivers of myself"—
these "love-spendings"—in order to beget "loving crops" of immortal successors upon the bodies of countless women. But this
Adam is more than the new world's archetypal breeder, for, says
the speaker, "sex contains all," not merely "All the passions, loves,
beauties, delights of the earth," but specifically all "songs" as well
(pp. 302–04). Similarly, "Enfans d'Adam 2" ("From Pent-Up
Aching Rivers") is overtly "the song of procreation," celebrating
all sorts of couplings, "the warp" and "the woof" of sex. Adam
is a "vessel" obeying God's commandment ("The general com-
manding me") to be fruitful and multiply, alleging, like a true
mystic, that the spirit operating within him is furthering a divinely

[19] *The Complete Works of Walt Whitman*, ed. Richard Maurice Bucke, Thomas
B. Harned, and Horace L. Traubel (New York: Putnam's, 1902), X, 40.

inspired "programme." And yet his "act-poems" of sex encompass
artistic creation—the translation of the sexual act into poetry, the
transmutation of phallicism into vocalism, of sex into song:

> From that of myself, without which I were nothing,
> From what I am determined to make illustrious, even if
>   I stand sole among men,
> From my own voice resonant—singing the phallus,
> Singing the song of procreation,
> Singing the need of superb children, and therein superb
>   grown people,
> Singing the muscular urge and the blending, . . . (p. 288)

Ambiguously, the poem's closing lines suggest that the persona's
"enfans" may be these very "Enfans d'Adam" poems emerging
from the mysterious darkness of the poet's passionate soul:

> From the night, a moment, I, emerging, flitting out,
> Celebrate you, enfans prepared for,
> And you, stalwart loins, (p. 291)

The "night" from which the Adam persona emerges in "From
Pent-Up Aching Rivers" is also central to the theme of "Enfans
d'Adam 6" ("One Hour to Madness and Joy"), in which the
moment of sexual and "mystic deliria" furnishes the speaker with
the spiritual and artistic nourishment on which he can "feed the
remainder of life." In diction that is histrionic, if not spasmodic,
and reminiscent of the manner in which Ahab speaks of himself
as a natural force, he declares:

> O furious! O confine me not!
> (What is this that frees me so in storms?
> What do my shouts amid lightnings and raging winds mean?)
> O to drink the mystic deliria deeper than any other man!
> O savage and tender achings! (pp. 307–08)

The persona's "achings" are sexual and parental, male and female;
through their release "the puzzle—the thrice-tied knot" will be
"untied and illumined" to bring him a godlike "nonchalance" and
to have "the gag removed from one's mouth." While that ungagging suggests the inherent decency of sex, it also implies that
sexuality liberates the persona's vocalism. Freed from the "gag"
he becomes an inspired utterer. His amorous spasm is "something
in a trance," which will allow him to "drive free," to gain the

sexual release and the mystic illumination which are the twin
sources of his poetry. Melodramatically, he cries out:

> To ascend—to leap to the heavens of the love indicated
> to me!
> To rise thither with my inebriate Soul!
> To be lost, if it must be so!
> To feed the remainder of life with one hour of fulness
> and freedom!
> With one brief hour of madness and joy. (pp. 308–09)

Only the strong element of sexuality separates Whitman's rendering
of the poetic moment from that in a well-known passage by his
"Dear Master," Ralph Waldo Emerson, who describes the poet,
aroused to a sense of beauty and hemmed in by "herds of daemons,"
saying:

"By God it is in me and must forth of me." . . . [A]nd as an admirable
creative power exists in these intellections, it is of the last importance
that these things get spoken . . . that thought may be ejaculated as
Logos, or Word.

Doubt not, O poet, but persist. Say "It is in me, and shall out." Stand
there, balked and dumb, stuttering and stammering, hissed and hooted,
stand and strive, until at last rage draw out of thee that *dream*-power
which every night shows thee is thine own; a power transcending all
limit and privacy, and by virtue of which a man is the conductor of the
whole river of electricity. . . . Comes he to that power, his genius is
no longer exhaustible.[20]

Presumably, Emerson's "river of electricity" did not convey the
sexual nuances that it did to Whitman, but Emerson's description
of ungagging the power of utterance, liberating the "*dream-*
power*," and retrieving poems out of the dark night resembles
Whitman's own.

In this light, two "Children of Adam" poems appear to capture
the precise instant when sexual ecstasy coexists with the "native
moments" of artistic inspiration. In "Enfans d'Adam 8" ("Native
Moments") this juxtaposition occurs in the poem's grammatical
and temporal present during a (possibly masturbatory) fantasy as
the solitary persona cries out for "libidinous joys only! . . . the
drench of my passions! . . . life coarse and rank!" and imagines
himself, at some later hour, carousing with coarse companions and

---

[20] "The Poet," in *Essays: Second Series* (New York: AMS Press, 1968), p. 22.

making love to a prostitute. Implying that his sexuality qualifies
him not only "to consort with nature's darlings" but to guide the
American masses, and yearning to release his libidinous tensions
in a fulfillment that will be poetic and quasi-political, he vows:
"O you shunned persons! . . . I come forthwith in your midst—
I will be your poet" (pp. 310–11).

Another juxtaposition of erotic and poetic elements occurs in
that dazzling whirligig of sexual images "Enfans d'Adam 5"
("Spontaneous Me") which, once again, plays out the persona's
self-stimulated sexual fantasies. His "spontaneous" self seeks sexual
and artistic release as he passively conjures up a catalogue ("the
negligent list") of acts of love and sexual phenomena throughout
nature:

> Beautiful dripping fragments—the negligent list of one
>   after another, as I happen to call them to me, or
>   think of them,
> The real poems, (what we call poems being merely pictures,)
> The poems of the privacy of the night, and of men like me,
> This poem, drooping shy and unseen, that I always carry,
>   and that all men carry,
> (Know, once for all, avowed on purpose, wherever are men
>   like me, are our lusty, lurking, masculine, poems, . . .
>   (p. 305)

Here the persona has equated the creation of the poem—and of
all "masculine poems"—with the phallus: it sends forth spermatic
words and makes the reader intimate with "the poems of the privacy
of the night," an expression suggesting both the persona's genitalia
and that mysterious chthonian world of the spirit from whose dark
depths he utters poems.

The ending of "Spontaneous Me," with its implications of the
persona's "relief, repose, content," and his satisfaction with work
well done, confirms that we have beheld the sexually charged
moment of poetic creation:

> The wholesome relief, repose, content,
> And this bunch plucked at random from myself,
> It has done its work—I toss it carelessly to fall where
>   it may. (p. 307)

The "bunch plucked at random from myself" suggests that the
persona's spermatic creativity has fashioned "Spontaneous Me" into

another poetic garland. Here, too, "bunch" operates as a code word for the male genitals, the symbolic outlet of the poet's seminal creativity. The phallus begets the song, and here it *is* the song. In calling the creative act "random," Whitman implies that it is something the persona can toss off "carelessly" whenever this exultant mood seizes him. Forever, he seems to say, will these "potent original loins" be charged with sperm and these "native moments" recur; forever will the spermatic poet pluck songs from himself.

"Spontaneous Me" implies that the orgasm, whether actual or imagined, is the poem and that the poem is the orgasm. Like the poem's imagery, the idea spins around and around. Despite Emerson's demand for "spermatic" literature and the frequent implications, in his essays and verses, that the moment of poetic inspiration involves an exhilaration akin to drunkenness or a drug-induced high, he did not equate the creative moment with the thrill of the sex act as Whitman did. Whitman's complaint that Emerson could not understand the importance of sex to Whitman's scheme of things meant, above all, that Emerson had denied the link between sexual ecstasy and artistic creation. It was as though Emerson had acknowledged a seminal art but denied a phallic art—had recognized what Pound would term the "great clot" of semen in the brain but rejected the clot of semen in the testes. Whitman insisted that Emerson "did not see the significance of the sex element as I had put it into the book" and that "if I had cut sex out" of *Leaves of Grass* the whole poetic scheme would have been "violated in its most sensitive spot"[21]—presumably in the genitals. The poet who wrote "I sing myself, and celebrate myself" also rejoiced in "singing the phallus" to express that element "of myself, without which I were nothing." For in Whitman's spermatic trope, the poet, his phallus, and his song merge into one harmonious utterance.

21 Traubel, *With Walt Whitman in Camden*, I (Boston: Small, Maynard, 1906), 51.

Index

Notes on Contributors

Aspiz, Harold (1921–)
Lewis and Clark (1950–51); California State University, Long Beach (1958–).
Walt Whitman and the Body Beautiful, 1980.

Bradley, (Edward) Sculley (1897–)
Pennsylvania (1918–1967).
Editor, *The Sonnets of George Henry Boker*, 1929; *Whitman's* Leaves of Grass *and Selected Prose*, 1947; (with Harold Blodgett), *Leaves of Grass*, 1965; (with Harold Blodgett, Arthur Golden, William White), *Leaves of Grass, A Textual Variorum of the Printed Poems*, 1980.

Buell, Lawrence (1939–)
Oberlin (1966–).
Literary Transcendentalism: Styles and Vision in the American Renaissance, 1973; *New England Literary Culture: From Revolution Through Renaissance*, 1986. Editor (with Sandra Zagarell), The Morgesons *and Other Writings by Elizabeth Stoddard*, 1984.

Hiscoe, David
University of North Carolina, Greensboro (1980–1984); Rice (1984–1986); Loyola University, Chicago (1986–).

Holloway, Emory (1885–1977)
Adelphi (1914–1937); Queens (1937–1959).
Free and Lonesome Heart: The Secret of Walt Whitman, 1921; *Whitman— An Interpretation in Narrative*, 1926. Editor, *Uncollected Poetry and Prose of Walt Whitman*, 1921; (with Ralph Adinari), *New York Dissected*, 1936.

Hoople, Robin P. (1930–)
South Dakota State (1955–1956); Iowa Wesleyan (1956–1958); Minnesota (1958–1961); Manitoba (1961–).

Killingsworth, M. Jimmie (1952–).
Tennessee (1979–1980); New Mexico Tech (1980–1986); Texas Tech (1986–).

Marki, Ivan
Hamilton College (1965–).
The Trial of the Poet: An Interpretation of the First Edition of Leaves of Grass, 1976.

Marks, Alfred H. (1920–)
Syracuse (1949–1953); Ohio State (1953–1956); Ball State (1956–1963); SUNY, New Paltz (1963–1985). Editor, *The Literature of the Mid-Hudson Valley*, 1973; (with Barry Bort), *Guide to Japanese Prose*, 1975; (with Edytha Polater), *Surimono Prints by Elbow*, 1980. Translator, *Forbidden Colors* by

Yukio Mishima, 1968; *Thirst for Love* by Ujkio Mishima, 1969; (with Thomas Kondo), *Tales of Japanese Justice,* 1980.

Mason, John B. (1946–)
Youngstown State (1976–1985); Western Washington State (1986–).

Myers, Henry Alonzo (1906–1955)
Harvard (1934–1935); Cornell (1935–1955).
The Spinoza-Hegel Paradox, 1944; *Are Men Equal?* 1945; *Tragedy,* 1956.

Scholnick, Robert J. (1941–)
William and Mary (1967–).
Edmund Clarence Stedman, 1977.

Stovall, Floyd (1896–)
Texas (1929–1935); North Carolina (1945–1955); Virginia (1955–1967).
Desire and Restraint in Shelley, 1931; *American Idealism,* 1943. Editor, *Walt Whitman,* 1934; *Whitman's Prose Works,* 1962–1963.

Tapscott, Stephen (1948–)
University of Kent (1976–1977); Massachusetts Institute of Technology (1977–).
Mesopotamia, 1976; *American Beauty: William Carlos Williams and the Modernist Whitman,* 1984. Translator, *One Hundred Love Sonnets* by Pablo Neruda, 1986.

Templin, Lawrence (1922–)
Bluffton College (1961–).

Library of Congress Cataloging-in-Publication Data
On Whitman.
(The Best from American literature)
Includes index.
  1. Whitman, Walt, 1819–1892—Criticism and
interpretation. I. Cady, Edwin Harrison. II. Budd,
Louis J. III. Series.
PS3238.05 1987 811'.3 87–8997
ISBN 0–8223–0752–9